REBUILDING
A LOST FAITH

D0898825

REBUILDING
A LOST FAITH

BY AN AMERICAN AGNOSTIC
John L. Stoddard

"Into Thy vineyard I come in haste,
  Eleven sounds from its ancient tower,
So many years have gone to waste,
  What can I do in a single hour?"

TAN BOOKS AND PUBLISHERS, INC.
Rockford, Illinois 61105

239
STO

Nihil Obstat: C. Schutt, D.D.
                  Censor Deputatus

Imprimatur: ✠ Edm. Canon Surmont
                  Vicar General
                  Westminster
                  March 21, 1922

Originally published in 1921 by P. J. Kenedy & Sons, New York.

Retypeset and republished in 1990 by TAN Books and Publishers, Inc.

The type in this book is the property of TAN Books and Publishers, Inc., and may not be reproduced, in whole or in part, without written permission of the publisher.

Cover photograph (Basilicas at Lourdes) by Leonard Von Matt.

Library of Congress Catalog Card No.: 90-71103

ISBN: 0-89555-410-0

Printed and bound in the United States of America.

TAN BOOKS AND PUBLISHERS, INC.
P.O. Box 424
Rockford, Illinois 61105
1990

"Too late have I loved Thee,
O Beauty ever ancient, ever new."
—*St. Augustine*

"Thou hast made us for Thyself,
O God, and our hearts
are restless
'till they rest in Thee."
—*St. Augustine*

CONTENTS

PREFACE

THE world of literature possesses many records of conversion to Catholicism which are more startling in their events, more powerful in their delineation and more pleasing in their language than this story. Yet the experience of every soul is after all unique, and I myself have gained much benefit from reading the accounts of those who have preceded me, as pilgrims to the Port of Peace. This book is the result of numerous requests to write an explanation of the motives, influences and arguments which brought me back to faith in God, the Bible, Immortality and the Christian Religion, and finally led me to enter the ancient, Apostolic, Catholic Church, whose Primate is the Pope. It has seemed best to preface this explanation with a brief account of my youthful religious experience, between which and my present standpoint there stretches, like a desert between two oases, a spiritual wilderness of more than forty years. Both of these widely separated mental states constitute kindred portions of my spiritual entity, the former having been to some extent the origin of the latter.

From a glance at the Table of Contents of this volume one might perhaps conclude that the book is intended to be controversial. It is true that many of the usual differences between Catholics and Protestants are here discussed, but not with a desire for controversy. As I formerly took a more or less public stand towards prominent religious questions—unhappily in opposition to what I now through God's grace recognize as truth—I feel myself constrained to state with equal frankness my present religious convictions. As possible readers, I have had in mind especially such Protestants and Rationalists as, like myself, have grown up under modern sceptical and materialistic conditions, with little or no conception of ecclesiastical authority. To them the point of view from which I have approached the study of the Catholic Church will seem familiar and natural, however much they may differ from me in my conclusions. To Catholics who may turn these pages, I would say in advance, lest they be disappointed, that the results arrived at by these arguments will offer to them nothing new. Yet possibly the story of the arduous journey I was forced to make to reach a land already so well known to them may have for them some interest. They will at least appreciate the fact that I was moved to write these pages by a desire to counteract the evil influence which my hostility to Christianity once exerted, and to undo to some extent the harm produced for more than two score years.

God can make use of even the humblest instrument, and He may deign to do so in this instance. In view of this possibility I prayed that His Divine blessing might accompany me as I wrote.

God grant that such has been the case.

—THE AUTHOR

Chapter 1

FROM FAITH TO RATIONALISM

Nothing would be done at all, if a man waited till he could do it so well that no one could find fault with it.
— JOHN HENRY NEWMAN.

In den Ozean schifft mit tausend Masten der Jüngling; Still, auf gerettetem Boot treibt in den Hafen der Greis.—SCHILLER.

MY EARLY training was extremely religious. Both my parents were of old Puritan stock. Their theology was Calvinistic and of the type denominationally known as "Congregational." Their lives were not made gloomy by their creed, though they were certainly serious. Family prayers, morning and evening, were observed by them, followed on Sunday evenings by the singing of some beautiful hymns, whose words and melodies are still dear to me. The musical accompaniment to these was furnished by my father, and those sweet Sabbath evenings, when the family group assembled thus in prayer and praise, remain among the most touching memories of my life.

> Dear, old-time tunes of prayer and praise,
> Heard first beside my mother's knee,
> Your music on my spirit lays
> A spell from which I should be free,
> If lapse of time gave liberty.
>
> I listen, and the crowded years
> Fade, dream-like, from my life, and lo,
> I find my eyelids wet with tears,
> So much I loved, so well I know
> Those plaintive airs of long ago!

1

My mother also used to talk to me in simple but impressive words about our Saviour, Heaven, and the truths of the Gospel; and after her death I gained through reading her journals an insight into the spirituality of her nature and her intimate life with Christ in God.

When I was twelve years old, there took place something in my parents' life which, though I could not fully understand it then, has never been forgotten. It is worth recording here, as a proof of one of the results of Protestantism, arising from its theory of the supremacy of individual judgment in matters of faith and doctrine. A new minister had been installed in our Congregational church, but not without difficulty. It was at that time customary for ministers of the Congregational, Presbyterian, Baptist and other denominations, before entering on a pastorate in any church, whose members had given them a "call," to pass a theological examination, not only in the presence of a select committee of neighboring clergymen, but also before the deacons and even the lay members of the parish. These theological inquisitors, scarcely two of whom would probably have agreed in their interpretations of either Scripture or dogma, compelled the wretched postulant to run, for several hours, a gauntlet of questions, criticisms and "observations," whose alleged object was to ascertain whether, in the judgment of this heterogeneous court, he was perfectly "sound in the faith." As a matter of course, some of the questioners always were dissatisfied with the candidate's answers, and doubts were thus aroused in the minds of listening parishioners, many of whom were incapable of weighing the arguments, and some of whom were nothing more than well-meaning religious eccentrics. Thus were the seeds of future discontent and disintegration inevitably sown. Nevertheless, the applicant was seldom rejected. Those who had found him "too Calvinistic," "old-school," "liberal," or "lax," usually gave way at last through motives of expediency, though not without some mutterings of doubt and ominous predictions. In the particular case referred to, the suspicions awakened by the examination of Rev. Mr. D. developed quickly into active opposition. Some members of his church, among whom were my parents, became alarmed at the way in which he spoke of the Saviour in his sermons. Just how he failed to satisfy them I do not now remember, but I have reason to suppose that he was thought to emphasize too much the human element in the Son of God, while laying insufficient stress on His divinity.

At all events, a schism in the church grew imminent. A formal protest was drawn up by the dissatisfied party, and the reading of this arraignment, in the presence of the unhappy minister himself, in a crowded "Friday evening prayer meeting" I well remember. It amounted to an ultimatum on the part of the complainants, who thought of course that they, as Protestants, had a right to protest. At all events, they insisted that either the Rev. Mr. D. must preach a different theology, or they would leave the church and found another of their own! Had not Luther set them a glorious example? A bitter controversy ensued, which caused a lamentable scandal among all good Christians, and excited the derision of the ungodly. Finally, a compromise of some sort was effected, but the Rev. Mr. D. soon betook himself elsewhere. Nothing could better illustrate, than this little incident, the natural process of disintegration which has been going on in Protestantism for the last four centuries—an extraordinary process truly, if Protestant sects are really representative of a Church, which Christ not only founded, but with which He promised to abide to the end of time!

When I was thirteen years of age, my mother died, leaving to me a blessed memory of piety and love. My father, also eminent in godliness, died two years later. At the time of this latter event, I was still at school, but soon left for a neighboring city, expecting to pursue a mercantile career. God willed it otherwise. During the following winter, largely through the influence of two sincerely religious friends, I passed through the spiritual crisis commonly known as "conversion." No special excitement attended it. There certainly was no "revival" in the neighborhood. But I have reason to believe that this experience, notwithstanding my subsequent apostasy, was the result of God's Spirit striving with my soul. I was at all events profoundly moved by the realization of my sinfulness and of the necessity of reconciliation with God, and I sought His forgiveness humbly through the sacrifice of Jesus Christ, the Saviour of mankind, resolving with His help to lead a Christian life.

When this great change had taken place, an ardent desire seized me to devote myself, as a minister—preferably as a missionary—to the preaching of the Gospel. This was not strange. In my ancestry ministers had been numerous. One of my father's brothers had recently died as a missionary in the Orient; another was an active and enthusiastic supporter of the cause of foreign missions. The latter, welcoming my zeal, and heartily approving my wishes, agreed to furnish me with funds sufficient to obtain a university education, and a few months later I forever abandoned a mercantile life, and reopened my books with the determination eventually to proclaim Christ and Him crucified either at home or abroad.

Soon after, with ten or twelve young people of about my own age, I made a public profession of my faith, and was received into the Congregational church of which my parents had been members. In connection with this ceremony I was baptized, as I had not received that Sacrament in childhood. This is a point worth special consideration here, for— unlike the original Church of Christ, which has always regarded Baptism as a necessary Sacrament, obligatory for children as well as for adults—the Protestant sect to which my parents belonged—and there are many like it—did not believe in Infant Baptism.

In fact, *apart from the tradition of the Catholic Church,* which Protestants disregard, it is difficult to find authority for this custom. In Scripture, faith is stated to be essential to the rite of Baptism, and every instance of Baptism mentioned in the Bible is of adults.

Infant Baptism was, however, practiced very early in the Church's history, and the Fathers justified it. St. Irenaeus, for example, says: "Christ came to save *all*, who through Him are born again to God, infants and little ones, boys, young men and the aged." (Iren. ii, 22,4). The usual Protestant belief is that Baptism bestows upon the infant a capacity for receiving this grace when it shall at the proper age have ratified the vows made for it by its sponsors. The Catholic doctrine, on the contrary, is that the grace is bestowed upon the baptized infant then and there. While many Protestants, principally Anglicans and Episcopalians, adopt this custom, fully as many reject it. Some even consider Baptism to be no Sacrament at all, but merely a rite, connected with admission into the Church! Others, although the institution was indubitably established by the Son of God, have actually condemned it as sinful! Great numbers of Protestants have, therefore, never been baptized.

It is difficult for me now to understand how devout Christians, like my parents, could have failed to recognize Baptism as an indispensable Sacrament—that is, an outward sign of an inward and spiritual grace, instituted by Christ Himself; for few of our Saviour's words are so emphatic as the following: "Verily, verily, I say unto thee, Except a man be born of water and of the Spirit, he cannot enter the kingdom of God." He likewise commissioned His Apostles to teach all nations, "*baptizing* them in the name of the Father, and of the Son, and of the Holy Ghost."

As for my youthful associates and myself, I am sure that we regarded our Baptism merely as a solemn ceremony, and had no notion whatever of the doctrine of the Catholic and Anglican Churches—that *it confers on the adult a special sanctifying grace, remits his sins, and makes upon his soul an indelible mark, or "character."* Yet of the truth that the Sacrament of Baptism is primarily intended for the remission of sins, we have abundant evidence: for St. Peter, as recorded in *Acts* 2:38, distinctly says: "Be baptized, every one of you, in the name of Jesus Christ, for the *remission of your sins*"; and the Nicene Creed states also: "I confess one Baptism *for the remission of sins.*" But of this and many other doctrinal points we youthful neophytes knew practically nothing, for our instruction in such matters had been very superficial.

In fact, ignorance of the fundamental dogmas of Christianity is the rule, rather than the exception, among Non-Conformists. Although my parents had brought me up religiously, I personally never had received the least instruction in the catechism, and I doubt if any of my companions were better informed than myself. What we knew of the creed of our Church we had "absorbed" from sermons, family prayers and Sunday school lessons. Nor were we, as postulants, asked any questions about doctrines! As I remember the scene, each one of us in turn was requested to relate his or her "experience," which naturally was a story of religious sentiment. We merely took for granted the truth of the creed, as we found it given in the constitution of that particular church in which we pledged ourselves to Christ and to His service.

The university years that followed were characterized by nothing specially worth recording. Surrounded by religious influences, it was not difficult for the professedly Christian students of my college to lead at least a nominal Christian life. This in my own case was distinguished neither by apathy on the one hand, nor special spirituality on the other. No serious doubts disturbed me, and I looked forward to the ministry as my career, though my original wish to be a missionary to the heathen had considerably diminished. Accordingly, without remarkable enthusiam, yet equally without misgivings or regrets, I entered, in my twenty-second year, the theological seminary of ——.

My fellow "theologues" were for the most part men of excellent character, though of moderate mentality. As scholars and as speakers, most of them were evidently doomed to mediocrity. So true was this of some of them, that I often wondered whether they would ever have adopted this profession if it had not been made so easy for them. The seminary was richly endowed, and offered gratis to such students as applied for aid, not only free instruction, but also comfortable rooms and board. Moreover, after their second year of study they always could earn money by preaching to congregations temporarily without pastors. Under such circumstances, men who are graduating from college without money, and who for the first time face the world's fierce struggle for existence, are easily induced to enter the ministry. In such cases it is a great temptation to choose the line of least resistance, and this, if it be the Protestant ministry, leads almost certainly to an assured livelihood. In America, it is true, the Protestant clerical profession is, as a rule, miserably paid (see Chapter XII), and in small country parishes ministers have often to endure real hardships; yet, if a youthful graduate from a theological seminary possesses pleasing manners and average ability, he will have little difficulty in obtaining a pastorate, in which no great amount of learning and oratorical skill is necessary. Especially, if he becomes an Anglican, or in America an Episcopalian, clergyman, he can usually make a desirable marriage and enjoy a good social standing, irrespective of his intellectuality.

One of the studies of the first year at this seminary was Hebrew, and I shall never forget the pitiful efforts made by some of my associates to master the difficulties of that language. The poor fellow at the desk adjoining mine was frequently the picture of despair, when asked to conjugate a Hebrew verb, or to translate a line of Genesis. Perhaps a third of the class derived some benefit from reading thus a moiety of the Old Testament in the original, but for the rest it was a mournful tragedy, and can have been no help whatever to them in their subsequent ministry.

The study of the New Testament in Greek was, of course, more beneficial, for all of us had read considerable Greek in college, and the familiar English version of the Bible made it impossible for the dullest student to fall or flounder in translation, as frequently was the case in Hebrew. Our interest in the study of the words of Christ and the Apostles was also naturally much greater than in that of the remoter and more difficult writings of the Old Testament. Moreover, in our professor of New Testament exegesis we had a clever, stimulating teacher. Yet it was precisely in connection with this study that I found my greatest theological difficulties.

The copy of the New Testament in Greek which I used as a textbook, was the valuable edition compiled by the celebrated Dean Alford. This had, as a rule, at the top of every page two or three lines of Greek, while much of the remaining space was filled, *in fine print,* with comments on the textual variations of those lines, as found in different manuscripts of the New Testament! Up to that time I had known little of the literary composition and transcription of the Scriptures, nor had I realized that between the date of the oldest New Testament manuscript in our possession and the death of Jesus stretches an interval of more than three hundred years. It is true, the interval between our oldest manuscripts of the classical writers—Homer, Plato, Cicero, Horace and others—and the date of *their* lives is a still greater one. Nevertheless it came to me as a shock to learn that we have not a single manuscript of the Gospel which takes us nearer to the time of Christ than we are to the age of Queen Elizabeth. The disappearance of the original manuscripts of the New Testament is, of course, not surprising, for the frail papyrus on which the previous words were originally written was extremely perishable; and later copies, made on vellum, also required the greatest care to save them from destruction. Moreover, some Emperors, like Diocletian, ordered that all obtainable Christian manuscripts should be burned. Of the researches of scholars in this matter, and of their ways of bridging over that time-interval by means of quotations from writings of the Fathers, I knew then next to nothing, for *no information was given us in the seminary on that subject.*

I was greatly disturbed, therefore, to find that in the New Testament manuscripts which we possess there are no less than 100,000 different readings! I have since learned not to exaggerate the significance of this fact, for in reality they are for the most part unimportant, and show an absence of collusion or dissimulation in the writing of the Scriptures which amounts to a historical guarantee of their genuineness. Many of these textual differences probably occurred through the carelessness of copyists, others were caused by the creeping into the text of footnotes made by previous transcribers, while others still may have been made intentionally by conscientious men, who thought that they could thus improve the older text, or at least explain its meaning. Mistakes could also easily be made because the Scriptures of the first ten centuries after Christ were written in large capital ("uncial") characters, without Greek accents or punctuation, and even without division between the words!

More serious, however, seemed to me the absence from the oldest manuscripts of some entire passages found in the later ones. Such paragraphs were, in my edition of the Greek New Testament, enclosed in brackets, to indicate that—being found only in later manuscripts—they were considered less authentic. In such cases the oldest existing manuscripts—the "Sinaitic," formerly in St. Petersburg; the "Vaticanus," now in Rome; and the "Alexandrinus," in the British Museum— are usually regarded as the most authoritative, but not invariably; for if *many* of the later manuscripts contain a reading, which the earlier ones lack, their united—even if more recent—testimony is sometimes thought to be more decisive than the negative attitude of the older codices. What the *precise* text of the lost originals was, we have no way now of determining, save as we find quotations from them in the writings of the old Church Fathers and their pagan critics. But such omissions do not necessarily prove that the passages are of an origin later than the early Gospels. They may have been intentionally omitted for some specific reason connected with the particular church for which the copy had been made; for at certain epochs and in certain places it seems to have been thought best by the Bishops (owing perhaps to the unusual prevalence in that city of some special heresy), that certain passages, liable to be misunderstood by the local church members, should be omitted from the manuscript ordered for that community.[1]

Copies of the Books of the New Testament were not invariably made then on the theory that every word of the original manuscripts *must* be reproduced. They were transcribed for definite purposes. During the first one hundred and seventy years after the birth of Christ, although those Books were certainly regarded as sacred and inspired, the Apostolic oral tradition was still so fresh, that written authority was less frequently appealed to.

Practical difficulties also contributed to the omission of certain portions of the text. The manuscripts were always in the form of narrow rolls, which—being of necessity unrolled to be read, and rolled again to be put away—were liable to be injured. They were, moreover, of a uniform length for convenience in handling, and sometimes, to avoid having too long a roll, or to economize the expense of another "Book," a sentence might be altogether omitted. I mention these difficulties, because, as a Protestant, I was much more disturbed by them than a Catholic would have been.

Catholics, as a rule, attach comparatively little importance to these textual discrepancies, for their theological system is built up, not from dead manuscripts alone, but from the history of the doctrines, the *traditions of the Fathers, and the infallible voice of the Living Church.* Protestants, on the other hand, who base their dogmas merely on conflicting texts, who have no other standard than the silent Book, and who acknowledge

---

1. Similarly, the Gothic Bishop, Vulpilas (+ A.D. 381), in his translation of the Old Testament, in the Codex Argenteus, intentionally omitted the Books of Kings, in order not to make his own warlike Gothic people still more predatory through reading of the martial exploits of David.

no authority but private judgment, are very seriously embarrassed by these differences, since many of their doctrines find their confirmation or refutation in the acceptance or rejection of a certain reading. Accordingly, it finally dawned upon me that *the Bible alone, without a competent interpreter,* cannot explain all that is necessary for religion; but where was I to find in Protestantism a competent authority which had the right to settle questions about doctrinal interpretation and textual authenticity? Individual opinions were as numerous among Protestants as the discrepancies themselves. Even my Professor could give me merely his private "view" as to which of a number of conflicting readings was the right one, but this and his idea of what dogmatic conclusion should be drawn from it had no authority whatever.

This seemed to me intellectual chaos. The Anglican Dean Farrar, in his *The Bible; Its Meaning and Supremacy,* states unmistakably that in order to ascertain what the word of God, contained in Scripture, really is, *we must find out for ourselves, and choose what satisfies our reason; for our own private judgment is our final court of appeal, to know how much of the Bible we can accept.* (pp. 118-29). But, if the Bible be a Revelation from God, how can it be interpreted by every individual to suit himself? Of what value is a heavenly manual which we may mutilate at will?

While I was thus floundering in my exegetical and *theological* difficulties, a work which deeply interested me was the "Examination of Canon Liddon's Lectures on the Divinity of Our Lord and Saviour Jesus Christ." The author of this volume announces himself anonymously as "A clergyman of the Church of England," and this fact proves what I shall soon again refer to—that Anglican clergymen differ so widely in their doctrinal beliefs, that they promulgate nearly every variety of Christian dogma. The book is, in fact, an adverse criticism of the biblical arguments brought forward by Canon Liddon to prove the Divinity of Christ; and its author argues that *it is impossible for an unprejudiced reader of the Bible to deduce from that source only the doctrine of Christ's co-equal deity!* "The really Scriptural position," he declares, "is that Christ fills, in the scale of being, a place not perfectly defined, but certainly above man, and *as certainly beneath God.*" (p. 307). "If," he asserts, "that doctrine be from God, facts of the plainest character appear to compel the admission that He has seen fit to promulgate it, *not through the Sacred Volume, but through the living voice of a divinely organized and divinely inspired Church.*" (p. 34). In other words, this clergyman of the Church of England attempts through more than four hundred pages to prove that St. Paul *disbelieved in the Divinity of Christ,* although assigning to Him a position higher than that of all other creatures. The fact that such a conclusion could be reached by a Christian clergyman by means of a critical study of the text of the New Testament, and that such ideas could be held and published by a regularly ordained priest of the Church of England, gave the last blow to my already tottering faith in the infallible text of Scripture, *as interpreted by private judgment.* Certainly something more was needed than a silent Book, if from its pages one clergyman of the Anglican Church can be led to "affirm with unhesitating confidence that Christ is *not* Very God," while another clergyman of the same Church asserts his firm belief that He *is* Very God!

I felt that some supreme and living authority must be found to settle these vexed questions, unless the Church of Christ were to dissolve and perish. When able students of the Bible come to such diametrically opposite interpretations of it, it is evident that this volume, precious as it is, is not so simple a book that everyone, learned or unlearned, can readily understand its meaning. St. Peter, in fact, says expressly that in St. Paul's Epistles there are some things "hard to be understood, which they that are unlearned and unstable wrest, as they do also the other Scriptures, unto their own destruction." (*2 Pet.* 3:16). The Bible, therefore, in and of itself can never take the place of a living and infallible teacher. It remains silent under all the tortures inflicted on its texts. The voiceless book and complicated manuscripts cannot alone decide the matters which disturb the soul.

Suddenly, as my heart cried out thus for a divinely appointed interpreter of God's Revelation, I realized for the first time that Christ Himself neither wrote a book, nor dictated a line of one to any of His disciples. What He had done was *to found a Church,* which He had promised always to remain with and to guide. If He had wished that His religion should be propagated and preserved by a book only, *why should He not have written one?* The truth is that Christianity preceded the New Testament. The Gospels and Epistles were written for the benefit of a Church *which already existed.* The Gospels were not composed until sixty years after the death of Christ, nor was the Canon definitely established till the Council of Carthage, A.D. 397. Hundreds of Christians never saw the Books of the New Testament; and before a line of them had been traced, "Christ and Him crucified" had been preached to thousands, many churches had been founded, and converts innumerable had been made among both Jews and Gentiles.

Why, then, did I not see that the original Catholic Church was precisely the divinely instituted Teacher and supreme Authority which I was seeking for? Because, like millions of otherwise well-educated Protestants, I knew then practically nothing of that Church, save what intolerant abuse or unfair criticism had given me. It is nothing short of amazing that Protestants, as a rule, not only know so little of the Catholic Church, but that they *wish* to know so little of it. It is deplorable that, although so many books explanatory of Catholicism are written and published, most Protestants refuse to open them, or even to hear a sermon from a Catholic preacher! Occasionally they ask a Catholic: "What is the present religious belief of the Catholic Church?" not realizing that, although one may appropriately ask about the "present religious belief" of the ever-changing Protestant sects, one cannot do so in regard to the Catholic Church, *for her belief does not change,* since she preserves inviolate the ancient teaching given her by Christ and the Apostles, which through the aid of the Holy Ghost has been retained and guarded by her from the beginning.

Little of this did I, as a callow theological student in a Protestant seminary, know. Nevertheless, I felt compelled to go to someone for advice, and naturally turned to one of my professors. He listened to me with probably as much sympathy as such a scholarly recluse could feel. He seemed, however, to think my case a serious one, particularly as my doubts were shared by one at least of my classmates. To obviate our difficulties, therefore, he kindly volunteered to give our class some lectures of his own upon the proofs of Christ's Divinity. This he soon did, and I well remember the significant looks and ironical laughter indulged in by our fellow students, as certain remarks and arguments of the lecturer were thought by them to disconcert and put to rout my comrade and myself. These lectures did not, however, remove my exegetical troubles, and others were soon added to them.

Once more I sought the aid of my instructor, but this time, if I had expected from him bread, I received only a stone. I recollect in particular asking him how he met the scientific difficulties connected with the Star of Bethlehem. Why, for example, should God have sanctioned a pseudo-science like astrology? And, since we know that every visible star is either one of our planets or else a mighty sun, separated from us by an inconceivable distance, how was it possible to believe that a stupendous mass of matter, probably larger than our own great luminary, could come within even a hundred million miles of our solar system without wrecking it completely? Moreover, how could such a gigantic body indicate with precision any portion of our tiny earth?

It would have been easy for the learned man to have pointed out to me the fact that the great astronomer, Kepler, had found a confirmation of the Gospel story in the condition of the stellar firmament in the seventh year before the Christian era, as we reckon it—the year accepted now by many scholars as the probable date of the Nativity. [More recent research supports the traditional date for Christ's birth, i.e., that He was born in the year 1 A.D.—*Editor, 1990.*] It certainly is most remarkable that in that year—repeated three times, in the months of May, October and December—there occurred a conjunction of the planets Jupiter and Saturn in the same constellation, and—more extraordinary still—that a conjunction of those two satellites with the planet Mars took place in the same year—a marvelous phenomenon, which occurs only once in 794 years! (see *Encyclopaedia Britannica,* Vol. 27, p. 80, and Vol. 13, p. 661). This was an incident sure to excite the amazement of Chaldean astronomers, since such an event would, according to the tenets of astrology, foretell terrestrial happenings of supreme importance. Even if this had been unknown to my professor, he could have cited, as a possible explanation of the Star of Bethlehem, the well-authenticated instances of new stars suddenly appearing in the heavens, and, after blazing for a time with variable splendor, vanishing again from sight. As for God's making use of such a phenomenon nineteen centuries ago, in connection with the then prevailing notion that such sidereal occurrences are associated with our human destinies, the worthy Doctor of Divinity might surely have reminded me that in God's manifestations to mankind He often uses methods suited to men's limited comprehensions and to the views and customs then prevailing; and if I had objected that the moment of the actual blazing up of the "new star" was probably several centuries previous to men's perception of it, because its waves of light, though traversing the awful void at inconceivable speed, could then first reach our distant orb, he could have answered, "What difficulty does such a preparation for the Nativity present to the Creator of this universe, to whom time is but one eternal Now?"

But nothing of all this did the professor deem it worth his while to mention. He merely smiled a trifle enigmatically, and gave me the advice to make as little reference in my sermons to that point as possible! This staggered me. Could it be true that in Christian theology there was an esoteric and an exoteric system, and must its teachers laugh, like Roman augurs, when they met professionally? Some of my readers may object that the case I mention was exceptional. I do not affirm the contrary. I merely tell my own experience.

Under these circumstances, therefore, it is not surprising that, a few months later, a member of the faculty called upon me and, with a manner that betrayed embarrassment, remarked: "Mr. ——, you know we are approaching the time when the students of your class will present themselves before the Board of Examiners as candidates for ordination. Now, just between ourselves, I want to advise you and your friend X not to appear there. Intellectually, both of you are qualified to stand the test; and, morally, to the best of my knowledge, you are both irreproachable. But" (he cleared his throat, and smiled) "you know there are some 'hard heads' on that board, who would scent heterodoxy in a moment, if you and X began to answer honestly their questions upon certain points. An uproar would ensue. Your licenses to preach would be refused. Worse still—for us—the matter would be mentioned and exaggerated in the newspapers, and the seminary would acquire a reputation for heresy."

This was a blow the effect of which he evidently perceived, for he continued with a confidential smile: "But after all, Mr. ——, why do you specially want to *preach?* You are much better fitted to be a professor. Why not go abroad and spend a year or two in study? Then you could very well return, and be yourself. . .a Professor of Exegesis! That is what *you* ought to do."

When he had left, I paced my room in agitation. After all these years of preparation, must I now turn back at the very threshold of the Christian ministry—not because I was incompetent as a scholar, nor on account of any perceived defect in either my morality or spirituality, but merely because my theological difficulties on certain points—largely dependent on disputed texts of Scripture—might, if disclosed to the Board of Examiners and the public, scandalize the seminary? Yet I was sure that, if my instructor were himself obliged to pass a similar examination, and to answer certain questions truthfully, he also would be liable to the charge of heresy. I felt instinctively that he shared my doubts. At all events, he made no effort to dispel them, nor did he tell me what he did believe. He merely expressed the wish that I should not inform the public of my scruples!

About this time I had a confidential conversation with a young minister of my acquaintance. He told me he was most unhappy. Doubts similar to mine had assailed him also during his course of study, but he had kept them to himself, had somehow managed to pass the examination for ordination, and now was bitterly conscious of the fact that he was preaching much that he did not believe! I never shall forget his mournful words. "Old friend," he said, "it is too late for me to act as you can do. I have worked all these years to be a minister, and *orthodoxy owes me now a living.* Moreover, I am married, and have settled down in a parish. To tell my people and the world that I no longer believe the doctrines I proclaim would bring down ruin on myself and family. I simply cannot do it. I therefore steer around the dangerous points, and get along as best I can. The people want a certain amount of emotional religious treacle given them once a week, and I am paid to furnish it. I therefore serve it out to them, mixed with such ethical ingredients and literary spice as I am capable of producing." This frank avowal of my friend not only shocked and saddened me, but filled me with alarm, lest possibly such a fate might yet be mine were I not true to my convictions.

Fortunately for me, at this very time there occurred, in the providence of God, a sudden change in my circumstances, which enabled me to suspend temporarily my theological studies, and to enter upon a career of teaching. At the end of the year, being still undecided in my views, and conscientiously unwilling to return to the seminary, I resolved to make a tour of the Continent and the nearer Orient, hoping to find from a new point of view some light as to the ultimate path I should pursue. This year of travel did not, however, smooth away my theological difficulties, and I was forced to ask myself whether I should adopt the profession of teaching permanently, or finish my theological studies in another way, and become a Unitarian minister.

Upon the latter point I determined to consult an eminent Unitarian clergyman, settled over a wealthy, fashionable church in the metropolis. After hearing my story to the end, he frankly said to me: "My advice to you is *not* to become a minister of this denomination. What can a young man now expect from the Unitarian Church? It is moribund. It has no future. *This is not the form of Christianity that is going to survive.* I am an old man, and shall remain where I am, but you had better keep out of Unitarianism."

Nearly half a century has passed since those words were addressed to me, but they still echo in my heart. I left that clergyman's house and kindly presence profoundly disillusioned. I called to mind the wish expressed by Thomas Jefferson in 1822: "I trust there is not a young many now born in the United States who will not die a Unitarian!" "Truly," I said to myself, "that ardent desire of the great American does not seem likely to be realized. On the contrary, this refined modern Arianism, like many other forms into which Protestantism has dissolved, is only one of numerous intellectual halting places between Rome and Rationalism. It is evident that I must choose one or other of these two extremes."

"Rome" seemed to me then, however, hardly worth considering; for I again confess with shame that up to that time I had never opened a Catholic book, and knew of the Catholic Church only what reading on the Protestant side had taught me. Nevertheless, I thought that so-called "knowledge" quite sufficient!

Though fairly well educated in matters of Church history

and theology—according to the superficial standards of my seminary—I, like most Protestants (the High Church Anglicans perhaps excepted), took it for granted that all the calumnies which I had read of "Rome" were true, and therefore I concluded that conditions which I had found unbearable in Protestantism would be much worse in Catholicism.

Accordingly, although it was a matter on which my soul's eternal welfare might depend, so great were both my ignorance and arrogance, that I made no attempt to investigate the claims and doctrines of the Catholic Church, but chose deliberately Rationalism, whose ardent advocate I then remained for forty years.

Chapter 2

IN THE WILDERNESS OF RATIONALISM

And that inverted bowl they call the Sky,
Whereunder, crawling, cooped we live and die,
Lift not your hands to it for help, for it
As impotently rolls as you or I.
                                    —OMAR KHAYYÁM.

Some day when Atheism has been tried and found wanting,
it [Society] will look around for a fixed point in the social chaos,
and will find nothing but the Catholic Church. —The
Unworthy Pact, p. 243.

Notre intelligence tient dans l'ordre des choses intelligibles le
même rang, que notre corps dans l'étendue de la nature.
                                    —PASCAL.

RATIONALISM DID not mean for me Indifferentism.
The world was then in intellectual ferment. Those
were the days of Bishop Colenso in South Africa,
of James Martineau in England, of Emerson in Concord.
The scientific and religious elements of the country stood
"at daggers drawn." Mankind was quivering under the impressions made upon it by Darwin in his *Origin of Species*
and *Descent of Man,* by Spencer in his *First Principles,* and
by Huxley in his daring exposition of Agnosticism. These
formed the great triumvirate of the new theology. Lesser
luminaries, with whom I came into closer contact through
sermons, lectures, books and conversation, were Moncure
D. Conway, Octavius Frothingham, Francis E. Abbott, editor of the Boston *Index,* Minot J. Savage, the radical Unitarian minister, also of Boston, and, finally, the mocking,
eloquent iconoclast, Ingersoll [considered to be the founder
of American atheism].

That was a time when young men like myself went every Sunday eagerly to listen to some scientific lecture, "Free Religious" address, or Unitarian sermon, and even in the week-time zealously frequented radical debating clubs, where papers were discussed on "Immortality," "Science and Religion," "The Bible," "Omar Khayyám's Philosophy," "Gnostics and Agnostics," and a score of similar themes. We had, in fact, what might be called *a positive enthusiasm for unbelief.*

It is true, this was not to any great extent embarrassed by definite knowledge; but all that was unknown to us we thought unknowable! Our great mistake was that we accepted without question, not merely all the positive truths which science brought to light, but also *all the radical deductions which certain scientists drew from them.*

We disbelieved in God and in His government of the universe because we *thought* that science proved their non-existence; yet in reality we based our unbelief on the authority of a few men, not much older than we were, who frequently disagreed among themselves. At the same time we ignored the statements of older and far greater scientists, and scornfully rejected the authority of the Church, and the traditions and testimony of 1,900 years!

A truthful picture of that time is given by Canon Sheehan, D.D., in his *Early Essays and Lectures:* "All sacred things of religion, names that were spoken with bared heads and bended knees, sacred stories that had so often brought comfort to the sorrowful, and sacred hopes that had so long had their consecrated shrines in the human heart, are made the subject of derision. The scoff of the unbeliever has degraded in the eyes of thousands the purest and holiest revelations of Heaven." (p. 57).

So far did we finally carry our hostility to the Christian religion, that almost any ideas which bore the stamp of flavor of Christianity were obnoxious to us. Many of the parables and precepts of the Gospels would have been lauded by us to the skies, had they been uttered by some Chinese sage, or couched in other words than those employed by Christ and His disciples. Not for the world would we have spoken of "God" or the "devil" as real entities, but we would talk complacently of "something Real that is Divine," or "something Real that is Diabolic," as if we could transform the nature of things by speaking of them in the abstract, or by writing their names in capitals! Thus did we cheat ourselves with words, and caught at every subterfuge, in order to avoid a reference to the Almighty as a Person. Thus did we turn our backs upon the Light of the World, to hail some tallow candle as the Morning Star, and to "explain Christianity by explaining it away."

There is much truth in the words of Father Benson: "The mind most impervious to the Church's influence is that of the tolerably educated; the young man who has studied a little, but not much, and that chiefly from small handbooks; the young woman who attends University Extension lectures, but not too many of them."

To the young and superficially educated there is special danger in having people older and better-informed than themselves assume, *as a matter of course,* that a belief in an intelligent Creator is obsolete, and that Materialism is to be the "religion of the future"; for untrained minds are wont to cower before the ridicule of anyone who claims superior knowledge, although his bold assertions may be mere assumptions. As a matter of fact, although we all talked much at that time about "Free Religion," in our hearts we wanted no religion whatsoever; and though we were forever clamoring for "religious liberty," what we really meant by that term was liberty to have no religion ourselves, and to discourage everybody else from having any. Spencer had stated in his *Sociology* that "a religious system is a normal and *essential* factor in every evolving society"; but we interpreted this as meaning that, when society had evolved enough, it would slough off its religions, as a snake discards its skin.

To counteract, if possible, this stream of scientific skepticism, the Protestant Churches founded lecture courses, and able champions of orthodoxy were engaged to refute the arguments of their opponents. These courses we attended, and afterwards discussed them fiercely. No doubt our minds were often too much prejudiced to form a fair decision, yet I recall those days with wonder, as I look about me at the present rising generation, and note its relative indifference to such subjects.

If skepticism was the characteristic of our youthful epoch, indifferentism is the "Religion" that prevails today. At present, youths as old as we were then could hardly be induced to attend a lecture—let us say, on "The Miraculous in the Bible," were one to be given. Some of them never hear a sermon of any kind. They prefer to play golf, or to "take a spin" in an automobile. I do not think it an improvement.

Bad as our skepticism was, it showed at least mental activity *in a realm higher than that of mere materialism.* The world today is intellectually active chiefly in mechanical inventions and the art of money-getting. The greatness of this age is material, not moral; rapid, not religious. But we are paying the penalty for this.

Mistaken as we were in many things, and absolutely wrong in our rejection of Christianity, we were at least concerned with themes of paramount importance. There was some hope for us, for we took interest in discussions which pertained to the immaterial and the spiritual. We may have been fools, but we were capable of becoming wiser, because we still read, thought, investigated and debated. There was some life in us for the Spirit of God to work on. The frozen callousness of today is less encouraging.

Our modern youths have practically no sense of spiritual values, since they have grown up in an age of self-indulgence and indifference to religious questions. Many of them are by inheritance what their fathers became through conviction— godless agnostics, or else materialists, who see in money, luxury and pleasure the only things worth caring for. It is not too much to say that at the present time millions of youthful men and women, who are to decide the future of Great Britain and America, are being brought up in ignorance of the Bible, of the teachings of Christ, and of the fundamentals of Christianity. Into their lives there enters neither worship, nor even serious reading! Their temples are the theaters, their shrines the "movies," their Scriptures the newspapers, their Sunday school books the Sunday "Comic Supplements"! If they were questioned on religious subjects, they would probably reply, that of the existence of God, personal immortality, or a future day of judgment they knew nothing and cared less. I doubt if thousands of them ever say a prayer. This state of things has brought about one of the most conspicuous characteristics of our age—*Irreverence,* especially for everything connected with religion.[1]

Instances of this fact are numberless, but the following is worth recording. In an antiquary's shop in Switzerland there was lately to be seen a beautiful old reliquary. It stood upon a pedestal, flanked by exquisite statuettes of Saints, while the summit was surmounted by a figure of our Saviour. In the center had once stood a crystal tube, five inches high, containing a sacred relic. The beauty and richness of the object can be estimated from the fact that it was purchased for 2,800 francs. The purchaser has, however, substituted for the relic-holder an. . .electric light bulb! It is to serve hereafter as a lamp upon his writing table. Viewed merely from the aesthetic standpoint, this is regrettable as an act of vandalism, but it is also sad to think of the lack of reverence thus exhibited. Of all the prayers which have been offered up to God before this precious shrine in memory of the saintly soul, a fragment of whose earthly vestment was once treasured here, its present owner doubtless never thinks. For him it is a pretty ornament—a lucky "find"; and in its consecrated

---

1. Among the advertisements which make hideous the landscapes of America, and are particularly conspicuous at night in letters of fire above the crowds of Broadway is one of almost inconceivable vulgarity and profanity, which urges the people to "BOOST JESUS."

center is now seen the typical symbol of our "progress"—an electric burner, by the light of which he may perhaps read Bernard Shaw's *Mrs. Warren's Profession* or Sir Oliver Lodge's *Raymond*!

Unfortunately, such acts of desecration multiply themselves continually. I know of a resident in a European capital, who acquired a silver altar-front from an old Benedictine abbey in Sicily. This he has actually set above his sideboard as a background for his fine liqueurs! The same man had the unhappy inspiration to use, as vases for bouquets of flowers, five old chalices, which had no doubt contained hundreds of times during the celebration of the Mass, the Holy Sacrament![2]

So far has our flippant, practically godless society drifted! Irreverence and materialism are acting like corrosives on its character, and are eating away its old foundations. We see their bad effects in much of our modern literature, where a desire to be "breezy" and to shock the reader's sensibilities in regard to sacred themes is thought to be a proof of genius, or, at all events, of originality. Yet flippancy in reference to God, immortality, or the religion of Christ is more than indecorous, it is indecent. Such writers and sensational preachers often seem to be the progeny of those who passed the Son of God upon the Cross, wagging their heads. Let us be charitable enough to believe that they "know not what they do."

My last station on the way to absolute infidelity was the philosophy of Auguste Comte in his singular paraphrase of religion, known as Positivism. This religious wraith, insofar as it represented Moderate Socialism, appealed powerfully to certain rare, ascetic souls, like Frederic Harrison and George

---

2. As an example of modern irreverence, bordering on blasphemy, it may be mentioned that a well-known professional dancer recently appeared—of course in a state of semi-nudity—in the Trocadero, Paris, in two new dances, representing "The Childhood of Jesus" and "The Redemption"! And, as if this monstrous impropriety were insufficient, the first performance of these dances was given on Good Friday!

Eliot, who were capable of being devoted to "Humanity" in the abstract. It can, however, never dominate the masses of mankind, and has found few followers. It is dying out. A wit described one of its services as being an assembly, where there were present "three persons and no God"! Curiously enough, much of the formal framework of Positivism is derived from Catholicism, for Comte was in early life a Catholic, and never entirely lost the influence of his youthful training. Huxley, in fact, called Positivism "Catholicism without Christianity."

The truth is, Comte saw plainly that *society cannot exist without a religion of some sort,* and furthermore that religion implies worship. Some object, therefore, worthy of worship had to be found by him; and, since according to Positivism there is no God, Comte deified the abstract notion of Humanity. In the elaborate scheme which he built up from this foundation philosophers were to replace priests, while inventors, scientists, poets and heroes were to be regarded as the Saints of Positivism. Paris was to be to them what Rome is to the Catholics, and Mecca is to Moslems; and a substitute for the Blessed Virgin was to be symbolized by a "woman of thirty, with a child in her arms"! In short, the "Religion" of Comte was a combination of noble ideals and great absurdities. C. Kegan Paul has said of it: "Positivism is a fair-weather creed, when men are strong, happy, untempted, or ignorant that they are tempted, and so long as a future life and its dread possibilities do not enter their thoughts; but it has no message for the sorry and the sinful, no restoration for the erring, no succour in the hour of death."

Nevertheless it attracted us for a time, as a novelty. We did not stop to ask ourselves why Comte and many other great men were agreed that man has a religious instinct, and must accordingly have a religion to give satisfaction to that instinct. Yet, if so, where did this religious instinct come from? If man *must* have some sort of a religion, his need must correspond to a reality. Hence *Atheism is antagonistic to a universal want and instinct of humanity.*

What we young men inevitably drifted into finally was arrogant infidelity and materialism. I do not know why we all derived great satisfaction from the theory that we had descended from an ape-like animal, but we certainly did. It was probably because we thought that it refuted the Biblical account of man's creation, and made the doctrine of his Fall and Redemption quite untenable. Anything like a Divine Revelation of man's origin and relation to God was, of course, rejected by our rationalistic circle with disdain, and, having lost our faith in such a Revelation, we came to lead a practically godless life.

I, at least, never went to church for public worship; Christianity was to me but one of numerous religions, all of human origin; the universe was an insoluble mystery; the existence of God was probable, but the term was meaningless; Christ was a noble teacher and examplar, but a man, who had been born and died like other mortals, with no resurrection; whether the soul existed separate from the body was a matter for conjecture; in any case, its conscious immortality was very questionable; reincarnation was a pleasing theory, which fairly well explained the presence here of suffering and evil, but the essential thread of *memory* was lacking to make a previous life of any real advantage; death was a matter hardly to be feared, since it was universal and as natural as birth; moreover, if it meant eternal sleep, it was a boon; if not, one could at least suppose, according to the theory of evolution, that our next stage of existence would be an improvement on the present one; and since the inhabitants of this planet, if they survived the dissolution of the body, would probably be kept together, wherever they might be transplanted, conscious reunion with our loved ones seemed not utterly unlikely.

Of all these things, however, I thought as little as possible; and, much as an ostrich thrusts its head into the sand to avoid the sight of coming danger, I lived on, apathetic, hopeless and apparently indifferent. Yet in my better moments I indulged in hopes and feelings which I was ashamed to reveal to anyone. In my portfolio lie several poems, some original, some selected, which well describe my doubts and sentiments, that would not die. Perhaps I cannot do better than to quote from one of them.

At The Monastery of Acqua fredda

By Acqua Fredda's cloister-wall
I pause to feel the mountain breeze,
And watch the shadows eastward fall
From immemorial cypress trees;

While mirrored peaks of stainless snow
Turn crimson 'neath the father shore,
And here and there the sunset glow
Threads diamonds on a dripping oar.

But now a tremor breaks the spell,
And stirs to life the languid air—
It is the convent's vesper bell,
The plaintive call to evening prayer;

That prayer which rises like a sigh
From every sorrow-laden breast,
When twilight dims the garish sky,
And day is dying in the west.

How sweet and clear, how soft and low
Those vesper orisons are sung
In Rome's grand speech of long ago,
Forever old, forever young!

So full of life of hate and greed,
So vain the world's poor tinselled show,
What wonder that some souls have need
To flee from all its sin and woe?

I would not join them; yet, in truth,
I feel, in leaving them at prayer,
That something precious of my youth,
Long lost to me, is treasured there.

Chapter 3

THE AWAKENING

The gods are just, and of our pleasant vices
Make instruments to scourge us.
       —SHAKESPEARE.

I know but one way of fortifying my soul against these gloomy
presages and terrors of mind, and that is, by securing to myself
the friendship and protection of that Being who disposes of events
and governs futurity.—ADDISON.

There is a fairer hope for nations animated by a sincere reli-
gious sentiment . . . than for a people who have lost all faith
in a future, and are living without any God.—DRAPER.

Nations plunged in the abyss of irreligion must necessarily
be nations of anarchy.—DRAPER.

THUS OUTWARDLY indifferent, but inwardly unhappy, I drifted on toward life's inevitable end . . . till
suddenly the spectacle of the unspeakable horrors of
the World War and the terrible débâcle of our boasted civilization aroused me from my torpor, like the trump of God.

The outbreak of hostilities in 1914 found me in one of
the European warring countries, and circumstances of a domestic nature retained me during the entire war not only in a
belligerent land, but actually in its inner war zone, often within
the sound of cannon and the fall of bombs. My purpose is
not to describe here, even briefly, the sufferings and privations which I saw and shared in regions bordering on that
belt of battle. If any of my readers have been overwhelmed
with horror, pity and dismay at merely reading in their
sheltered homes of such conditions thousands of miles away,
they can perhaps imagine what it meant to live, day in, day

out, for nearly five years with the dying and the dead, the wounded and the crippled, the widows and the orphans, and thousands upon thousands of brave youths departing. . . never to return. Those were five years of well-nigh universal wretchedness, and sometimes of complete despair. My wish is to relate how this encampment at the gates of Hell, this sojourn in the valley of the shadow of death, slowly but surely drew me back to God.

Life is a great teacher, but death is a still greater one. To know that thousands of brave souls are being hurried into eternity, day after day and every hour of the day, not "somewhere" far away, but just beyond that range of hills and inside the horizon's verge; to learn that some of those poor, slaughtered boys were my own friends, or sons of friends; to see their parents meet the awful news; to look upon the ghastly wrecks of what but yesterday were stalwart youths; and then to note the ever-lengthening line of shrouded forms and read the lists of desolated homes—to see, to feel, to know all this, and not to ask my soul some searching questions about God and immortality, was impossible.

Hence, little by little, a mysterious Power, which I now humbly recognize as the grace of God, constrained me to confront once more the awful problems I had shunned so long. Tomorrow I, too, might be dead; my dear ones also might be slain; my own home might be shattered to a mass of ruins. Surely the time had come for me to settle once for all my attitude toward the omnipotent Maker of the universe, one tiny part of which was my own soul. However hopeless the attempt, I nevertheless felt forced to make it.

At the outset it was clear to me that the scientific skepticism which had been my philosophy for forty years could neither aid nor comfort me in this catastrophe. It had sufficed thus far to narcotize my soul, but now it had no more effect. I looked at "civilized" Europe, and beheld entire nations slaughtering one another by land, by sea and in the air with the most frightfully destructive means that science had been able to invent.

I saw still other millions of the human race—the aged, the infirm, women, children, infants—threatened with starvation! And, all the while, the Frankensteins of modern times, the mighty agencies of printed words, emitted floods of falsehoods, hate and malice, which spread a terrible miasma through a blighted world! I saw besides all this, and partly as a result of it, society itself dissolving in indecency; public and private morals rapidly degenerating; hideous diseases eating out the marrow of the race; revolting realism in art and drama breeding a public taste for filth; the old ideals of honor, truth and even common honesty trampled under foot, accompanied by indifference to religion and open disbelief in God and immortality. Home life, the very nucleus of Christian civilization, seemed in many places a thing of the past. A letter from a friend in America assured me: "No one here cares any more for a home. Hundreds of fine houses are closed, and the owners travel, or live in hotels. They would not take a 'home' as a gift, if they would thereby be compelled to live in it. What they desire most is an automobile which will pass all others on the road. What will the coming generation be, under such homeless conditions on the one side, and insensate luxury and perilous amusements on the other?"

As to the latter, the mere perusal of the titles of many of the dramas placed today upon the stage will convince anyone, in whom a remnant of morality and decency still remains, that the tendency among playwrights and managers alike is to place before the public plays which are sexually suggestive, morally unwholesome, vulgar and degrading. Their themes are all too frequently picked out of the moral garbage boxes of humanity. Yet, if we turn from these unwholesome exhibitions of indecency to the still more baneful influences of the cinematograph shows, we reach an even lower level. A New York editor writes: "It is not an exaggeration to say that today the dominant purpose of the movie-picture industry is to commercialize some form of immorality. Even pictures not morally objectionable seek popularity by adopting titles which hint at and promise indecency. The moving picture is a standard menace to the morals of our children."

This condemnation is not confined to "Puritan America." The president of the juvenile court in Brussels (in Belgium there exists a special magistracy for youthful criminals) has also published a most interesting report, in which he states that cinematograph shows have a pernicious influence on children's morals. "The daily proofs of this," he says, "are striking. The cynicism of the little criminal is astounding; he confesses that he steals in order to be able to go to the kino, and that it is the kino itself that incites him to steal. The cinematograph surpasses every other agency for ruining our youth; it is even more deleterious than the reading of detective stories, because in this case at least the effort of reading is necessary. The cinematograph, as a rule, excuses and glorifies murder and crime, suggests suicide, embellishes adultery and incites to theft." In fact, all who are acquainted with the subject recognize that this amusement, which might be of so much educational value, is becoming more and more a breeding place for vice and immorality.

Is it any wonder, therefore, that at last a tidal wave of disillusionment and discouragement has overwhelmed the world? One suffers from a kind of spiritual nausea; and what accentuates one's mental anguish is the realization that most of us have been egregiously deceived; that, in our deification of inventive cleverness, we have been worshipping the wrong gods; that much of our loud-vaunted "progress" is merely acceleration; and that our boasted civilization is a thin veneer, concealing a substratum of appalling barbarism.

We have believed that our *mechanical inventions* formed the principal test of man's advancement; but now we are beginning to perceive that the only real criterion of civilization and progress is *character;* and that greater personal comfort, better facilities for communication, and an immense increase of marketable products through machinery, can no more help a man whose character is deteriorating, than a new suit of clothes can cure an individual suffering from cancer. In short, we have been living in a fool's paradise. Our standard of measurement has been wrong. What we have needed was progress in things spiritual, not in things material.

Appalling also is the fact that most of our so-called progress means increased capacity for...wasting the earth's resources! Each year has brought forth new contrivances, by which to throw away on senseless speed the planet's ever-dwindling stores. But when earth's coal and oil shall have been exhausted, no more can be produced. Our capital, though originally large, is limited; yet, although almost every new invention has led to fresh extravagance, we have all hailed it as a triumph! We have indeed learned to fly like birds, and to plough the ocean's depths like fishes; but we have used these last achievements chiefly to destroy our fellow men, or else to blow to atoms what has been amassed through centuries of toil.

Meanwhile we have made the acquisition of wealth and physical indulgence the principal end and aim of life, and in our rush for riches and pleasure have thrown our old ideals of morality to the winds, and most of our religion to the scrap heap. Yet, with all this, our "progress" has not made us happier. We had supposed that happiness consisted either in making or in spending money, but now we have discovered this to be a miserable delusion. There never was a time in human history when men possessed so little happiness and peace of mind as now. Our modern unbelief brings with it no relief from the intolerable burden of the world, but rather an increasing discontent with present conditions, assuaged by no consoling vision of the future. Truly the cup of all this godless and material prosperity has bitterness in its dregs!

We once supposed machinery to be our slave; it has become our master. It has relieved us of some manual toil—with little real benefit to the joyless laborer—but it has heaped upon us overwhelming burdens; for our desires increase a thousandfold with every new invention, and with them come those fiends of modern life—competition, envy, hatred...War!

All this I finally perceived, and realized that this reign of Hell on earth was the inevitable nemesis of our misconduct. We had discarded God, and *He was letting us see how we could live without Him.* We had ignored religion in our families, schools and governments, and the result had been the breakdown of a civilization we had thought secure.

In the great Belgian Exposition a few years ago, above the entrance to the Hall of Modern Mechanical Inventions was placed the inscription: "Man as God." These words express the sentiment of many of the leading men of Europe at the present time. Yet we can see what many of the machines produced by "Man as God" have thus far done for him! Our "godlike" mechanism is maddening some, murdering others, materializing all of us. We boasted once that our inventions had made rapid transit so secure, that famines were no longer possible; but later wonderful machines have changed all that, and never have the inhabitants of Europe suffered so acutely from undernourishment and hunger-typhus as precisely in the last few years, when thousands of infants and the old and feeble have died, and are still dying (1920), from lingering inanition!

I also recognized the fact that merely secular education is not sufficient for the preservation of society. The notion that some years of schooling, *with no instruction in morals and religion,* is a panacea for all social ills, is a delusion. The acquisition of mere secular knowledge often means the power of gaining wealth illegally, or gratifying vice more easily. It may make children "smarter," and young men still more cunning in the art of money-getting, but it makes some of them clever anarchists and criminals. The man of brightest intellect, *unbalanced by moral and religious forces,* often is a godless knave. In such a case his glittering accomplishments resemble iridescent colors on a putrid pool. What is the use of learning facts concerning physics, chemistry, biology, history, languages and mechanics, if there is wanting in the youth who masters them a *moral character,* to guarantee us that this education, which we tax ourselves to give, shall not be used against the commonwealth? As "grafters," corrupt legislators, venal editors, demagogues and Bolshevists, the *educated* scoundrels are more dangerous than the same men would be if uneducated; and history plainly teaches that the continued prosperity, often the very existence, of nations largely depends upon the vigor of their moral and religious life, and on their faithfulness to public and private *duty.*

I am aware of the difficulty of making taxpayers, who belong to different faiths, agree upon the kind of religious instruction to be given to their children. But surely some agreement can be reached by rational men upon at least the simplest principles of Theism, which none but atheists and anarchists would probably reject. There is at present a total lack of even ethical instruction in our schools, in consequence of which we have a growing generation of youthful materialists who possess a very meager moral code, look upon wealth and pleasure as the only gods worth worshipping, admire the "grafter" and the "plunger," if they are successful, acknowledge only the "eleventh commandment"—"Thou shalt not be found out"—and later on may hire conscienceless lawyers to help them circumvent the law or bribe the Legislature.

A New York lawyer has recently written: "Our children may be taught the lives, the wars and the amours of every god and goddess of pagan mythology, but the name of Jesus Christ must not be spoken in the schoolroom. The walls of the schoolhouse may show the pictures of real or fabled heroes of Greece and ancient Rome, but no picture of the Saviour of men or of His Mother may be shown, lest some squeamish soul in this Christian country be sore offended!"

"It cannot be doubted," writes a pastor in the *Katholiken Korrespondenz,* "that the exclusion of religion from the instruction and education of millions of children must cause a gradual lowering of the moral formation of the people. It is inevitable that, if there is a lack of a positively taught, reli-

gious conception of life, greed for money and abandonment
to low pleasures will more and more cause the life of the
people to degenerate, and that unscrupulousness and corruption will gain the mastery. Phenomena of fearful significance
in American life prove this clearly. The State is being under-
mined." (Prague, February, 1920).

This condition of affairs reacts unfavorably even on purely
secular education. If there was one thing of which the people
of America were formerly proud, it was the educational system prevailing in at least some of the United States; but, judg-
ing from the salaries at present paid to most of the teachers
there, education is valued much less than material pleasures,
luxuries and vices. Dr. Claxton, Commissioner of Education
in the American Republic, says: "The negro porter on a Pull-
man car makes more than two-thirds of the high-school
teachers in the United States; while a good stenographer, with
no more than a high-school education, may make more than
the maximum paid for a teacher in the grades." Accordingly,
he estimates that there is now a shortage in the United States
of 50,000 teachers, and that *"not less than 300,000 now in service
are below any reasonable standard of ability and preparation"!*

Worse than this, however, are the conditions prevailing in
some American colleges and so-called universities, where the
professors are so badly paid that they often cannot afford
to hire a servant, and are obliged, in case of the illness of
their wives, to do the housework themselves, *including standing at the tubs, and doing the family washing!* The writer has absolute, documentary proof of the truth of this almost incredible
statement, and it is beyond question that scores of gifted men,
who have the higher education of American youth in charge,
are, at a time when the world stands aghast at American luxury, living in extreme poverty, and struggling with hardships,
privations and harrowing anxieties.

Meantime the void so noticeable in our modern education
is filled with such ethical standards as are discoverable. . .in
the newspapers! Fifty years ago, Carlyle declared that the press

had replaced the pulpit. If that is still the case, God help us! One could not find a more appalling illustration of the prostitution of truth, honor and morality than is seen in the press of a considerable portion of the world today.

For years it has lent itself to the work of murder, and has kept the fires of international hatred burning at white heat, for the sake of profits gained from the patronage of a sensation-loving public, or from parties interested in the publication of prejudiced descriptions or absolutely false reports. A considerable portion of the press is now an ominous danger to public morals, since it has shown itself to be both vile and venal, and willing to deceive and brutalize mankind.

The depths to which its employees are frequently reduced is seen in the judgment passed upon the calling of the American journalist by a New York editor, John Swinton, during an annual dinner of the New York Press Association. It certainly is a frank confession: "There is no such thing as an independent press in America, if we except that of little country towns. You know this and I know it. Not a man among you dares to utter his honest opinion. Were you to utter it, you know beforehand that it would never appear in print. I am paid one hundred and fifty dollars a week [The reader will bear in mind that this book was first published in 1920, at which time this would be a very tidy sum.—*Editor, 1990.*] so that I may keep my honest opinion out of the paper for which I write. You, too, are paid similar salaries for similar services. Were I to permit that a single edition of my newspaper contained an honest opinion, my occupation, like Othello's, would be gone in less than twenty-four hours. The man who would be so foolish as to write his honest opinion would soon be on the streets in the search for another job. It is the duty of a New York journalist to lie, to distort, to revile, to toady at the feet of Mammon, and to sell his country and his race for his daily bread, or what amounts to the same thing, his salary. We are the tools and the vassals of the rich behind the scenes. We are marionettes. These men pull the strings, and we dance. Our time, our talents, our lives, our capacities are all the property of these men; we are intellectual prostitutes."

Philip Francis, for years an editorial writer of great influence in America, and who has had for forty years an intimate connection with journalism, writes: "With a few honorable exceptions, the big papers and magazines of the United States are the most ignorant and gullible, as well as the most cowardly and controlled press, printed in any country in the world. The majority of the owners are mere financiers, who look upon their magazines and newspapers simply as money-making mills, and who, whenever it is a question between more coin and good, honest, patriotic public service, will take the coin every time." (*The Poison in America's Cup*, p. 31).

What adds to the peril of this capitalized Press—which is, of course, not confined to any one country—is the deplorable fact that millions of the people of all lands *find in their newspapers their only mental food,* and form their opinions on practically all subjects by reading insincerely written editorials. Some even have time only for the headlines!

Reverting now to the absence of religious education among the present rising generation, we find in France the testimony against the system of secular training prevailing there still more damaging than in America. For many years, as is well known, the policy of the French Government was not only anti-Catholic, but also anti-religious. At one time it nearly succeeded in destroying the belief and practice of Christianity among the men of France at least. Already in 1863, the following picture of the state of France was drawn by a friendly critic: "A sad infidelity appears to me the prevalent tone of feeling among the French of all ranks. In the railway carriages, from officers, merchants, laborers, travellers of all ranks and degrees, when no priest or nun was present, I have heard nothing but sneers at the weakness of those who believed in *la mythologie* of Christianity. A vast proportion of the people are atheists. The French seem divided into two classes—

those who believe everything, and those who believe nothing." (*Once a Week,* No. 233, 1863). Not long ago, on a rainy Sunday afternoon, in the vast hall of the Trocadero in Paris, an audience of 5,000 assembled to declare their adhesion to atheism, and to listen to speakers who mocked at "the dead God, on whom priests live"!

These evils were foreseen and pointed out, already forty years ago, by statesmen like M. Jules Simon. To realize how atheistically the French authorities ventured even then to speak in public, we have but to consult the records of that time. Thus, in 1882, a president of French schools said to the children: "People pretend that we wish to have schools without God. But you cannot turn a page of your books without finding there the name of a god—that is, of a man of genius, a benefactor, a hero of humanity. In this point of view we are true pagans, for our gods are many"! (*Dieu, Patrie et Liberté,* p. 350.) Another president, addressing a body of schoolteachers, said: "Religious teaching plunges him [the student] fatally into an obscure night and into an abyss of lamentable superstitions." (*idem,* p. 351). Another president, quoted from the same source by Cardinal Manning *Miscellanies,* said: "Young citizenesses and young citizens, you have just been told that we have driven God out of the school. It is an error. *Nobody can drive out that which does not exist. God does not exist.* We have suppressed only emblems." (Vol. 3, p. 63). The "emblems" referred to were sacred pictures and especially crucifixes. These the Prefect of the Seine in the Senate called "school furniture"! The same could be said of the Courts of Justice throughout France, from which the crucified figure of the Saviour and future Judge of mankind, which formerly confronted every witness and juryman, has also been removed. Paul Bert, the Minister for Public Instruction under Gambetta, in 1881, and for years a leading exponent of the French atheistic school, proposed to sell all Bishops' palaces, seminaries for priests, and nunneries, belonging to the State, and openly declared: "Others may occupy themselves, if they like, in seeking a nostrum to destroy the phylloxera; *mine shall be the task to find one that shall destroy the Christian religion."*

We cannot wonder, therefore, that the French Abbé Bougaud says in his book, *Le Grand Péril*, "Our people are not hostile to religion; they are ignorant of it; they live bowed down to the earth. You speak to them, but they do not understand." (p. 70). This is an awful responsibility for any nation to take upon itself, and is ominous for the future, when one or two generations more shall have come and gone in godlessness! The Abbé also says: "If warned by the lightning which foreruns the storm, they return to God...the people who are now wandering may be brought back. ...If, on the contrary, they are obstinate, we must wrap our mantle about us, and let the storm pass over. It will be terrible." (p. 83). Have not his words been mournfully fulfilled? Poor France, of course, is not the only land where godlessness has made such open and official progress.

In Italy similar causes have produced in many places similar results. Italian priests have told me that frequently men whom they encounter on the streets take a malicious pleasure in uttering in their presence the most shocking blasphemies. In a newspaper, published in Northern Italy, I recently read a communication signed by a "Group of Fathers." In this the charge was made that two schoolteachers in the town of Guanzate had distinguished themselves by their virulent hostility to Christianity. A dialogue between one of these teachers and a pupil is quoted: "Where have you been?" "In the church to be taught my catechism." "May you and your God go to perdition in your church!" Another dialogue was as follows: "What book is that?" "The catechism." "What a little fool you are to learn those absurdities!" With these words the teacher seized the book from the child's hands, and tore it in pieces. One day, another of these teachers became suddenly infuriated by the sight of the Crucifix in the hall. He therefore attacked it with fury, tore it from the wall, and, with an accompaniment of oaths, kicked it through the schoolroom toward the stove, with the intention of burning it. Fortunately, a pious hand was able to rescue in time the figure of the Divine Sacrifice. These facts are stated by the group of Fathers to be absolutely true and authentic, "as many witnesses can testify." Moreover, these acts and words of sacrilege were done and said, not before older lads, who would perhaps have resented them, but before innocent little children of the primary grades. Accordingly, on the 3rd of April, 1920, a formal protest to the Italian authorities was made by some of the inhabitants of the place, including numerous fathers and two hundred mothers, who declared that they wished that their children should be brought up as Christians.

Guanzate is, of course, only one of thousands of Italian towns where religious teaching is today either refused or neglected; and the teacher, guilty of kicking the Cross of Our Lord through the schoolroom, has doubtless many actual or would-be imitators. The citizens of that one community have openly protested, but in how many other villages are the people silent, either intimidated, or rendered infidels themselves by such impiety!

In England and America such acts of violent hostility are rare, but there are many atheists in those enlightened lands who, believing that theirs is the "religion of the future," desire to instruct their children in the coming creed. Accordingly, in London, Liverpool and other British cities, as well as in some American ones, Sunday schools have been instituted by Radical Socialists for that purpose! The Rev. Dr. N. D. Hillis, of Brooklyn, stated recently that there are in New York City alone about 12,000 *children taught every Sunday in Socialist or Anarchist schools that there is no God,* and that the precepts and doctrines of the Christian religion are absurdities!

A textbook is used in these Sunday schools, in which occur, among many others, the following questions and answers:

Question: What is God?
Answer: God is a word, used to designate an imaginary

being, which people have themselves devised.

Question: How did man originate?

Answer: Just as did all animals, by evolution from lower kinds.

Question: Has man an immortal soul, as Christianity teaches?

Answer: Man has no soul; it is only an imagination.

Question: Is it true that God has ever been revealed?

Answer: As there is no God, he could not reveal himself.

Question: What is heaven?

Answer: Heaven is an imaginary place, which churches have devised to entice their believers.

Question: Who is Jesus Christ?

Answer: There is no God, therefore there can be no Son of God.

Question: Is Christianity desirable?

Answer: Christianity is not advantageous to us, but harmful. *It is the greatest obstacle to the progress of mankind; therefore it is the duty of every citizen to help wipe out Christianity.*

Question: What is our duty when we have learned there is no God?

Answer: We should teach this knowledge to others.

Question: Do you owe a duty to God?

Answer: There is no God, and therefore we owe him no duty.

This is indeed an appalling state of things, the full significance of which will be seen only *when an entire generation* shall have grown to manhood without belief in God and immortality; for such a training substitutes for the hitherto accepted code of morals one that incites to crime or bestial degradation. If God is totally excluded from the popular mind, and if the masses are persuaded that the life beyond the grave is a mirage, that there will never be a dispensation of rewards and punishments by Almighty God, and that man's only duty is to grab the most of earth's good things—then civilization is to cease, and man will soon degenerate to savagery. We see this in the utterances of these modern anarchists. In the

Umanità Nuova, the paper of the Italian anarchist, Enrico Malatesta, appears the following: "*So long as a sorrow-stricken woman kneels down before an altar and derives therefrom any comfort and relief, we shall never be able to make a revolution effectively;* so long as children shall be reared on the knees of such mothers, those children will never be the men who are called to form the new humanity, but idiots, such as we see around us in such numbers today!"

Now true humanity, whether old or new, has hitherto regarded a *mother's pious love* as the most sacred thing on earth. The humanity of the future, however, is to rid itself of such weakness and idiocy! One marvels that a man can write such words without a chill of horror creeping over him and paralyzing the hand that holds the pen. In such monsters we comprehend at last the horrible cruelties of atheistic Bolshevism. Materialism, Socialism, anarchy—these are three steps which logically follow one another—rocks, onto which a rising tide of lawlessness is driving us. Much of the so-called "Socialism," which is undermining the religion and morality of the masses, is atheistic. Its radical leaders frankly admit it. "The future," says one of them, "must belong to atheism." It is significant that the French Socialist, Proudhon, who affirmed that "Property is theft," also wrote: "The first duty of an intelligent and free man is to drive incessantly from his mind and conscience the idea of God; because God, if He does exist, is essentially hostile to our nature, and we elevate ourselves in proportion as we rid ourselves of His authority. Each step we take is a victory, in which we crush the Deity!"

The sun of humanity at present seems to be eclipsed, and what is threatening us is not only atheistic anarchy, but hopelessness and blank despair. We seem already to have entered the penumbra of this spiritual obscuration, and to be suffering from incurable pessimism. When the great Roman Empire sickened under such a malady, a new and virile race was in reserve to give it fresh vitality; but *there is no new race at hand for us.* Society has grown so old that godlessness will

now prove fatal to it, if it gains supremacy. The globe is cir-
cumnavigated; the races are so unified that even mental sick-
nesses are now contagious; and from the taint of atheism no
people could be long immune. One cannot, therefore, view
the future without apprehension.

"Never in the history of man," says a writer "On Theism"
in an English Review, "has so terrific a calamity befallen the
race, as that which all who look may now behold advancing
as a deluge; black with destruction, restless in might, up-
rooting our most cherished hopes, engulfing our most precious creed, and burying our highest life in desolation. The
floodgates of infidelity are open, and atheism is upon us."

Donoso Cortez, the eloquent Spanish writer and diploma-
tist, well said: "*A combination of material wealth and religious poverty* is invariably followed by one of those immense
catastrophes, which write themselves forever on the memory
of man." Are not these words being verified today before
our eyes? Evil forces, originating from Mammonism, luxury
and godlessness, have overmastered us, and are now beating
down, or undermining, our "Towers of Babel" and "Gardens
of Lucullus," leaving us naked, disillusioned and bereaved,
with millions of the finest specimens of our manhood—the
victims of the World War—rotting in human shambles! To
some this means the total loss of faith in God and in religion;
to others, on the contrary, it proves that *God is the only thing
essential—the want of which is killing us.*

As for myself, I felt convinced, through close acquaintance
with a war-cursed, irreligious world, that we had come into
this lamentable state through our neglect of God and through
a lack of moral and religious training; and I was therefore
anxious to be one of those who turned their faces upward
toward the Divine and Supernatural, rather than one of those
who in despair were ready to "curse God and die." Hence,
having reached this point, consistency compelled me to go
further, and to seek material for the reconstruction of my
long-lost faith.

Chapter 4

SEARCHING FOR LIGHT
(THE EXISTENCE OF GOD)

Where wast thou when I laid the foundations of the earth? Tell me, if thou hast understanding. Who hath laid the measures thereof, if thou knowest? or who hath stretched the line upon it? Upon what are its bases grounded, or who laid the cornerstone thereof, when the morning stars praised me together, and all the sons of God made a joyful melody? Who shut up the sea with doors. . .and said, Hitherto thou shalt come, and shalt go no further, and here thou shalt break thy swelling waves. . .Where is the way where light dwelleth? And where is the place of darkness? Shalt thou be able to join together the shining stars the Pliades, or canst thou stop the turning about of Arcturus? —JOB 38:4-11,19,31.

For I will behold thy heavens, the works of thy fingers:
The moon and stars which thou hast founded.
What is man that thou art mindful of him?
Or the son of man that thou visitest him?
                                        —PSALM 8:4-5

It is absolutely certain that we are in the presence of an Infinite, Eternal Energy, from which all things proceed.
                                        —HERBERT SPENCER.

We are unmistakably shown through Nature that she depends upon an ever-acting Creator and Ruler.—LORD KELVIN: Presidential Address British Association, 1871.

FIRST OF ALL, could I believe in God? The words of Immanuel Kant recurred to me: "Two things overwhelm me with awe—the starry heavens and man's accountability to God." The study of astronomy had always been to me the most elevating and attractive of all intellectual pursuits. Schiaparelli well named it the "Science of Infinity and Eternity." With Kant's impressive words in mind, one cloudless night, I took occasion to survey a portion of God's stellar universe, with the determination, under its enthralling influence, to hold communion with my soul.

Never before had the mysteries of the sidereal worlds appeared to me so awe-inspiring. In that immeasurable realm of space, in which a hundred million suns pursue their solitary paths, what beauty, order and precision were discernible! I knew that all that area was occupied with matter in perpetual motion, either as interstellar ether, vibrating with waves of light or electricity, or else in various stages of evolution or devolution—stardust transforming itself slowly into suns and planets, and these resolving finally again to stardust.

I knew that some of these celestial bodies are still gaseous, others solid; some inconceivably hot, others comparatively cooled; while others still are absolutely frigid, burned out and black, with all their planets tenantless—the darkened orbs more numerous probably than the shining ones; for all the stars which we can see are merely those which at this stage of their careers happen to be for the time so highly heated as to be luminous.

Beyond that obscure, lifeless stage, however, there seems to be another; for, as those solar bodies doubtless had a fiery origin, so they will ultimately have a fiery end.

"As surely," says Sir William Thompson, "as the weights of a clock run down to their lowest position, from which they can never rise again, unless some energy is communicated to them from some source, not yet exhausted, so surely must planet after planet creep in, age by age, toward the sun." The same planetary decrepitude and cosmical death also awaits our solar orb itself, if it be true that it is likewise moving round some vastly distant center of attraction. In fact, it has been demonstrated that this stupendous universe, as we know it, once had a beginning and must have an end. Between that beginning and that ending some mighty scheme is evidently in a process of progression, and *we are a part of it!* Order, beauty and sublimity are everywhere discernible in this process. Many of the glittering points of fire, at which we gaze from the thin rind of our relatively tiny globe, are "double" or even "multiple" stars—huge orbs revolving round a central point of gravity with stately motion, in dual, treble or even quintuple unions, which become still more marvelous from the fact that they have frequently different and even complementary colors! What shall we say, too, of the stellar clusters, which telescopes resolve into groups of thousands of suns, unquestionably bound together in some wonderful affinity; wheeling about each other in gigantic orbits, yet in their inconceivable remoteness from our earth, seemingly massed in one unbroken blaze, like jewelled mitres of supernal splendor?

I gazed long also at the amazing Milky Way—the "ground plan of the universe," the "broad and ample road, whose dust is gold," the pathway of innumerable suns, perhaps the equatorial zone of the whole stellar universe! In this vast, shoreless sea of space we—earth-imprisoned voyagers—find ourselves on the surface of a tiny satellite, whirling upon its axis at the rate of a thousand miles an hour. Although we feel no motion, not only are we turning thus, but are also being borne along our planet's path around the sun with a velocity of 1,080 miles a minute, or *one and a half million miles a day!* Moreover, in addition to all this, our entire solar system is sweeping onward through infinity at a rate of 400,000,000 miles a year, and entering thus continually new regions of sidereal space! Yet is there no appreciable danger of collision; for our solar colony, vast though its limits are, is but a point in a gigantic solitude. Our isolation is almost inconceivable. Our nearest astral neighbor moves at a distance of 275,000 times the earth's distance from the sun, which is itself 92,000,000 miles! Yet this star is exceptionally near!

And what *we* do in our small corner of the universe, millions of other suns and satellites are doing—swinging in perfect equilibrium millions of miles from one another, and moving with such perfect regularity that most of their vast changes can be foretold to a minute centuries in advance, or ascertained at any date of the historic past!

Yet the same law that guides the motion of Arcturus regulates the falling leaf. The same Divine hand paints the sunset glory and the petals of the rose. Proofs of design and wisdom, which overpower one in his study of astronomy, are just as evident in every other sphere of science. The revelations of the microscope are as marvelous as those of the telescope. The same supreme Intelligence is discoverable in the infinitely small as in the infinitely great. The ornithologist finds an adaptation of means to ends in the wonderful structure of birds; the zoologist traces it in every form of animal life; the botanist is filled with reverence and admiration in his investigation of the fertilization of flowers; the worker in the laboratory is lost in wonder at the mysteries of chemical affinities; and if "an undevout astronomer is mad," so also is an undevout investigator of the universe in any field of knowledge he may enter.

Thus I was recently much impressed by reading in an old British Review some facts and statistics in regard to that essential requisite for life of any kind upon our planet—*irrigation*. Water is really the lifeblood of our earth, yet we accept its rhythmical migration from sea to sky, and from the sky to sea again, as lightly as we do the circulation of the vital fluid through our veins. How wonderfully perfect is the process of evaporation, forever going on from all the lakes and oceans of our globe—as from those mighty reservoirs the solar heat draws moisture upward in the form of vapor! For water, being many hundred times heavier than air, could in no other form be lifted several miles above the earth. Yet this supply, prodigious though it be, floats lightly in the empyrean in the shape of clouds—huge, sunlit galleons, filled with precious cargoes, waiting patiently to be unloaded. These vaporous ships are filled and emptied without human hands; and sail to their respective ports without a helmsman, chart or compass. Currents of air, like currents in the sea, convey them far into the hearts of continents, that they may there discharge their freights over the very fields in which stand waiting husbandmen. The total quantity of water thus distributed in rain or snow is inconceivable. Sometimes a single cloud contains thousands of tons of liquid, which, if released at once, would sweep away both vegetation and the soil itself; yet with what delicate precision is its distribution usually effected! True, cloudbursts do sometimes occur, as if to remind man what might always be the case, but for the care of Providence; yet, as a rule, nothing can be more gentle than the fall of moisture to the earth. The rain sifts through the atmosphere in billions of small drops, as if poured through a finely woven sieve, alighting from a dizzy height without the crushing of a leaf or flower; and, on its way, cleansing the air of its impurities, as later on, in the form of rivers, it will sweep them to the sea. Man can do nothing to determine the delivery of this essential element; but at the touch of some cool mountain peak or by the contact of a chilling wind the magic "Open Sesame" is spoken, and the rain descends! Suppose we saw all this for the first time, instead of being accustomed to it from our childhood, and hence accepting it, like so many other blessings, as a matter of course: could we then fail to see in this impressive scheme the plan of an intelligent Creator?

Filled with these thoughts, I turned back to my library, and looked through books which, fifty years before, had seemed to me a new evangel. I took down Spencer's writings—not his *First Principles* this time, but his last—found in his mournful autobiography. Here I read: "Behind these mysteries lies the all-embracing mystery—*whence* this universal transformation, which has gone on unceasingly throughout a past eternity, and will go on unceasingly throughout a future eternity? And along with this rises the paralyzing thought—what if, of all that is thus incomprehensible to us, there exists no comprehension anywhere! *No wonder that men take refuge in authoritative dogma."* I also turned to the remarkable passage concerning Spencer in Henry Murray's Memoirs: "Walking up and down the lawn. . . I told him [Spencer] what a load of personal obligation I felt under to his *First Principles,* and added that I intended to devote the reading hours of the next two or three years to a thorough study of his entire output. 'What have you read of mine?' he asked. I told him. 'Then,' said Spencer, 'I should say that you have read quite enough.' He fell silent for a moment, and then added: *'I have passed my life in beating the air.' "*

I turned to my old notebooks, and found records there, which I had once inserted, without appreciating their full significance. Among them were these words from Sir Isaac Newton: "The whole variety of created things *could arise only from the design and will of a Being existing of Himself.* This exact machinery of suns and planets could not originate except from the plan and power of an intelligent and mighty Being." Another page contained these words from Darwin: "Another source of conviction for the existence of God—connected with reason rather than with feelings—follows from the extreme difficulty, or rather *impossibility,* of conceiving this immense and wonderful universe, including man, with his capacity of looking forwards far into futurity, as the result of blind chance or necessity. When thus reflecting, *I feel impelled to look to a First Cause, having an intelligent mind* in some degree analogous to that of man." Moreover, in his "Fertilisation of Orchids" Darwin speaks of "beautiful contrivances" and "marvellous adjustments"—words which clearly point to a directive Intelligence. The great astronomer, Kepler, said: "My supreme desire is to find in myself the God, *whom I find everywhere outside."* No less remarkable are the words of Sir W. Siemens, uttered in 1884: "We find that all knowledge must lead up to one great result—that of an intelligent recognition of the Creator through His works." Sir Francis Bacon, who had one of the keenest intellects ever given to man, declared in his essay on "Atheism": "I had rather believe all the fables in the Legend, and the Talmud and the Koran, than that this universal frame is without a mind." Lord Kelvin, one of the greatest of modern scientists, has affirmed that "Overpowering proofs of *intelligence and benevolent design* lie around us, showing us through Nature the influence of a free will, and teaching us that all living beings depend upon *one everlasting Creator and Ruler.*" Dr. Bence Jones, in his *Life of Faraday,* says of that great discoverer in chemistry and electricity: "His standard of duty was supernatural...It was formed entirely on what he held to be the Revelation of the will of God in the written word, and throughout all his life his faith led him to act up to the very letter of it."

Why, then, did we poor, amateur investigators of half a century ago always prefer the latest atheistic school of scientists for our teachers, rather than master minds, like those which I have quoted, many of whom were also our contemporaries, and whose researches led them, not to blank agnosticism, but to the adoration of their Creator? I do not know, unless we thought the newest theory must always be the truest, and that the latest word of some experimentalist must also be the final word of science. At all events, we were quite positive that we knew already, or would soon discover, all the secrets of the universe which the human mind could grasp! Yet Lord Kelvin said, as recently as 1896, in Glasgow: "One word characterizes the most strenuous efforts for the advancement of science that I have made perseveringly for fifty-five years—that word is *failure.* I know no more of the electric and magnetic forces, of the relation of either to electricity and ponderable matter, or of chemical affinity, than I knew and tried to teach my students in my first session as professor!" The truth is, that, in spite of such achievements as determining the speed of light and the composition of the stars, we are still unable to explain the origin and essence of the simplest life, whether it be our own, or that of the "flower in the crannied wall."

We have discovered only externals. To explain *essentially* the simplest phenomena of light, heat, force, electricity and gravitation is beyond our power. Thus Newton said: "I know the *laws* of attraction, but if you ask me *what attraction is,* I cannot tell." Professor Tyndall also said, in reference to the waves of sound that reach the brain along the auditory nerve— there, as it were, to be translated into thoughts: "*Why* the motion of that nervous matter *can thus excite our consciousness* is a mystery which the human mind cannot fathom. The prob- lem of the connection of body and soul is as insoluble in its modern form as it was in the prescientific ages. . . If you ask him [the materialist], what is this 'matter' of which we have been discoursing; who or what divided it into molecules; who or what impressed upon them this necessity of running into organic forms, he has no answer. . . Science also is mute in reply to these questions."

But if Professor Tyndall thus concedes his ignorance of material causes, he ought not to imply, as he did in his ad- dress before the British Association, that material causes alone are sufficient to produce, not merely the material world, but also the world of reason and intelligence; and to say that he can see in matter "the promise and the potency of every form and quality of life," including therefore *human* life, with all its intellectual capacities. What is the reason of this preference on the part of many scientists to recognize such "promise and potency" in matter, rather than in mind? Whence comes their apparent satisfaction in giving to mankind a material, rather than a spiritual origin?

> *O star-eyed Science, hast thou wandered there*
> *To waft us home the message of despair?*

For with that grim solution of the riddle of the universe, we lose belief in God and personal immortality, and Tyndall himself speaks of coming generations still trying to compre- hend earth's mysteries, "ages after you and I, like streaks of morning cloud, shall have melted into the infinite azure of the past."

But when we thus attempt to banish the Creator from the universe, we forget our mental limitations. Even in our perception of phenomena we live in very narrow limits. Sound-waves, which fall too slowly or too fast upon our ears, we cannot hear. Their loudest echoes leave our auditory nerves unmoved; and there are lightwaves, which for similar reasons do not register themselves upon our brains. Two-thirds of the rays emitted by the sun fail to awaken in the human eye the sense of vision, but move entirely outside the power of our optic nerves to apprehend! But if such waves of light and sound continually pass our eyes and ears without imparting the least intimation of their presence, *there must exist around us, outside of that small zone of apprehension dominated by our senses, another world of physical phenomena,* moving to other ends than ours.

How large this unseen, silent world may be we cannot tell; but since it is an actual reality, why should it be so difficult to believe that there is also a *spiritual* realm, lying beyond the capacity of our present *spiritual* powers to perceive? Is not our gross materialism due principally to the fact that we forget our limitations and the infinite distance between creature and Creator? Though we cannot create the lowliest flower, alter the essential character of the smallest seed, comprehend the primary forces hidden in a tiny acorn, or explain the origin of the humblest form of life, which floats within the sea or flutters in the sun, we often act as if we were capable of criticizing and instructing the Creator of the acorn and . . . Arcturus!

In those old days, with what incredible assurance we ignored God; finding indeed a million stars, but not the least proof of their Maker! "Evolution" and "protoplasm" were then words to conjure with. But granting everything that evolutionists have a right to claim, there must have been originally an *Evolver;* and there may be an evolution obedient to Divine arrangement, as well as one obedient to blind necessity. The former is indeed the sublimest possible theory of the Divine method. Allowing that the primal germ contained all possible potentialities, the question still remains: *"Who made that germ, and gave it those potentialities?"* An infinite Volition must have started matter on its journey, and ordered the direction of its evolution. What matters the *modus operandi,* whether by ages of development, or by special creation, provided we acknowledge a Divine Mind as the great Originator? To call a substance "Protoplasm" is not an explanation of the origin of life, nor does that substance obviate the need of a First Cause.

Is it any easier or more rational to believe in an eternal, unintelligent Protoplasm, than to believe in an eternal and intelligent God? Even if we refer man back to a primeval cell, we must acknowledge that *a cell that can become a man— with all his endowments, moral, mental and physical—is more mysterious than the man himself.* "Without the hypothesis of a presiding mind, directing its processes, the doctrine of evolution is a greater mystery than that of special creation." (Maccoll, *Christianity in Relation to Science and Morals,* p. 21).

Professor Wallace, who shares with Mr. Darwin the credit for discovering the theory commonly known as "Darwinism," affirms that there are at least three stages in the development of the organic world, *where some new cause or power must necessarily have come into action.* The first stage is the change from inorganic to organic, when the earliest vegetable cell. . .first appeared; the second stage is that of the introduction of consciousness—animal life; the third is that of the advent of Man, with his powers of rational thought and speech.

To call the argument from design old and "obsolete" is easy, but to answer it is difficult. For this reason men profess to be tired of it, and try to lessen its effectiveness by juggling with words. The argument *is* old, because the vast majority of mankind have always recognized the evidences of design in Nature; but it will never become obsolete, so long as telescopes and microscopes exist, and human minds perceive and reason on the marvels thus revealed. The argument *is* old, but so is the coming of the dawn; and as the one will always force itself upon the vision, so will the other force itself upon the mind, until the universe shall wax old like a garment, and "all the host of the heavens shall pine away, and the heavens shall be folded together as a book." (*Is.* 34:4).

The famous skeptic, Hume, accepted the argument from design, and said: "The whole frame of Nature bespeaks an intelligent Author; and no rational inquirer can, after serious reflection, suspend his belief a moment with regard to the primary principles of Theism and Religion." To look upon the laws which regulate the universe as entities, that need no God, and "of themselves" worked out their wondrous combinations, is but a desperate effort to accept any hypothesis, however unreasonable, *rather than believe the only rational explanation—that of a Creator.* As Huxley says, the laws of Nature are not *agents,* but merely *records of experience.* Moreover, reason demands for laws a Law-Giver; design necessitates a Designer; an adaptation of means to ends calls for an Adapter; and world-building implies a World-Builder. We are compelled to choose between believing that this vast, orderly universe is governed by Intelligence, blind autonomy, or chance. But in the face of all the proofs of an *intelligent Personality* in Nature, the notion of impersonal autonomy becomes untenable, while the idea that chance in such a universe as this can take the place of a Creator is still more incredible, and by all the laws of probability impossible.

When we walk through our gardens and behold the tender blossoms of the apple trees, the tendrils of the ripening vines, the delicate veinlets of the iris, and the exquisitely tinted petals of the rose, can we persuade ourselves that all that floral loveliness of form and color has come to us by chance, or through "unconscious chemistry"? Nay, would not such an origin be infinitely more improbable than one attributable to the will and purpose of a wise, beneficent Creator? Alas! too many of us never think at all about the origin of all these marvelous phenomena. We have become so thoroughly familiar with them that we accept them as a matter of course, and look upon them with the heedlessness of animals. It is a mournful commentary on our superficial natures, that familiarity with such wonders breeds indifference. "If," says Emerson, "the stars should appear only one night in a thousand years, how would men believe and adore, and preserve for many generations the remembrance of the City of God, which had been shown."

In the consideration of this subject, one thing impressed itself upon my mind with constantly increasing emphasis. It was the absolute impossibility of believing that in this limitless expanse of flaming suns and countless constellations, *no one understands its origin and mysteries more than we do;* and that our feeble, finite intellects form the highest limit of intelligence existing in this wondrous scheme of things!

That thought is blasphemous in its conceit, and paralyzing in its influence. We may talk academically of a "Godless world," but when we really face its possibility, we find that there is nothing more appalling in its horror than the conception of a boundless universe, eternally evolving in perfect order and in full activity...*without a Mind to comprehend, or Will to guide it!* "Man," says Disraeli, "is made to adore and to obey." When we conceitedly survey our puny selves, we fain would disbelieve this statement; but when we look off from our darkened planet into starlit space, we know that it is true.

Chapter 5

THE MORAL LAW

By the verdict of his own breast no guilty man is ever acquitted.
                                                    —JUVENAL.

God, Immortality, Virtue are the three pillars on which the universe rests.—JEAN PAUL RICHTER.

ACCEPTING REVERENTLY this proof of an All-wise and an All-powerful Creator, I asked myself if there were also other evidences of His being. Again I called to mind the words of Kant: "Two things overwhelm me with awe—the starry heavens and *man's accountability to God.*"

Was there, then, inward evidence also of a God? Yes; for implanted in us is a Moral Law, whose incorruptible interpreter is conscience. Of this I am as well aware as of my own existence. This monitor is, to some extent, innate in all men. The lowest member of the human race has *some* intuitive knowledge of the difference between right and wrong; and there is in him an instinctive feeling of obligation to do the former, rather than the latter. However callous criminals become, that inward voice still speaks within them; and after committing murder, deeds of excessive cruelty, and acts of base ingratitude, they are conscious of guilt.

This monitor does not entreat or argue with us; it *commands*. It says imperiously: "This is right, that is wrong; do the former, do not do the latter." As a free agent, I can disobey its mandate, but, though I do so, I well know I *ought* to have obeyed it.

Utilitarian moralists tell us that conscience is nothing but a state of mind, acquired from inherited notions of what was beneficial to our savage ancestors; that the moral sense in man is not innate and God-implanted, but merely a phenomenon, which varies under different circumstances; that general utility is the highest test, and that morals are but generalizations from experience. If this were so, our moral code would be dependent on tradition, environment, political exigencies, climate and geography; respect for God would disappear; fear of His judgment would be replaced by dread of the police court; and public opinion would become our sole criterion of morals.

How dangerously all such standards shift from age to age, and place to place, is only too well known. It is one thing to utter such statements academically, but quite another to introduce them as principles of everyday life. Woe to the generation that descends to that low level! If self-gratification and utility are our sole reasons for "morality," society will inevitably degenerate, principle will succumb to pleasure, the moral fiber will be weakened, and man's divinest attribute, the spirit of self-sacrifice, will be annihilated.

If we deny the existence of certain fixed, eternal distinctions between what is radically right and what is radically wrong, hideous deeds, like old-age slaughter and infanticide, could be legitimately encouraged for the welfare of the State or family. If happiness were declared to be the only ethical standard, whose family would be safe, whose property secure? There would be speedily inaugurated a system of Socialism, which has been well defined as a scheme "to take from the worthy the things they have labored for, in order to give to the unworthy the things they have not earned." Under such conditions a mob of selfish Communists would make short work of our possessions, and social anarchy would soon prevail. We see this proved, not only by a hundred instances in history, but actually now (1919-1920) in many parts of Europe.

There artful demagogues have roused the dregs of the population to raid, rob, plunder, and even to destroy, from a mere lust for destruction; and there we see the sanguinary triumph of a godless mob, whose crimes, in respect to the torture and murder of aristocrats, priests and the educated part of the community, surpass the worst atrocities of the French Revolution. These lawless masses do what they have always done, whenever they have made their violent inroads into the domain of history. They talk at first of liberty, equality and fraternity, but speedily create their own despotic idols of an hour, whose tyranny becomes atrocious. At last they usually fall to fighting among themselves, and order is restored at a further cost of blood and treasure. One of the most pronounced characteristics of these anarchists is their hatred to every form of religion and their persecution of the Church; and when the restraining influences of belief in God and a future life have been weakened or destroyed, society retrogrades to barbarism, as is actually the case in many sections of Europe today.

Evils resulting from the utilitarian code of morals are not, however, entirely confined to revolutionary mobs. In social morals also its results are frequently appalling. Indeed, upon that theory of ethics what is the use of being virtuous, even on Becky Sharp's "ten thousand a year," if the "roses and raptures of vice" are more alluring? What is the strength of virtue, based on motives of expediency only? Young people, urged to lead an upright life, will naturally say: "Why should we do so, if the Moral Law is fluctuating, and derived from nothing higher than a chain of experiences starting in an anthropoid ape?" It is all very well for passionless ascetics to declare that they can be just as pure and noble without a belief in a Supreme Judge, as with one; but the great majority of men and women will certainly ask themselves: What is the use of being good, if there is no one in the universe who knows or cares? Moreover, even though admitting that a certain course of conduct, gradually evolved by man, is necessary for society in general, the *individual himself will always want to be an exception to the rule.* Under the pressure of temptation, considerations for the "welfare of society" will prove frail barriers of defense.

A striking illustration of moral degeneracy may be seen

at present in a European capital, where a few wealthy visitors from the New World have founded a society which practically advocates free love. The real significance of its theories is partly veiled in its printed literature, the circulation of which would otherwise be prohibited; but in the society's meetings, which are attended by persons of both sexes, married and single, young and old, language is used which is unmistakable. The priests and priestesses of this strange cult assert that every woman has the right to choose for herself a partner of the other sex. If she prefers to do so through the conventional mode of marriage, well and good; but if in some other way, it is equally well and good. If she is subsequently disappointed in her choice, she could be quite at liberty to choose another companion, or. . . several others. Her first partner, even though he be called her husband, should make no opposition to this "natural selection," but on the contrary should aid her with his counsel and approval! Under no circumstances should individual freedom be restrained or subject to reproach. One advocate of this moral bankruptcy is the father of two daughters; yet, incredible as it would seem, he claims that these young girls will, later on, be justified in following the precepts of free love! Unfortunately, the supporters of this pernicious system are not content to keep it to themselves, but carry on a propaganda for its doctrines with the expenditure of considerable sums of money. Naturally its baneful influence is as contagious as leprosy, and its results upon the individuals contaminated by it will be ruinous, as similar customs in the past have always proved. How many families will be wrecked, how many innocent lives forever blasted, how many children ruined and abandoned through its influence, can be imagined!

Already among the members of this club there has been at least one instance of attempted suicide; for even those who deny the existence of an intuitional conscience, must know that evil-doers frequently experience remorse, if not despair. Yet, after all, if pleasure and utility are the sole criteria of morality, what is there strange or illogical in such conduct? If there exists no higher standard than that of "happiness" to determine what is right, the noble qualities of self-denial and self-sacrifice become absurdities, and the satisfaction arising from the consciousness of having done one's duty is an illusion.

Why should one risk one's fortune, happiness and life for others for some great cause? In order to acquire glory? That is an evanescent dream, and must in any event be paid for dearly. To win the approval of posterity? What does it matter? We shall know nothing of it. To enjoy the esteem of the public? What does the clever and successful rascal—whether political, financial or social—care for that, provided his ambitions or desires have been gratified? On the other hand, the motives of self-sacrifice and duty have produced the noblest characters of which the race can boast. These motives Christ especially appealed to: "Whosoever will be chief among you, let him be your servant; even as the Son of man came not to be ministered unto, but to minister, and to give His life a ransom for many." Accordingly, the Church can point to thousands of her children who, through a sense of duty toward their fellow men, as well as to God, have made their lives a record of complete self-abnegation. Abandoning riches, social eminence, and comforts, her saints have voluntarily turned their backs upon the world, assumed a rough, uncomfortable dress, and embraced lives of poverty, hardship, fasting and humility, in order to devote themselves to a lifetime of wearisome teaching, or to the service of the sick and wretched—often carrying Christ's Gospel even to colonies of lepers, though certain of being ere long fatally infected!

The French author, Frédéric Soulié, was cared for in his last illness by a Sister of Charity, to whom he often spoke jestingly on the subject of religion. Touched by her great devotion and sincerity, the skeptic one day asked her seriously: "Are you really convinced of the truth of your religion?" "Do you think," she replied, "that if I were not, I should be here, sacrificing my liberty and health in your service?" This dignified response impressed him deeply. The Sister saw it, and took occasion to speak to him of the welfare of his soul. The sick man listened attentively, was soon after reconciled with God, and died, pressing the crucifix to his heart.

Utilitarianism, on the contrary, which recognizes no criterion of morality save self-interest, produces no such characters. It cannot logically explain innumerable evidences of self-abnegation—from the incomparable sacrifice of Calvary to the deed of many a shipwrecked hero, who has yielded up his place of safety in the lifeboat to another, and turned back calmly to inevitable death.

It must not be forgotten, also, that the great philosophers of paganism were believers in the existence of conscience and the Moral Law. Seneca, for example, wrote: "Every man has a judge and witness within himself of all the good and evil that he does...The foundation of true joy is in the conscience...God is nigh to thee, He is with thee, He is within thee. I tell thee, Liculius, a sacred spirit is resident in us, an observer and guardian both of what is good and what is evil in us." Socrates also remarked: "If the rulers of the universe do not prefer the just man to the unjust, it is better to die than to live." Cicero also speaks of that Moral Law which "no nation can overthrow or annul. Neither a senate nor a whole people can relieve us from its injunctions. It is the same in Athens and in Rome; the same yesterday, today and forever." Epictetus declared: "When we are children, our parents deliver us to the care of a tutor...When we are become men, God delivers us to the guardianship of an implanted conscience. If you always remember that God stands by, as a witness of whatever you do, either in soul or body, you will never err, either in your prayers or actions, and you will have God abiding with you. Never say, when you have shut your door and darkened your room, that you are alone; for you are not alone, but God is within, and your genius is within; and what need have they of a light to see what you are doing?" Aristotle, too, considered it the special attribute of man that he is a moral being, able to distinguish between good and evil, justice and injustice; in other words, that the final bases of right and duty are to be found, not in comfort and utility, but in a perception of the eternal distinctions between right and wrong; and if so, then the Moral Law is something independent of the ephemeral race of man. *"It is an essential quality of God, existing before all worlds were made; and from the consciousness of moral obligation, which we find implanted in us, we reason back to its eternal Source—the Infinite and Perfect."*

To deny these doctrines, which belong alike to Christianity and to the highest pagan philosophy; to say with Hobbes that "Good and evil are names that signify our appetites and aversions"; to claim that conscience is nothing but an echo of ancestral selfishness; and that the notion of accountability to God is a superstition—all this is a very comfortable view of life, but it rests upon no solid foundation, and is opposed to the entire course of justice, which man has found it necessary to establish on this earth.

Unless this world is the result of chance, man must have been created for some definite purpose. What can that purpose be? It certainly is *not* a search for happiness, for all experience shows us that there is no surer way to lose one's happiness than to seek it. The object of one being here seems to be, rather, *the development of character.* This also is not only Christian doctrine; it was the view of many of the noblest spirits of antiquity. Seneca, for example, asks: "How comes it to pass that good men labor under affliction and adversity, and wicked men enjoy themselves in ease and plenty? My answer is that God deals by us as a good father does by his children; He tries us, hardens us and fits us for Himself. . . . As the master gives his most hopeful scholars the hardest lessons, so does God deal with the most generous spirits; and we are not to look upon rebuffs of fortune as a cruelty, but as incidents in a contest. How many casualties and difficulties have we dreaded as unbearable evils, which upon further consideration proved to be mercies and benefits! When we are visited with sickness and other afflictions, we are not to murmur, as if we were badly used. It is a mark of the general's esteem if he puts us in a post of danger. We do not then say—My captain uses me ill, but that he does me honor. . . No man knows his strength or value except by being put to the proof. The pilot is tried in a storm; the soldier in a battle; the rich man in poverty. Providence treats us like a generous father, and brings us up to labors, toils and dangers; whereas the indulgence of a fond mother makes us weak and spiritless." Epictetus writes in a similar manner: "Difficulties show what men are. Hereafter, when a difficulty befalls you, remember that God, like a trainer of wrestlers, has matched you with a rough antagonist."

It is remarkable how closely the views of the great Roman moralists coincide with those expressed in the New Testament. St. Paul, for example, in speaking of a Christian, uses frequently the metaphor of a soldier. "Endure hardness as a good soldier of Jesus Christ." "Fight the good fight of faith." "The time of my departure is at hand; I have fought a good fight, I have finished my course, I have kept the faith." Many of the parables of Christ also represent man as a steward, who eventually must give an account of his stewardship. Especial emphasis is also laid upon the fact that our position toward God is that of *children toward a Father,* who, while He loves us, disciplines us by trial and purifies our characters through affliction. St. James declares: "Blessed is the man that endureth temptation; for when hath been proved, he shall receive the crown of life." (1:12) St. Paul also writes: "My son, neglect not the discipline of the Lord, neither be thou wearied white thou art rebuked by him; for whom the Lord loveth, he chastiseth; and he scourgeth every son whom he receiveth. If ye endure chastening, God dealeth with you as with sons. Now all chastisement for the present seemeth not to bring with it joy, but sorrow: but afterwards it will

yield...the most peacable fruit of justice. (*Heb.* 12:6, 11).
In the Book of Revelation also the Spirit saith unto the
Churches: "Such as I love, I rebuke and chastise." (*Apoc.* 3:19).

Pagan and Christian moralists, therefore, are agreed in
representing this world as a battlefield, an arena, or a school,
where we are trained for something better. "That this world
is intended for man's education," says Emerson, "is the only
sane solution of the enigma." But such a system of discipline
proves that man is worth training. So much effort to improve
us would not be expended on ephemeral creatures, with no
future. It is rational, therefore, to conclude that, just as children are instructed for a higher grade in school, so is the
human race prepared here for a higher life; partly in contest
with the elements, since most of us must earn our bread by
manual labor; but chiefly in the increase of our *mental* strength
by study, our *moral* strength by resisting temptation, and our
spiritual strength by a devout obedience to the will of God.
Failing this, we miss the aim of our creation.

It is true, to most of us the Master's orders and restrictions
seem very different from the methods which we ourselves
should have chosen, precisely as the tedious duties of the
schoolroom, the needful discipline at home, strict prohibi-
tions in regard to dangerous pleasures, or the giving of distasteful medicine appear to children foolish and tyrannical
infringements of their liberty. This comparison appears to
modern Mammonists absurd. According to them, men are
not children, but demigods. Christ, however, declared that
unless we become as "little children," we cannot enter the
kingdom of Heaven.

We have His word for it that these respective standpoints
are irreconcilable. "Ye cannot serve God *and* Mammon."
Stripped of superfluous phrases, Mammonists maintain that
we are on this planet to make money and to spend it. God,
on the contrary, informs us that our life consists *not* in the
abundance of things which we possess, and says to the self-
complacent rich man: "Thou fool, this night thy soul shall

be required of thee." Mammon measures progress chiefly by mechanical inventions for man's greater comfort and for greater speed. God's voice within us measures it by the extent to which society is dominated by His Moral Law. Mammon doubts or denies the existence of Deity. The Bible asserts that only "the *fool* hath said in his heart there is no God." Mammon declares that men "shall be as gods." The Bible ascribes those words originally to the devil. Mammon destroys man's reverence for the Supernatural. Christ, on the contrary, promulgates, as the "first and great commandment" —"Thou shalt love the Lord thy God with all thy heart, and with all thy soul, and with all thy mind."

Moved by all these considerations, it seemed at last to me both rational and necessary to believe, not only that the Creator of this universe is All-wise and Omnipotent, but that He is also the Author of a Moral Law, by which mankind is to be trained and tried, and which is shown to us by conscience in an *intuitive sense of right and wrong, antecedent to and independent of experience and utility.* It is unnecessary to ask if the Author of this Moral Law is Himself a Being of perfect goodness. A contrary supposition would imply that Infinite God, having proposed to man the highest ideal of moral conduct, cannot or will not Himself live up to it!

"And yet," objects the skeptic, "if God is really the personification of perfect justice and goodness, how can you account for the presence here of so much suffering and evil?" That is, of course, the oldest and most profound of mysteries. That God *allows* evil to exist here is indisputable; but it is evidently part of the great scheme of giving man free will. Man's freedom of choice leaves the door open to the possible entry of evil, and to a certain extent explains its presence.

There is no doubt that much the greater share of human misery and degradation is the result of man's own wickedness and folly. His own deliberate choice makes of this earth too frequently a scene of cruelty and crime. That our will is free is one of the most indisputable facts of our inner consciousness. Upon that supposition is based the entire scheme of human legislation, which holds that men are responsible for their conduct. How could society be preserved on any other hypothesis? If man is a mere automaton, his responsibility ceases, and no court could justify him. But the commands of Christ and the mandates of conscience both appeal directly to the will. Its freedom also forms the basis of all religion, for any *real* homage of the soul must of course be voluntary. Virtue, to be worth anything, must involve the possibility of having been rejected for vice by a free agent. We talk sometimes of "irresistible motives," but we know at heart that we *can* do, or can leave undone, any given act, however strong the temptation may be. It is upon that hypothesis that we associate daily with our fellow men. To deny this is to contradict one's individual consciousness. It is our liberty of will that makes us *persons,* and we know it.

Moreover, it is man's proudest distinction. Everywhere else in nature we see a blind obedience to law. The rhythmic movement of the tides, the punctual reappearance of the lunar disc, the regular recurrence of the seasons, the tireless heartbeat and the falling leaf—all illustrate compulsory obedience. There is no absolute liberty of choice to obey or disobey God's mandate, save in man. He alone can be disobedient, if he will; and, as a matter of fact, he *does* will it frequently. He says with Ovid:

Video meliora, proboque,
Deteriora sequor.

But, on the other hand, man sometimes wills to sacrifice himself, to suffer voluntarily for others, and even for their sake to encounter death; and this is recognized as the best and noblest in man's character, precisely because, *being free to make the sacrifice or not, he chose to make it.* Man has it, therefore, in his power to prevent, or greatly to alleviate, much of the earth's wretchedness and suffering. If he would only live in conformity to the law of Christ, he could confer upon

his fellow men and on the animals, which he so often wan-
tonly destroys or tortures, lives of peace and happiness. The
guilt for an immense amount of suffering inflicted on dumb,
patient beasts rests on the cruelest of all creatures—man
himself!

As for the pain and misery over which man has no control,
let us concede that this presents a problem that we cannot
solve. Why God permits great natural catastrophes and many
kinds of suffering in men and beasts, remains for us a mystery. But we may recollect that to most children many acts
of their parents seem no less cruel and mysterious, which
nevertheless are for their good. Do we object to being classed
as children? Let us recall the previously quoted words of Newton and Lord Kelvin, and realize how profoundly ignorant
we are of practically everything except phenomena. *If the words
of these scientists do not mean that we are, in the sight of God and
His government, dependent, ignorant children, what do they mean?*

At all events, which is more rational—to believe that a
malevolent demon rules this universe, or that it is governed
by a benevolent Deity, *whom we in most things know to be beneficent and good, but all of whose designs and ways we cannot yet completely comprehend?* There can be but one rational answer to
that question. To think that the Creator and Preserver of this
wonderfully appointed cosmos is a malignant Spirit, bent on
torturing His creatures, or capable of neglecting them, is revolting to our reason; and equally so is the supposition that the
universe is a vast, unintelligent mass of matter, dragging us
automatically on to ends unknown to any mind. In any case,
how do the pessimists help us with their hopeless theories?
Do they make our present existence more endurable? Do they
render its mysteries any more comprehensible? On the contrary, to what a hideous and irrational view of the world
do those condemn themselves, who mock at man's accountability, make moral standards rest on selfishness, and disbelieve
in God's existence! Of course if we repudiate the testimony
of history, philosophy and Divine Revelation, and hold by

preference that conscience is "inherited," that morals have no higher sanction than expediency, and that unconscious fate or an evil principle rules the world—then truly nothing is left us but despair. But happily we have something better; for in our souls abides the inborn, irresistible conviction that God is good, as well as great, and that right *must* be rewarded, and wrong punished, *if not here, then elsewhere.*

Chapter 6

IMMORTALITY

The spirit of man, which God inspired, cannot perish with this corporeal clod.—MILTON.

The seed dies into a new life, and so does man.
—GEORGE MACDONALD.

When I go down to the grave, I shall have ended my day's work, but another day will begin next morning. Life closes in the twilight; it opens with the dawn.—VICTOR HUGO.

> *Alas for him who never sees*
> *The stars shine through his cypress-trees;*
> *Who, hopeless, lays his dead away,*
> *Nor looks to see the breaking day*
> *Across the mournful marbles play;*
> *Who hath not learned in hours of faith*
> *The truth to flesh and sense unknown,*
> *That Life is ever Lord of death,*
> *And Love can never lose its own.*
> —WHITTIER.

The day which thou fearest so much, and which thou callest thy last, is the birthday of an eternity.—SENECA.

THE CONCLUDING sentence of the previous chapter—"If not here, then elsewhere"—brings us to the theme of immortality.

What means this endless flood of souls, arriving who knows whence, departing who knows whither; these inconceivable billions passing, like grains of sand in an hourglass, through countless centuries that are gone, and through unnumbered centuries yet to come? Is man's life really nothing but "a sigh between two silences"; a narrow strand between two oceans of nonentity; a moment between an infinite past, of which we know a little, and an infinite future, of which we know nothing? Is Omar's philosophy the right one?

Ah, make the most of what we yet may spend,
Before we too into the dust descend;
Dust into dust, and under dust to lie,
Sans wine, sans song, sans singer, and...sans end!

Judged from a purely physical basis, death seems to be the end of all; but when we fix our thoughts upon that tiny spark of consciousness within us, which is endowed with the capacity of "reading God's thoughts after Him" in laws which govern the sidereal universe, of recognizing the Moral Law within our breasts, and even of asking the questions: "Whence have I come?" and "Shall I live again?" *that* makes another solution of the problem probable.

The materialist, of course, denies the existence of the soul. To him thought is a function of the brain, and nothing more. He tells us that "the brain produces thought, as the liver secretes bile," apparently unmindful of the fact that bile is a material substance, while thought is immaterial. "If by some accident," he says, "your skull is injured, or if you lose a little of its contents, you cannot think as once you could, your memory is impaired, or you no longer give to things their proper names. This proves that thought is a product of matter, or at least is absolutely dependent upon it, and that there is no such thing as a soul."

A psychist, however, reaches a very different conclusion. According to him, that accident has injured merely the *instrument* of the soul, but not the soul itself. As Beethoven could not have properly played one of his own symphonies, if an octave had been broken out of the keyboard of his piano, so he could not have composed that symphony, if he had lost a considerable portion of his brain. The injured instrument fetters the action of its master. And it is easily injured.

Dr. Maudsley, Professor Carpenter, Professor Schultze, and

other famous physiologists tell us that a fragment of the gray substance of the brain, *though not larger than the head of a pin,* contains many thousands of commingled globules and fibers! Of ganglion globules alone, according to the estimate of Meynert, there cannot be less than 600,000,000 in the convolutions of a human brain! No words can adequately describe the surpassing delicacy and minuteness of the structure of the brain and the intricacy of its arrangement. And what is still more wonderful, with every action of the mind some structural change takes place in the brain-substance. Its globules are not only incalculably numerous, but are in a state of constant birth, growth, decay and reproduction! The action of the mind occasions this; for the transmission of mind-force through the globules is accompanied by the decomposition of the pulp of the nerve threads, which meander among them in all conceivable directions. Scientists confess that "there is no glimmering of the way in which the energy, evolved thus by the destruction of the brain pulp, is changed into the phenomena of consciousness; no explanation how pulp-vibration is transformed into thought and feeling; and an unfathomed abyss still stretches out beyond the most advanced ground won by the most adventurous physiologists." In fact, *eliminate the idea of a spiritual force—the soul—behind that brain-pulp, and no explanation is possible.*

Professor James, however, has taught us that we may consider the brain not merely as a *producer,* but as a *transmitter.* The ruin of the transmitter would not affect the existence of the spiritual force behind it, which supplies our consciousness, any more than the destruction of a telephone instrument would mean the annihilation of the person using it. That spiritual force behind the brain would still remain intact, and might after death adopt still other methods of transmission—perhaps a spiritual body. The conclusion is irresistible that the moral and intellectual faculties of man belong to a region for which physical science has no explanation, and that this wonderfully complicated brain is a material instrument, on which an immaterial master plays. Of this, indeed, we are conscious. We *know* that *we* and the brain pulp are not the same entities. We *know* that there is an absolute difference between our personal consciousness and a mass of gray matter, however intricately fitted out with nerves.

Moreover, although every particle of matter in the human brain is changed repeatedly during man's lifetime, nevertheless *through that continual ebb and flow of molecules man's thread of consciousness remains unbroken from his infancy till death.* The same immaterial master continues to preside over the instrument, although the latter has had to be continually repaired. In other words, amid the flux of matter and the decay and renovation of corporeal particles, *our personal identity, consciously recognized, remains immutable.* In that unchanging thread of individual consciousness we find a proof of the existence of an immaterial soul, which is independent of material changes, and presumably therefore is independent also of the body's decomposition.

Marvelous to relate, this soul can also summon up by a mere mandate of volition numberless points along that thread of consciousness, another name for which is memory. The molecules of the brain, the eye, the ear and other sections of the bodily sensorium are not the same as when the incidents, thus recalled, made their impression on the sensitive nerves, *yet the enduring soul, which has survived those changes, can remember them!* Faces and landscapes, voices and words, music and even subtle odors—all present themselves; for, though the tablet on which they were registered has changed its composition, the soul can read at will the record, as heat brings out upon a faded manuscript words once inscribed there with invisible ink.

What also is that higher power which scans some dots or crooked letters on a printed page and apprehends from them at once exquisite music, inspiring poetry, or even the Word of God Himself? Is this capacity nothing but a function of matter? And what of the power which *originally wrote* those dots and crooked characters, expressed in them those noble sentiments, and left in them a deathless meaning that can thrill the hearts of millions? Is not that power something absolutely and essentially different from both the printed matter and the hand that prints?

Of all terrestrial beings man alone looks off from this thin rind of cooling earth into the depths of starlit space, and asks what it all means; he is the only one who feels that where his thought and imagination penetrate, there his soul may pass. It is usually said that the soul's survival of the dissolution of the body cannot be *scientifically* proved. Well, be it so; but *are physical and scientific methods the only ones by which that can be proved?* The materialist declares that there is no soul, because it cannot be discovered in dissecting the body, which is as unreasonable as to disbelieve in God because we cannot detect His presence in the lines of the solar spectrum. Let us remember that if science cannot prove that the soul DOES survive the body, it also cannot prove that it does NOT survive it.

All scientists agree that *matter* is indestructible, since its component parts, its atoms, never perish. But if dull, senseless matter thus persists, is it unreasonable to suppose that what is *spiritual* is also indestructible? Of course God can by His omnipotence annihilate the soul, but is it likely that He should desire to exterminate the spiritual life which He called into being? In view of the fact that *man's endowments fail here of their full development,* does it seem consonant with the wisdom of Almighty God that, after innumerable years of preparation, He will let the race die out, without fulfilling somewhere the potentialities which are inherent in it? Here they are certainly unfulfilled. Is it not, therefore, natural to expect another opportunity for their fulfillment? If man's capacities end merely in the grave, God's work appears to be imperfect. If this brief life be all, then man, who hopes for something better and higher than his present lot, who feels a love which triumphs over death, and longs for a reunion with the loved ones he has lost, is mocked by a mirage, as maddening as it is illusive. On this hypothesis the history of humanity is a tragedy, and man's soul is purposeless. Those who look forward to no other life, and hold that death is merely equivalent to

Quitting mortality, a quenched sun-wave,
The All-creating Presence for his grave,

may well despair, as did the gifted authoress of those lines, George Eliot [pseudonym of Mary Ann Evans, an English novelist—1819-1880], who from a once-devout Christian had become a disbeliever in Christianity. How mournful is her confession to a friend: "I see no hope for humanity but one grand, simultaneous act of suicide!"

In truth, of what use are our scientific discoveries, if all we ascertain, beyond the knowledge of phenomena, is the sterile fact that we, a colony of God-forsaken waifs, are floating on a planetary derelict in an uncharted sea, doomed to inevitable annihilation, without a notion of who started us upon our hopeless voyage, or where our shortlived barque will founder? Of what use are our spiritual longings, our intellectual achievements, and our deathless loves, if the brief period of human life upon our planet be nothing but an interval of fevered consciousness, a hyphen in that planet's history between one billion years of fire and another billion years of frost?

We have within us practically limitless capacities for acquiring knowledge, and *we crave that knowledge.* Yet in this life we can, as Newton said, pick up a few shells only on the shore of the ocean of truth. It is as if a man, who had with difficulty learned to read, had opened his first volume and deciphered a few lines, when he was smitten with blindness! In all the countless forms of animal and vegetable life around us, everything fulfills its purpose. In man, however, we have a being who scarcely has begun his work, before he has to leave it! The noble pagan moralist Plutarch says: "God is a trifler, if He makes so much of creatures in whom there is nothing permanent, nothing steadfast, and nothing which resembles Himself. . . For Him to spend His care on creatures such as these would be to imitate those who make gardens in oyster shells."

A somewhat similar idea is expressed by Goethe in his criticism of *Hamlet*—"A mighty purpose in the human soul is like an oak, planted in a china vase. The vessel is inevitably shattered by the expansion of the seed within. So is it, if we limit man's existence to the narrow period between the cradle and the grave. Is the growing plant to wither as soon as the vessel is filled or broken by it?" Even the skeptic, Buckle, wrote that the belief in a future state approaches more nearly to certainty than any other belief, and that its destruction would drive most of us to despair. In order to justify the introduction of man upon this planet by a Being of infinite wisdom and goodness, we feel that man's life should not be left incomplete. Our undeveloped powers, therefore, are prophetic of their own development, *although not necessarily in this world.*

If any further essential evolution of man upon this earth had been intended, there has been plenty of time for its commencement to have been observed in the last two thousand years. We are told that man's progress now is intellectual, not corporeal. But even so, it must be said that man has made very little real intellectual progress in the last two millenniums. Eliminating mechanical inventions and purely scientific discoveries (which, grand and wonderful as many of them are, *are not of the highest order of mentality,* and do not make man either better or more spiritual), we seem to have retrograded since the days of Sophocles and Aristotle, when, it is generally conceded, the Athenians reached the highest intellectual level yet attained by any people. There is scarcely a great modern idea (outside the realm just mentioned), which was not once the property of the ancients. The genii of the past still dominate a mighty portion of the intellectual world. Pythagoras is the father of our pantheism; Democritus the inventor of the atomic theory. "Out of Plato," says Emerson, "come all things that are still written and debated among men of thought." Praxiteles and Phidias are still unrivalled; Homer is still the "Father of Poetry"; Demosthenes is the model of orators; Seneca, Epictetus, Plutarch, and Marcus Aurelius, as moralists, are unsurpassed. According to the theory that man's evolution is now purely intellectual, we ought to have had by this time many masterminds; but the contrary is the case.

It may be even fairly questioned whether the power of the human brain has kept its former average, now that its strength is dissipated by the immense diffusion of intellectual culture over many fields. Gladstone stated it as his opinion that the brains of the modern generation of Britons showed a deterioration of power, as compared with those of the Elizabethan age. The *entire stock* of the world's knowledge is, of course, enormously increased, but the brain-power itself is decreasing, partly because of the vast amount of knowledge to be acquired, partly because of the superficial way in which we hurry over it. If, then, we cannot see here any essential evolution in mankind, either corporeally or intellectually, in the space of two millenniums, may we not reasonably hope that the next step toward the realization of man's possibilities will be taken by him on another stage, the lowly door to which is death?

The science of evolution points the way to this [To be precise, biological evolution is rather a theory than a science, and research continues to pile up evidence against the theory. As the author explains, man's lack of evolution on this earth supports the idea that he can be perfected in a life after death.—*Editor,* 1990.], and Christ Himself assures us of it. "Because I live," He says, "ye shall live also." How sublime, too, are the words of St. Paul: "There are bodies celestial, and bodies terrestrial; but one is the glory of the celestial, and another of the terrestrial. . . So also is the resurrection of the dead. It is sown in corruption; it shall rise in incorruption; it is sown in dishonour; it shall rise in glory. It is sown in weakness, it shall rise in power. . . For this corruptible must put on incorruption; and this mortal must put on immortality." (*1 Cor.* 15:40, 42-43, 53).

Think for a moment of the grave, and try to imagine yourself, your soul, your aspirations, your capacities, as ending
there! We feel instinctively that *we* are something higher than
our bodies, and are destined to survive them, as we survive
the parting with an outworn garment.

It is inspiring also to remember that, in holding a belief in
a future life, we are companioned not by Christians only, but
also by the noblest spirits of the pagan past. Socrates held that
death gave to the soul a happy release from the body. "I am
persuaded," he said, "that I am going to other gods, who are
wise and good; and also, I trust, to men departed, who are
better than those I leave behind; therefore I do not grieve, as
otherwise I might, for I have good hope that there is yet something awaiting the dead, and a far better lot for the good than
for the wicked." "You may do with my body what you will,"
he also said, "provided you do not imagine that to be me."
Cicero declared that he was filled with joy at the thought of
the bright day, which should transport him to that meeting
place of upright souls, whither his loved ones had preceded
him. Seneca also wrote: "This life is only a prelude to eternity...The day will come that shall separate this mixture of
soul and body, of divine and human. My body I will leave
where I found it; my soul I will restore to Heaven, which would
have already had it but for the clog that keeps it down...Let
us live in our bodies, as if we were only to lodge in them to-
night, and to leave them tomorrow...Let us measure life by
deeds, not by time. To die sooner or later is not the main concern, but to die well or ill; for death brings us to immortality.
Our bodies must perish, as being only the covering of the soul.
We shall then discover the secrets of nature; darkness shall be
dispersed, and our souls shall be irradiated with light and
glory—a glory without a shadow; a glory that shall surround
us, and from which we shall look down, and see day and night
beneath us. If we cannot lift up our eyes toward the lamp of
Heaven without being dazzled, what shall we do when we
come to behold the Divine light in its illustrious original?"

Another powerful argument for a future life is furnished by the conviction, which most of us instinctively and necessarily feel, that *God's great Moral Law must ultimately triumph.*

This craving for a compensation for the inequalities of justice in this life is undeniable. We see it even in our wish that fiction and the drama should display the final victory of the good and kind, the punishment of the bad and cruel. If such is not the end, we are dissatisfied. A pessimistic ending may be "true to life" and more "artistic," but we do not like it. We feel it is unjust. Our human life may well be likened to the opening act of a drama, the plot of which is not yet clear. Hence we desire and expect to see its further development. There is indeed a sense in which the verdict of mankind anticipates God's final judgment, for in the long run history usually gives its honors to the good and loyal, while the tyrannical and treacherous are detested. Martyrs, religious or political, seldom fail eventually to be revered, while those who murder them are execrated. Criminals also, as a rule, are brought to justice; "murder will out" in a majority of cases; nor are the guilty often happy in their guilt, even though sin may have rendered them materially prosperous. Remorse is at times a very real and terrible consequence of crime. We also see the effects of sin upon our *characters.* Good actions tend to make us better, nobler and stronger; bad actions, on the contrary, debase us. There is no escape from this spiritual result. In this respect, whatsoever a man soweth, that *must* he also reap. His sin may be forgiven him by God, but it will leave its stain upon his memory, its taint upon his thought, a weakness in his will, an evil tendency in his impulses. And *the spiritual record stands!*

> *The Moving Finger writes; and, having writ,*
> *Moves on; nor all your piety nor wit*
> *Shall lure it back to cancel half a line,*
> *Nor all your tears wash out a word of it.*

What is this but the application of the inexorable law of

cause and effect to the immaterial world—that is to say, to the soul?

But for the average man the verdict of posterity is too remote, the instances of retribution are too few, and the effects of sin upon the moral nature not enough, to satisfy his craving for God's perfect justice. Nevertheless he still has confidence that the books of God will ultimately balance. Why is this? Whence comes it that, despite so many facts which militate against it, man still believes in his accountability to God, and feels assured that justice will prevail at last, dispensed by a personal God, or by an impersonal force, called destiny, or karma? Even our modern pantheists and agnostics cannot wholly give up the Greek idea of an inevitable nemesis for crime. They scoff, it is true, at the supposition of a personal God, yet they retain the more incredible notion of an impersonal fate as the awarder of even-handed justice, or as the avenger of wrongdoing!

What is the origin of this irresistible conviction? It comes not from experience, for much of our experience is not of the kind of which we have just spoken. Retribution does not *always* follow guilt and strike the guilty one. In this world crime is frequently successful; the criminal is often undetected; sometimes the innocent actually suffers for the guilty. Plainly a faith in ultimate justice, therefore, must be born in man, together with the Moral Law itself. It is easy to assert that, since God tolerates injustice here, He will continue to tolerate it hereafter, but the heart cries out against such an idea, and reason finds that it would be illogical. The very fact that man's desire for the triumph of God's justice is *sufficiently strong to form one of the principal grounds of his belief in immortality,* is in itself a reason for believing in that triumph; and since it is indisputable that the vast majority of mankind does look forward to that reign of righteousness, we may feel sure that what is so instinctively and universally demanded by the human soul, must have a basis in reality.

Besides all this, however, to minds amenable to the argument from Revelation comes the overwhelming testimony of Christ Himself. *His entire teaching rests upon the theory that our souls are deathless,* and He continually alludes to the future life, as being that for which we here are to prepare ourselves. He does not, it is true, attempt to demonstrate this, but takes the fact for granted, as one assumes the existence of one's native land, when speaking of it in a foreign country. "My kingdom is not of this world," *(John* 18:36). He says. "In my Father's house there are many mansions. If not, I would have told you: because I go to prepare a place for you. And if I shall go, and prepare a place for you, I will come again, and will take you to myself; that where I am, you also may be." *(John* 14:2-3). He presents indeed the future life *as the complement and justification of this one,* and lays great emphasis on the fact that in that coming life there will be a Divine Judgment of men, according to the deeds done by them in the body.

It is, in fact, *Christ Himself* who is to come in the clouds of Heaven and in the glory of the Father *to judge, reward and punish the deeds done in the flesh!* Not only did Jesus teach this in such parables as those of Dives and Lazarus, the tares and the wheat, the wise and the foolish virgins, and many more; the direct and explicit language which He used in regard to a future judgment is unmistakable. When we read, for example, the solemn words contained in the Gospel of St. Matthew, beginning with the declaration, "When the Son of man shall come in his majesty," *(Matt.* 25:31-46), etc., and other kindred passages, there can be no doubt whatever as to the message that Christ intended to convey. Its truth indeed is recognized by all Christians who repeat sincerely the sentence of their creed: "Whence He shall come to judge the quick and the dead."

Moreover, Christ distinctly bade the poor in spirit and those who are persecuted in this world for righteousness' sake, to rejoice and be exceeding glad, for great shall be their reward in Heaven. This meets the longing of our souls. When we survey this world, with its appalling crimes and manifold injustices, we feel it is impossible that men can be allowed to pass triumphantly through careers of iniquity, and then slip out of all accountability through annihilation, eluding thus the justice of Eternal God. We also feel that it is utterly incredible that nothing in the future will reward the virtuous who have suffered here, and compensate God's children who have here been wretched. Instinctively we place our confidence in the Divine assurance: "And God shall wipe away all tears from their eyes; and death shall be no more, nor mourning, nor crying, nor sorrow shall be any more; for the former things are passed away." (*Apoc.* 21:4).

Nevertheless, in spite of these considerations and the unequivocal statements of Christ, we have to face a fact which Dr. William Osler mentions in his *Science and Immortality*. He writes: "Without a peradventure it may be said that a living faith in a future existence has not the slightest influence in the settlement of the grave social and national problems that confront the race today." Well, so much the worse, then, for the race. The fact that many at the present time seem wholly indifferent to the question of immortality, and have no faith in any future system of rewards and punishments, *has nothing to do with the truth or falsity of the dogma.*

Probably most of those Indifferentists have not seriously thought upon the subject, or do not wish to think of it. They should, however, bear in mind (as has already been observed) that though it be impossible to prove scientifically that the soul *does* survive the body, it is equally impossible to prove that it does *not* survive it. Hence, the *possibility* of a future existence must be reckoned with, even by those who hold that death ends all. They cannot be certain that their view is the correct one. In fact, the only future event of which they can be absolutely certain is that of death, which cannot under ordinary circumstances even be foreseen. If it be true that millions are today indifferent to the question of a future life, it proves how far our prevalent materialism has lowered man's moral standards, but it does *not* prove that a future life is impossible.

Certain it is that, in the case of all of us, the time is short before the question must be settled for us, individually and alone. We may for a few years keep this greatest of all subjects from our thoughts by clogging them with worldly cares, or by a mental opiate of dissipation; but not always. We can for a time refuse to lift our gaze above the glare of the electric light; yet overhead still wait for us the starry heavens, and in our souls abides the sense of our accountability to God. A time will come—may come at any moment—when this ephemeral existence, with its business occupations, wealth and pleasures, must be left. Some callously declare that they shall then expire like the beasts, and pass at once to nothingness. But, in the face of man's unsatisfied desires and potentialities, of his instinctive longing for the reign of perfect justice, and of the positive words of Christ in reference to a future judgment, how do they *know* that they will pass thus into annihilation, untried, unrecompensed, unpunished? They do *not* know it. They cannot know it. *The fact that they desire it does not make it true.*

And if they do not find annihilation at death's portal, but on the contrary confront their Maker and their Judge there, well, what then? One thing is sure—of all that they desired here—rank, riches, pleasures, personal beauty, power, fame—they can take nothing with them. All that will go with them into the future life will be—not what they *have,* but what they *are.* To all men, therefore, it must seem possible, to most men probable, and to Christians certain, that this life is not all; that this world's sorrow, suffering and bereavement are *not* the meaningless precursors of annihilation; that all the great achievements of the human mind will *not* end uselessly upon a lifeless orb; that earth's injustices will *not* rest unavenged; that worthy, pious and self-sacrificing deeds will *not* go unrewarded; and, above all, that Heaven is *not* a mere mirage, nor God a myth, nor immortality an idle dream.

Chapter 7

REVELATION

One God, one law, one element,
And one far-off, divine event,
To which the whole creation moves.
                              —TENNYSON.

First, I would ask: What do you believe? Put it in words.
Conceive it in thought. Fix your mind's eye upon it. Put it
in writing in some silent hour; know at least what it is. As
you value your eternal soul. . . be not content to abide in uncer-
tainty and indefiniteness concerning the truth, which you know
to be vitally necessary to your salvation.
                              —CARDINAL MANNING.

God's Revelation of Himself is a drawing back of the veil
or curtain, which concealed Him from men; it is not man find-
ing out God, but God discovering Himself to man.—TRENCH.

THE TESTIMONY of Jesus Christ to the reality of a future life and a final judgment of mankind was either the utterance of a fallible human being, or it was part of the Divine Revelation, which He brought to this world.

My next inquiry, therefore, was whether such a Revelation had been made, and if so, whether the nature of the message and the messenger were of such a character that I could accept them as Divine. As for the inherent probability of a Revelation being made by God to man, I asked myself, if it were rationally conceivable that such a God as I had come to believe in would set in motion this amazing piece of mechanism, called the Earth, and then deliberately leave it to its fate, neglecting in particular the finest and most delicate portion of it all—the human soul. It absolutely contradicts the character of such a Being that He should let this human colony rush aimlessly through space upon a relatively short-lived globe, with no instruction from Him whatsoever, and no Revelation of His will concerning it. If man has been created for some definite purpose, as is to be supposed from an intelligent Creator, how can he learn the nature of that purpose, the goal assigned to him; and the conditions of attaining it, unless he has received from God some indication of His wish and some commands as to man's life of conduct?

That some Divine Revelation would be given to mankind is, therefore, antecedently probable; and such an expectation was cherished by many of the noblest intellects of antiquity. Centuries before the multitude heard from the lips of Christ the Sermon on the Mount, Socrates said to Alcibiades: "It seems to me necessary to wait *until someone comes to instruct us how we ought to conduct ourselves toward God and men."* Seneca also wrote: "No man is in a condition to help himself; *someone above him must stretch forth his hand and raise him up."* To those great souls it did not seem consistent with God's character that, having made us and so carefully prepared a home for us, He should abandon us to total ignorance.

Nor has He done so. First, the impressive Revelation of His power and wisdom through His works has been sufficient, almost universally, to prove to man that God exists; and this belief is strengthened by the Revelation of the Moral Law, implanted in the human breast, which also leads man to believe that God is righteous, and will ultimately usher in the reign of justice, which we all desire. These two great Revelations were, for centuries, all that the vast majority of the race possessed, and by *their* modicum of light, not ours, will that majority no doubt be judged. St. Paul (*Rom.* 1:20) affirms that those who reject these proofs of God's existence are without excuse; and if by careful searching we could find (which is exceedingly doubtful) a race of men with no belief in God whatever, they would assuredly be the most degraded of the human species, with whom it were no honor for a modern atheist to be allied.

The Christian religion, however, claims that God has made to men a much more definite and perfect Revelation of Himself than those of natural religion and conscience. Is this true? That was the next essential point for me to settle.

Newman has nobly said of this Revelation: "It comes to you recommended and urged upon you by the most favorable anticipations of reason. The very difficulties of nature make it likely that a Revelation should be made; the very mysteries of creation call for some act on the part of the Creator, by which those mysteries shall be alleviated to you or compensated. . .*You cannot help expecting it from the hands of the All-merciful,* unworthy as you feel yourselves of it. It is not that you can claim it, but that He inspires the hope of it; it is not that you are worthy of the gift, but it is the gift which is worthy of your Creator. . .The very fact that there is a Creator, and a hidden one, powerfully bears you on, and sets you down at the very threshold of a Revelation, and leaves you there, looking up earnestly for Divine tokens that a Revelation has been made."

That a Divine Revelation will contain no mysteries we cannot, of course, expect. If it had none, it would not be a Revelation. A Revelation from God must reveal something which man's unaided reason could not possibly have ascertained; for if the truths revealed could have been gained by human reason, what was the need of the Revelation? It follows that a Divine disclosure of truths, otherwise unattainable, should be accepted, not critically and skeptically, but as a message from God, and in that childlike spirit which Jesus pronounced necessary for entering the kingdom of Heaven.

A revelation, however, implies a revealer; a message necessitates a messenger. Christ claimed to be that messenger. His words upon this point are unmistakable. He stated repeatedly that He had come from His Father, as the Son of God, for a special purpose. "For this was I born, and for this came I into the world; that I should bear witness unto the truth."

(John 18:37). His teachings, therefore, were the Revelation which His Father had commissioned Him to bring to mankind. "The Son of man *is come* to seek and to save that which was lost." *(Luke* 19:10). "He who honoureth not the Son, honoureth not the Father, who *hath* sent him."*(John* 5:23). "I *am come in the name of my Father,* and you receive me not." *(John* 5:43). "And the Father himself who hath sent me, hath given testimony of me." *(John* 5:37). "I must work the works of him that *sent* me, whilst it is day." *(John* 9:4). "Father, the hour is come. . .*I have finished the work which thou gavest me to do." (John* 17:1, 4).

Where, then, is the record of this Divine Revelation, brought by Christ to mankind, to be found? Unquestionably in the New Testament and in the teaching of the Church which He founded. Returning first, therefore, to a study of my long-neglected Bible, what was I to say of it? Certainly nothing disrespectful. To speak even flippantly of the Bible is to show oneself an ignoramus. In a merely literary sense the writings it contains are unsurpassed; and were we to eliminate from literature that Book of books, with all that is connected with it, or has been inspired by it, the void would be appalling. After thousands of years it still remains the most perfect form in which religious sentiment ever expressed itself. Renan declares: "Hebrew literature *is* the Bible—the Book *par excellence,* the universal study. Other literatures of the East can be read and appreciated only by the learned. Israel alone, among all the Orientals, had the privilege of writing for the whole world. Millions of men, scattered throughout the world, know no other poetry." *(Rev. des Deux Mondes,* November, 1855). The precepts of the Vedas, the ethical teachings of Buddha, Mencius, Confucius, and the Stoic philosophers Marcus Aurelius, Seneca and Epictetus, are admirable, when taken by themselves; but, placed beside the words of Christ, they are like ordinary stones compared with precious gems.

What, then, was the essence of Christ's teaching? First, He proclaimed the *Fatherhood of God.* He does not represent God

as a vague, impersonal Entity, "an enduring Power, not ourselves, that makes for righteousness," as Matthew Arnold defines the Deity; but rather that God is our living, loving Father,
to whom we are to pray precisely in these terms, "Our Father, Who art in Heaven." This Father, Christ assured us, has
not abandoned us, but, on the contrary, loves us and cares
for us continually, and He affirmed this not speculatively but
"with authority, and not as the scribes."

Secondly, He revealed the Godhead in the solemn mysteries of His own Sonship, and of the nature and office of the
Holy Ghost, "the Comforter," whose coming He promised,
to complete His own Revelation.

Thirdly, He declared repeatedly man's accountability to God,
and prophesied a final judgment of mankind and a never-
ending life beyond the grave.

If He gave little information about that future life, it is
probably due to the fact that to us, with our present limitations, its conditions would be incomprehensible. This He im-
plied in the words: "If I have spoken to you earthly things,
and ye believe not: how will you believe, if I shall speak to
you of heavenly things?" (*John* 3:12). How indeed can we
comprehend a spiritual existence, where all the bodily appetites, which constitute such a large and dangerous element
in our earthly lives, shall have become extinct, and where
wealth, power and social eminence, as we know them, shall
have no more value? Christ exercised certainly, in regard to
all details about the future life, a serious, and no doubt intentional, reserve. He even discouraged too much curiosity about
it. When one of His disciples tried to obtain some special
information in reference to the future, the Saviour answered
him: "So I will have him remain till I come, what is it to
thee? follow thou me." (*John* 21:22).

Very significant, however, is one illuminating utterance
which He made to the Sadducees, when they had cynically
asked Him whose wife would be in the next world the woman
who had had in this one several husbands. Jesus replied to

them: "In the resurrection they shall neither marry nor be married; but shall be as the angels of God in heaven." (*Matt.* 22:30). In other words, *not physical and animal, but incorporeal and spiritual conditions there prevail.*

Yet ignorance of the characteristics of the "heavenly country" and of the "city which hath foundations, whose builder and maker is God," is no argument for their non-existence. On the contrary, in view of Christ's positive assurances on the subject we can be certain that they do exist, although no mortal eye hath ever seen them. Our ignorance of the future life has indeed one positive advantage—it keeps us relatively humble. If there remained no mysteries for us to stand in awe of, how utterly unbearable would be man's pride and arrogance, when even now he thinks he can exclude his Maker from the universe, and often speaks of the conditions of the life beyond the grave in terms of vulgarity and levity.

The principal characteristics of Christ's Revelation, therefore, are: God—an Eternal Spirit, our Creator and Father; the Incarnate Son of God, sent by the Father to redeem the human race; man's accountability to God, and the certainty of a future life and of a judgment to come. Added to these, as parts of His Divine mission, are also the code of morals taught in His parables and in His Sermon on the Mount, and the founding by Him of a Church, which was to preach and to preserve His teachings till the consummation of the world.

When one reflects upon it, it is truly a fearful thing that there are still so many in the world who disbelieve the fact that God once sent His Son upon this mission, and who, scoffing at His Revelation, deem the Incarnate God simply a mortal like themselves! Still are the mournful words of St. John true: "The light shineth in darkness, and the darkness did not comprehend it (1:5)...He was in the world, and the world was made by him, and the world knew him not"! (1:10). At the present time, the enemies of Christ are exulting over what they term the failure of His so-called mission and the "breakdown" of Christianity.

It is unquestionable that something has failed and broken down, but *that something is not Christianity; it is Christendom.* The words are not synonymous. Christianity is a spiritual appellation, Christendom a political or geographical one. The religion of Christ is not to blame for what self-designated "Christian" nations make of it. The world would be relieved, as if by magic, from its sin and misery, if men would only honestly receive Christ's Revelation as the guide of their lives, and obey its precepts. If the "Christian" world is not yet better, *it is because it is not Christian.* The fault lies, not with the Founder of Christianity, but partly with the millions who reject Him, and partly with those of His professed adherents whose lives form frequently a fatal obstacle to the acceptance of His Gospel. Countless instances could, of course, be cited to prove this, both in the history of nations and individuals. Suffice it now to mention the indisputable fact that the progress of Christianity in the less civilized portions of the world has been greatly hindered, precisely because so many nominal Christians there have robbed, brutally treated and murdered helpless natives. Such conduct makes the very name of Christ abhorred by the poor, hapless "heathen" victims who inevitably associate the men who torture, exploit and enslave them with the religion taught by missionaries of the same race and color. What shall we say, too, of the "Christians" who manufacture in Europe, in large quantities, bronze and iron idols and send them out to Asia, Africa and Oceania in the very ships which carry thither Christian missionaries and the publications of the Bible Society?

When men proclaim the "breakdown of Christianity," therefore, what do they mean by "Christianity"? Much of what passes under that name is nothing but hypocrisy, and much of it is "Rationalism" wrongly labelled. That sort of thing has unquestionably broken down; but that, I repeat, is not Christianity, but Christendom. Moreover, as Mr. Mallock reminds us, even if Protestantism or distinctively Rationalistic

Christianity should prove a failure, that would by no means prove that Christianity, *as a whole,* had broken down.

These do not constitute the only part of Christianity. "We have still," he says, "the Church of Rome to deal with, which is Christianity in its oldest, most legitimate and most coherent form." Now the Church of Rome will certainly *not* break down. We have Christ's word for that. Continually attacked by new enemies, it is as constantly defended by new recruits. Hence Catholics always have this ancient, impregnable, God-protected fortress to fall back upon, however fiercely storms of infidelity may beat upon it.

Protestants, however, when once their faith in an infallible book is lost, have nothing left. Their ethical societies, numberless antagonistic sects, and national establishments—all differing and without authority—are, when a tidal wave of skepticism strikes them, like ships without a rudder, that either drift as derelicts, or go to pieces on the shoals of doubt or the reefs of unbelief. The Catholic Church, on the contrary, stands where it has always stood, changeless in form, uncompromising in its dogmas. The Pope still speaks with authority, as he has always done, in matters of faith and morals. If the world shuts its ears to his benignant voice, or shouts it down with blasphemy, and rushes on to godlessness and ruin, it may indeed have failed, but *the Catholic Church has not failed!*

From the contemplation of murderous, godless Christendom, as it stands today, mankind must learn the need of turning from the pitiful travesty of Christianity, which has too long prevailed, to find once more the real Christianity in the Revelation of Jesus Christ. To Him and to His teachings the weary, disillusioned world must come, if it is not to perish. Most of us think that we know and understand these teachings of Christ, but do we? Let us re-read His words thoughtfully and, above all, prayerfully. In doing this, after an interval of many years, I personally found that the Gospels were to me practically a new book. Scales fell from my eyes, and beauty, truth and spiritual sublimity—voiced in Divine simplicity—revealed themselves throughout their pages. So powerfully indeed was I impressed by the change in my appreciation of Christ's language, that I was constrained to kneel in prayer and ask for further light and guidance from the Maker of my soul. It seemed impossible that *that* petition should remain unanswered; and my request expressed itself in Newman's touching lines:

> *Lead, kindly Light, amid the encircling gloom;*
> *Lead Thou me on!*

Chapter 8

"WHAT THINK YE OF CHRIST?"

What think ye of Christ?—MATT. 22:42.

Not even now could it be easy, even for an unbeliever, to find a better translation of the rule of virtue from the abstract into the concrete, than to endeavour so to live, that Christ would approve our life.—JOHN STUART MILL.

Whatever else may be taken away from us by rational criticism, Christ is still left, a unique figure, not more unlike all his precursors than all his followers.—JOHN STUART MILL.

I TURNED NOW from the message to the Messenger, and put to myself the question which Jesus put to the Pharisees: *"What think ye of Christ?"* (Matt. 22:42).

I knew what I *had tried* to think of Him for many years, but that humanitarian view of Him now seemed to me impossible. Again I studied His extraordinary life. What were the facts disclosed? Born in a manger; of a lowly origin; dwelling for thirty years not only in a conquered country, but in Galilee—an insignificant province of that country, and in one of the obscurest and least-esteemed villages of that province—Nazareth; a member of a narrow and self-centered race; speaking, not one of the world's great languages, Greek or Latin, but a dialect of Aramaic; pursuing the humble occupation of a carpenter; leaving no record of His personal appearance, or of His views concerning science, history, art, literature, or philosophy; associating all His life with simple, poor, uneducated people; having no wealth, and wishing to acquire none; winning His followers by no earthly favors; taking no part in politics; protected by no influential friends in either the Roman government circles or the Jewish priesthood; on the contrary, denouncing many of Jerusalem's aristocrats as "whited sepulchres, hypocrites, and broods of vipers"; selecting His disciples and future Apostles among humble fishermen; founding no philosophical school; never writing a line Himself, or dictating a line to others; leaving behind Him not a trace of personal correspondence; living for only three years in the public gaze; and, finally, before reaching middle life, dying by the shameful death of the Cross, between two thieves, and owing His place of burial and even His cerements to the bounty of a stranger! Could anything seem less likely than such a record to transform the world? Yet, in spite of all these apparently insurmountable obstacles to success, Jesus of Nazareth has affected human thought, human character, human ideals, and human history more deeply than all the other children of mankind combined; has won the adoring love of countless millions; and has been worshipped as the Son of God for nineteen hundred years!

And this not undesignedly or by chance; for, while He was still on earth, He claimed to be the Son of God, and predicted: "I, if I be lifted up, will draw all men unto Me." This He—and He alone—has done through all the ages, in all lands, and among innumerable myriads of men. His life and death mark the turning point of the history of the world, of which He is the central figure.

Lamartine has truly said that Christ's tomb was the grave of the old world and the cradle of the new. Moreover, the stream of spiritual energy which came from Him has never spent itself. Even Strauss says: "Christ and Christianity represent the highest moral ideas to which the world can ever expect to attain"; and Renan declares: "Jesus will never be surpassed. His religion will forever grow young again. All ages will proclaim that among the sons of men there has not been born a greater than Jesus. Jesus is without a peer. His glory remains intact. In Him was concentrated all that is good and elevated in our nature. Each of us owes to Jesus all that is best in him. Jesus remains an inexhaustible principle of moral regeneration for humanity. The Sermon on the Mount will never be excelled. The foundation of true religion is verily His work. The morality of the Gospel...is the most beautiful code of perfect life which any moralist has traced." He also speaks of Christ as "that sublime person, who still presides perpetually over the destiny of the world." (*Vie de Jésus*).

Buddha is sometimes thought to bear a closer resemblance to Christ than any other prominent figure of the past. In gentleness, humility and charity this probably is true. The mighty multitude of Buddhists in the world attests the fact. But there is still a heaven-wide difference between their respective attitudes. Buddha advanced no claim to be either God or the Son of God. He longed for death, and taught his followers to long for it, and to extirpate from their souls the will to live, because the miseries of life were too intense to be endured. Christ, on the other hand, while recognizing all the sin and misery of earthly existence, did not proclaim annihilation to be man's greatest boon, but pointed to a life hereafter, as the compensation and justification of the present one. Buddha believed and taught that human blessedness could be obtained only through the extinction of man's desires— which are alike the origin of temptation and the source of suffering. Jesus, however, was "led up *by the Spirit*" (that is, *by God's will*) "to be tempted in the wilderness."

He was, in fact, "tempted in all points like as we are, yet without sin." *Human character, perfected through suffering and through resisting temptations—not through escaping it by mental apathy or moral numbness*—that is the ideal of Christ, the cornerstone of Christian doctrine.

Many also have compared Christ, as a teacher of morals, with other ethical teachers, such as the Stoic philosophers. Jesus was, however, not only infinitely more than a teacher of morals, but, even as such, He represented an entirely different point of view. The aim of the Stoics was to hold themselves erect in hours of adversity, and to defy unflinchingly the blows of fate; but the strength thus gained was not to be exerted in behalf of the weak and suffering. The poor, the slaves, the outcasts of the world were not the objects of their care. Christ, on the contrary, announced His mission to be pre-eminently "to seek and to save the lost," and "not to be ministered unto, but to minister"; "He that is greatest among you shall be your servant." Here indeed is something unique in history. Jesus asked nothing of the world in temporal advantages; it could give Him nothing. *He* it was who had *something to give;* and what? His life, "a ransom for many"! There is something superhuman in this absolute independence of the world, and in the calm assumption that the gift of His life would be such a ransom; and that, when lifted up upon the Cross, He should draw all men unto Him.

He showed not the slightest doubt of being able to fulfill these words. In reading them, we feel that we are hearing someone who is not of this planet. We have indeed already seen that Christ used frequently the expression: "I am *come*" to do this or to fulfill that; and in these words "I am come" there is something awe-inspiring. For *if* He has come, WHY has He come? Whence, and for what purpose? How does He propose to save the lost, for whose ransom He will give His life?

His method is at once simple and sublime. *He founds a kingdom*—not an impersonal, figurative sovereignty, but one that is vital and intensely personal. At the head of this kingdom He places Himself. He is its personal Ideal, its Master, "the Way, the Truth and the Life." His followers are to "follow" Him. "I am the door," He said; "by me, if any man enter in, he shall be saved." (*John* 10:9).

The test of Christianity, therefore, is *loyalty to Christ personally;* and His question to St. Peter, before He conferred upon him his commission, was: "Lovest thou Me?" It is evident, therefore, that Christ's Kingdom is not of this world. It rests not upon grandeur, but on humility; not on the wisdom of men, but upon childlike faith; its power consists not in force, but in weakness; not in supremacy, but in service;

not in severity, but in affection. Its King subdues His subjects by His love for them. Earthly potentates shed the blood of others to acquire and maintain their thrones; Christ sheds His own!

The great historical scholar, Professor Harnack of the University of Berlin, although a radical free-thinker, uses in regard to Christ such phrases as the following: "A ray from His light transforms a man inwardly." "His Gospel cannot be replaced by anything." "It stands above all rivals of that time and all time." "He performed many wonderful, and in part still unexplained, deeds." "With perfect calmness He lived and breathed in a religion which He Himself had created in its essence." "He felt and thought with constant reference to God." "In liberty and serenity of soul none of the prophets approached Him by comparison." "His preaching has lost nothing in freshness during the centuries." "The appearance of Christ is and remains the unique foundation of all moral civilization." Yet these are tributes paid to Christ by one who regards Him merely as a *man!* What, therefore, should be thought of Him by those who hold Him to have been Divine?

Other great intellects, from whom we hardly should expect such testimony, have been even more outspoken in their admiration of the Founder of Christianity. Reopening the *Memorial of Saint Helena,* I read again the impressive words uttered by the dying Napoleon in reference to the Divinity of Christ: "I know men, and I tell you that Jesus Christ is not a man. Superficial minds see a resemblance between Christ and the founders of empires and the gods of other religions. That resemblance does not exist. There is between Christianity and whatever other religion the distance of infinity. Between Christ and whomsoever else in the world there is no possible term of comparison...His birth, the history of His life, the profundity of His doctrine, His Gospel, His apparition, His empire, His march across the ages and realms— everything is for me a prodigy, a mystery insoluble...Here I see nothing human...His Revelation is a Revelation from an Intelligence which certainly is not that of man...With what authority does He teach men to pray!...You speak of Caesar, of Alexander; of their conquests, and of the enthusiasm they kindled in the hearts of their soldiers; but can you conceive of a *dead* man making conquests with an army faithful and entirely devoted to his memory? My armies have forgotten me, even while living, as the Carthaginian army forgot Hannibal. Such is our power. A single battle lost crushes us, and adversity scatters our friends...How different is the power of the God of the Christians, and the perpetual miracle of the progress of the faith and government of His Church! Nations pass away, thrones crumble, but the Church remains...It is true, that Christ proposes to our faith a series of mysteries; but He commands with authority that we should believe them, giving no other reason than those tremendous words—*I am God!* What an abyss He creates by that declaration between Himself and all the fabricators of religion! What audacity, what sacrilege, what blasphemy, if it were not true!...Behold the approaching fate of him who has been called the great Napoleon! What an abyss between my profound misery and the eternal reign of Christ, which is proclaimed, loved and adored, and is extending over all the earth! Is this to die? Is it not rather to live? The death of Christ! It is the death of a God!"

Another remarkable tribute is that of the rationalist historian, Lecky. In his *History of European Morals* (Vol. 2, p. 9), we read: "The utmost the Stoic ideal could become was a model for imitation, and the admiration it inspired could never deepen into affection. It was reserved for Christianity to present to the world an ideal character, which, through all the changes of eighteen centuries, *has inspired the hearts of men with an impassioned love;* has shown itself capable of acting on all ages, nations, temperaments and conditions; has been not only the highest pattern of virtue, but the strongest incentive to its practice; and has exercised so deep an influence, that it may be truly said that the simple record of three short years of active life has done more to regenerate and soften mankind than all the disquisitions of philosophers and all the exhortations of moralists." The same author, in his *History of Rationalism,* says of the Founder of Christianity: "*There is indeed nothing more wonderful in the history of the human race* than the way in which that ideal has traversed the lapse of ages, acquiring a new strength and beauty with each advance of civilization, and infusing its beneficent influence into every sphere of thought and action...*This is a phenomenon altogether unique in history.*" (Vol. 2, p. 312).

Another wonderful apostrophe to Christ I found in the works of the Spanish diplomat, Donoso Cortez, who represents the Divine Master as thus addressing humanity: "It is I who, before appearing before kings, revealed Myself to shepherds; and who, before calling to Myself the rich, summoned to Myself the poor. It is I who, when I was on earth, restored health to the sick, sight to the blind, healing to the lepers, activity to the paralyzed, and life to the dead. It is I who, standing between rich and poor, called to Me with a tender voice poor, ignorant and humble fisherman. To them I devoted Myself entirely; I washed their feet; I gave to them My body for their nourishment, and for their drink My blood. To that point even did I love them! The sovereign Lord of all things, I stripped Myself of everything in order to become one of you. It is to one of you also, and not to some prince of this world, that I confided the government of My holy Church; and before conferring this supreme power upon him, I did not ask him what he possessed or what he knew, but...*if he loved Me!* I did not inquire whether he was a scholar or a learned teacher, but *if he loved Me more than the others did.* A woman was My mother, a stable My lodging, a manger My cradle. I passed My childhood in obedience and work. I lived in the midst of tribulation, I ate the bread of charity, I had not a day of rest. The wicked overwhelmed Me with their insults and contempt. My prophets even gave to Me the title of the 'Man of Sorrows.' I chose for My throne a cross, and I was laid in a stranger's tomb. In giving up My spirit to My Father, I called upon you all to come to Me, and ever since that time I have not ceased to call you. See; both My arms are outstretched on the Cross to give a welcome to you all."

Now, *of what other person, since the world began, have such words as these been written and spoken?* For whom else could such claims be made? Who else in all the course of history has justified such language, save He, who won and has retained for nineteen hundred years the love and adoration of unnumbered millions, not as a saint or teacher, but as very God? And this, too, not from the simple and uneducated only, but from countless specimens of man's highest intellectual powers—who have received the Christian Revelation with the humility of little children.

In his admirable little book, *Christ in the Church,* the Rev. Robert Hugh Benson (himself a convert to Catholicism, though his father was the highest prelate of the Anglican Church, the Archbishop of Canterbury) mentions the conversion in England, within the space of five years, of a "Professor of Greek in one University, of a Professor of Science in another, and of a Judge on the bench, famed for his keenness in sifting evidence," all of whom, after long thought, had submitted like children to the Church, and had knelt at the same altar rail "with their servants and the poorest Irish." This is the more remarkable, since the opponents of the Catholic Church usually maintain that Catholics are, for the most part, not only financially but also *intellectually* poor. In the time of Christ, however, it was also said that "the common people heard Him gladly"; but converts such as those above mentioned, as well as the well-known brilliant lights of French literature—Brunetière, François Coppée, Paul Bourget and Huysmans, prove that men of the highest intelligence can and do accept the doctrines of Catholicism. Those who assert that what the common mass of men believe cannot be true, should bear in mind that any genuine Revelation of

God ought to be made so simple in its grand essentials, that "the wayfaring man, though a fool, may not err therein." Its truth should be as all-embracing and transparent to the humblest peasant as the sunlit atmosphere, which—simple though it seems—is to the savant awe-inspiring, as being the home of interstellar ether, reaching to infinity.

Those who deny that Catholics can be men of intellect forget that almost all the world's great theologians, jurists, poets, historians, painters, sculptors, architects, discoverers, sovereigns, statesmen and scientists *for 1,500 years were Catholics;* while very many of such men, in the last four centuries, have also been children of the Church of Rome. It was the most illustrious of modern French scientists, Louis Pasteur, who said: "The more deeply I investigate the mysteries of nature, the simpler becomes my faith." Accordingly, it is not strange that he remained to the last a sincere Catholic, and died while clasping to his breast a crucifix—the symbol of his faith that "God so loved the world that He gave His only begotten Son, that whosoever believeth in Him should not perish, but should have everlasting life."

But not only are the words which have been spoken and written *about* Christ absolutely unique; His own declarations in regard to Himself are without a parallel in history. Unless indeed he were mad, who that was *merely man* would ever utter sentences like these? "I am the Way, the Truth and the Life; no man cometh unto the Father, but by *Me.*" "He that hath seen *Me,* hath seen the Father." "I and the Father are one." "He that believeth in *Me* shall not perish, but shall have everlasting life." "*I* am the light of the world." "Before Abraham was *I* am." "*I* am the bread of life; he that cometh to *Me* shall never hunger, and he that believeth on *Me* shall never thirst." "*I* am the living bread, which came down from Heaven; if any man eat of this bread, he shall live forever; and the bread which I will give is *My flesh,* which I will give for the life of the world." "If God were your Father, ye would love Me, for *I proceeded forth and came from God.*" Jesus said to a man whom He had healed: "Dost thou believe on the Son of God?" He answered and said: "Who is He, Lord, that I might believe on Him?" Jesus said unto him: "Thou hast both seen Him, and *it is He that talketh with thee.*" "I am the resurrection and the life; he that believeth in *Me,* though he were dead, yet shall he live, and whosoever liveth and believeth in *Me* shall never die." "Come unto *Me,* all ·ye that labor and are heavy laden, and *I* will give you rest. Take *My* yoke upon you and learn of *Me,* for I am meek and lowly of heart, and ye shall find rest unto your souls." "And now, Father, glorify thou Me with Thine own self with the glory *which I had with Thee before the world was.*" Surely one who speaks thus must be either a madman, a conscienceless impostor, or Divine.

This is equally true in regard to those words of Christ which reveal His perfect sinlessness. The claim to be sinless, if made by any other man whoever lived, would certainly offend us. Such an assumption on the part of even the most saintly person would appear a blemish on his character. The purest of mankind have usually been most aware of their defects, and have acknowledged them with sorrow. One of the noblest of them all—St. Paul—confessed himself the chief of sinners. We may be, therefore, sure that Christ, the very personification of humility and purity, would have bewailed His faults, and longed for greater holiness, *had it been necessary for Him to do so.* But there is not in the Gospels a single word to indicate that He ever regretted or repented of one of His utterances or deeds! His sermons, parables and prayers betray no consciousness of an accusing conscience. He even puts the direct question to His adversaries: "Which of you shall convince me of sin?" (*John* 8:46).

Such an attitude is itself one of the proofs of His Divine Sonship. It has been well said: "Piety without one dash of repentance, without one ingenuous confession of wrong, one tear, one look of contrition, one request to Heaven for pardon—let any one of mankind try this kind of piety, and see how long it will be ere his righteousness will prove itself to be the most impudent conceit." (Bushnell, *Nature and the Supernatural,* p. 286). Nevertheless, for two thousand years Jesus has been regarded as the one perfect man who has ever lived on earth, and not a word or action of His life belies His character as such.

It is impossible to suggest for Him a single virtue that is wanting in His flawless record. Yet He, while living on the earth, was subjected to the closest and most hostile scrutiny. The Scribes and Pharisees were always watching to discover something in His conduct, by which they could condemn Him. But all their efforts were in vain. No doubt they urged the traitor, Judas, to reveal to them some sin or weakness in his Master, which could be used against Him; but Judas could not do this, and his despair at last lay in the realization that he had "betrayed innocent blood." The only accusation which His enemies could bring against their Victim, with any show of success, was that of blasphemy—namely, the fact that He had really assumed the character of sinlessness, in having made Himself the Son of God.

Now what are we to say of this unique and perfect personality? Can the story be legendary? If so, *who could have invented such a character*—so stainless, so harmonious, so superhuman! And those marvelous words of His, which have transformed the world, *who was the author of them, if not Jesus?* Could ignorant Galilean fishermen have attained to such supreme distinction? But if not they, who was the unknown genius who conceived that unexampled life and published for all time such matchless utterances? Why have we not some record of the author of this deathless narrative? It is because there was no such author, other than Jesus Himself. It is easier and more rational to believe that Jesus lived and spoke, as He is recorded to have done, than to believe that humble fishermen, or some anonymous writer, created that portrayal of the Man of Sorrows which has touched, as nothing else has ever done, the feelings of humanity for two millenniums.

Channing has admirably said: "When I can escape the deadening power of habit, and can receive the full import of such passages as the following: 'Come unto Me, all ye that labor and are heavy-laden, and I will give you rest'; 'I am come to seek and to save that which is lost'; 'He that confesseth Me before men, him will I confess before My Father in Heaven,'. . . I feel myself listening to a being such as never before and never since spoke in human language. I am awed by the consciousness of greatness, which these simple words express; and when I connect this greatness with the proofs of Christ's miracles, I am compelled to speak with the centurion: 'Truly this was the Son of God.'"

Pondering all these things, I also made the words of the centurion my own. I felt it was more difficult to believe that such a unique character as Jesus was an ordinary man, than to believe Him to have been God Incarnate. Yet, even so, I feared that there would still remain for me some difficulties as to His Virgin Birth, His miracles and the nature of His Incarnation; but when I had once accepted Jesus as the Son of God, those dreaded difficulties vanished. I asked myself: If God desired, as Jesus claimed, to give to man a Revelation of Himself; and if in truth He sent to earth His only begotten Son to teach and to redeem mankind; *is it not reasonable to suppose that the advent on this planet of the Deity in human form would constitute an event out of the natural order of things—in other words, that it would be miraculous?* Would it not have been amazing, had such a marvelous occurrence not have been of a supernatural character? And how could the union of the Divine and human in one personality have been better effected than in the manner told us in the Gospel narrative? Let cavillers suggest a plan more worthy of reverence by human reason. Birth from two human parents for such an advent would have been inadmissible. But once concede the fact of the Incarnation, and Christ's supernatural birth becomes a matter of course, and the touching story of the Annunciation and the Blessed Virgin's wonderful Magnificat of praise seem quite in harmony with the coming of Divinity. Equally natural and probable also, after the advent of the Son of God, would be His miracles—mostly works of healing—all of which He performed as simply and naturally as He breathed, and for the very purpose of arresting the attention and winning the adhesion of a skeptical and heedless world. Finally, the crowning miracle—His Resurrection—was the logical and necessary consummation of His mission. Convinced, therefore, that Jesus was in truth Incarnate God, my next step was to ascertain what He had done to ensure the continuance of His kingdom upon earth, to perpetuate His teachings, and to remind mankind continually of His Revelation, and of the love and sacrifice of Deity.

Chapter 9

THE CHURCH OF CHRIST

That they all may be one; as thou, Father, art in Me and I in Thee, that they also may be one in Us, that the world may believe that Thou hast sent Me.—JOHN 17:21.

She [the Catholic Church] was great and respected before the Saxon had set foot on Britain, before the Frank had crossed the Rhine; when Grecian eloquence still flourished in Antioch, and when idols were still worshipped in the temple of Mecca...Extremes of thought and culture met in her bosom, and there blended into unity. Ancient civilization and modern barbarism had hurled their force against her, and each in turn had knelt at her feet. Empires had passed away, yet the Catholic Church stood erect amid the ruins.—MACAULAY.

The enemies of the Church themselves die and disappear, but the Church itself lives on, and preaches the power of God to every succeeding generation.—ST. AUGUSTINE.

If Christianity is historical, Catholicism is Christianity.
—CARDINAL MANNING.

IN WHAT way, then, did the Incarnate Son of God, before departing from this earth, provide for the continuance and advancement of His kingdom?

One thing is certain—He did not write a book, nor did He order one to be written. Instead of doing that, He *founded a Church,* against which He declared the gates of Hell should not prevail, and with which He promised to be present while the world should last. This being so, it is evident that every faithful follower of Jesus should become a member of that Church.

But which of all the Churches that profess to be Christian is the one which Christ established? Unquestionably the

Roman Catholic Church, *for this alone goes back to the Saviour's lifetime.* This was the Church which naturally succeeded Judaism; this was the Church whose early history is chronicled in the Acts of the Apostles, and this is still the only Church which, since the days of Christ, has maintained an uninterrupted life of nearly two millenniums. Her documents, history and traditions all go back to the age of the Apostles. From her all other forms of Christianity have been derived. The authors of the Gospels, Acts and Epistles were members of that original Catholic Church, and she it was that finally selected, from the manuscripts which had been written by her sons, the books of the New Testament, and was for centuries their sole custodian. But since this Church existed sixty years at least before the writing of those Scriptures was completed, and more than three hundred years before the Canon of the New Testament was definitely fixed, there must have been, during all that time, some other guide and guardian of the Church besides the Bible. What was this?

Evidently Tradition—that mighty link between the past and present, consisting of the oral instructions, interpretations and ecclesiastical observances, handed down in the Church from generation to generation from the very days of the Apostles. Thus St. Paul wrote to the Church of Corinth: "Keep the *traditions,* as I delivered them to you." (*1 Cor.* 11:2). To Timothy also he wrote: "The things that thou hast heard of me among many witnesses, the same commit thou to faithful men, *who shall be able to teach others also."* Those "faithful men" undoubtedly did teach others, and these taught others still. Origen, the great representative of the Church at Alexandria, said: "Let the ecclesiastical teaching, handed down by order of succession from the Apostles, be observed. That only is to be believed to be the truth, which in no way differs from ecclesiastical and Apostolic tradition."

Protestants often deride the authority of Church tradition, and claim to be directed by the Bible only; yet they, too, have been guided by customs of the ancient Church, which find no warrant in the Bible, but rest on Church tradition only! A striking instance of this is the following: The first positive command in the Decalogue is to "Remember the Sabbath Day to keep it holy," and this precept was enforced by the Jews for thousands of years. But the Sabbath Day, the observance of which God commanded, was our Saturday. Yet who among either Catholics or Protestants, except a sect or two, like the "Seventh Day Baptists," ever keep that commandment now? None. Why is this? The Bible, which Protestants claim to obey exclusively, gives no authorization for the substitution of the first day of the week for the seventh. On what authority, therefore, have they done so? Plainly on the authority of that very Catholic Church which they abandoned, and whose traditions they condemn.

Again, Anglicans and Episcopalians repeat those old confessions of the Catholic Church, known as the Nicene and the Apostles' Creeds. They do this, however, not because those Creeds are found in the Bible, for they are not there, but because those formulas of belief were composed and commanded by the Catholic Church. How was the Canon of Scripture itself settled? Certainly not by anything decisive on that subject in the books themselves. The question, which books were to be admitted to the Canon, was decided by the Catholic Church (no doubt under the guidance of the Holy Ghost) in accordance with the testimonies and traditions of the Fathers. Even when finally the various books of the New Testament had been composed, tradition must still have been for centuries the paramount influence in the Church, since the number of Biblical manuscripts was exceedingly limited, and millions of Christians could not have read them, even had they been accessible.

Those were the years when the Church was struggling upward from the catacombs to the conquest of the world, when she was preaching the Gospel to the heathen, converting Europe, sacrificing her martyrs, producing her Saints, and forming that magnificent liturgy, whose words are still pronounced at every Catholic altar in the world. During those centuries not only countless individuals, but also entire nations, learned and accepted Christianity, not by a book, but solely *by the teaching of the Catholic Church.* In fact, when, in the sixteenth century, the Bible (interpreted by private judgment) was proclaimed to be man's *only* sufficient guide, the Scriptures instantly became the source of strife and schism.

Accordingly, having now resolved to join some Christian Church, I had no difficulty in deciding which one. In this respect I shared the sentiments of the Unitarian preacher Dr. James Martineau, who, in his *Seats of Authority in Religion,* says of the Roman Catholic Church: "Her plea is that she has been there *all through;* that there has been no suspension of her life, no break in her history, no term of silence in her teaching; and that, having been always in possession, she is the vehicle of every claim, and must be presumed, until conclusive evidence of forfeiture is produced, to be the rightful holder of what has rested in her custody. If you would trace a Divine legacy from the age of the Caesars, would you set out to meet it on the Protestant tracks, which soon lose themselves in the forests of Germany and on the Alps of Switzerland, or on the great Roman road of history, which runs through all the centuries, and sets you down in Greece or Asia Minor at the very doors of the churches to which the Apostles wrote?" (p. 169).

Of all the Protestant sects, from which a selection could be made, I saw none which I wished to enter. A space of 1,500 years lay between even the oldest of them and the origin of Christianity, and experience had already taught me to expect in them no ecclesiastical unity, no real authority, and no doctrinal agreement. Moreover, even since my youthful days their number had decidedly increased. One day, in talking on this subject with a friend, he mentioned that his father was a *Christ*-ian. I thought at first that he had mispronounced the word, but he assured me that there was a sect called "*Christ*-ians," to distinguish them from ordinary

Christians. What their particular doctrinal divergence was I have forgotten, but I remember that, although my friend's father was a "*Christ*-ian," his mother was a Campbellite Baptist, his wife a Universalist, and he himself a Unitarian! This led me to investigate the number of divisions into which Protestantism had thus far resolved itself. The following list, though doubtless incomplete, and referring almost entirely to England and America, gives some idea of its disintegration.

"Advent Christians."
"Adventists."
African Methodist Episcopal.
African Union Protestant
    (Non-Episcopal).
"Age-to-Come Adventists."
American Episcopal Church.
"Amish Mennonites."
"Anabaptists."
"Apostolic Mennonites."
"Arminian Baptists."
Associate Kirk.
Associate Presbyterian Synod
    of North America.
Associate Reform Presbyterian
    Churches.
Associate Reform Synod of
    the South.
Bible Christians.
British Methodist Episcopal.
"British Wesleyans."
"Calvinistic Baptists."
"Cameronians."
"Campbellite Baptists."
"Christadelphians" (who have
    several churches in London).
"Christian Disciples."
"Christian Eliasites."
"Christian Israelites."

"Christ-ians."
"Christian Scientists."
"Christian Unionists."
"Church of God."
"Church of God Adventists."
"Church of Living God."
"Church of Progress."
Church of Scotland in
    England.
"Coarse" Mennonites.
Colored Methodist Episcopal.
"Congregationalists."
Congregation Methodist
    (Non-Episcopal).
"Countess of Huntingdon's
    Connexion."
"Covenanters."
Cumberland Presbyterian
    Church (colored).
Cumberland Presbyterian
    Church (white).
"Disciples in Christ."
"Dowieites."
"Dunkard Brethren"
    (several varieties).
Eastern Reformed
    Presbyterians.
"Evangelical Adventists."
Evangelical Association.

"Evangelicals."
"Evangelical Unionists."
Evangelist Missionary.
"Family of Love."
Free Church of England.
Free Kirk of Scotland.
Free Methodist
    (Non-Episcopal).
"Free-Will Baptists."
"General" Baptists.
"General Baptists, New
    Connexion."
"General Conference
    Mennonites."
"Hicksite Quakers."
"Hyper-Calvinists."
Independent Methodists
    (Non-Episcopal).
"Irvingites."
"Jezreelites."
"Life and Advent Union."
Lutherans (many varieties).
Mennonites (plain).
Methodist Church, Canada
    (Non-Episcopal).
Methodist Episcopal.
Methodist Episcopal, South.
Methodist Protestant
    (Non-Episcopal).
Methodists.
"Millerites."
Moravians.
Mormons ("Latter Day
    Saints").
New Connexion Methodists.
"Old Amish Mennonites."
Old Church of Scotland.
"Old Mennonites."
Original Seceders or

"Auld Lichts."
Orthodox Quakers.
"Other Mennonites."
"Paedo-Baptists."
"Particular" Baptists.
"Pentecostal Dancers."
"Pillars of Fire."
"Plymouth Brethren."
"Presbyterian Baptists."
Presbyterians.
"Primitive Baptists."
"Primitive Friends Quakers."
Protestant Episcopal Church.
"Refined" Mennonites.
Reformed Episcopal Church.
"Reformed Mennonites."
Reformed Presbyterian Church
    in North America.
Reformed Presbyterian
    Covenanted Church.
Reformed Presbyterians.
Reformed Zwinglians
    (four varieties).
Reform Kirk.
Reform Union Methodists.
"Regular Mennonites."
Relief Kirk.
"River Brethren."
"Salvation Army."
"Schwenckfeldians."
Secession Church of Ireland.
Secession Kirk.
"Separate Baptists."
"Seventh Day Adventists."
"Seventh Day Baptists."
Shakers.
"Six Principle Baptists."
Socinians.
Spiritualists.

Swedenborgians.
"Temperance Methodists."
"The Agapemone."
"The Apostolics."
"The Baptized Believers."
"The Benevolent Methodists."
"The Bible Defense
Association."
"The Brethren" (who baptize
each other).
"The Bryanites."
The Church of England
(Broad, High and Low).
"The Eclectics."
"The Followers of the Lord
Jesus Christ."
"The Free Christians."
"The Free Evangelical
Christians."
"The Free Gospel and
Christian Brethren."
"The Free Gospellers."
"The Free Grace Gospel
Christians."
The Glassites.
"The Glory Band."
"The Hallelujah Band."
The "Holy Ghost and Us"
Society.
"The Holy Jumpers."
"The Hope Mission."
"The Humanitarians."
"The Inghamites."
"Theistic Church."
"The Kilhamites."
"The Muggletonians."
"The New Wesleyans."
"The Old Baptists."
"The Open Baptists."

"The Peculiar People."
"The Primitive
Congregation."
"The Primitive Methodists."
"The Progressionists."
"The Protestant Trinitarians."
"The Ranters."
"The Rational Christians."
"The Recreative Religionists."
"The Salem Society."
"The Secularists."
"The Separatists"
"The Spiritual Church."
"The Strict Baptists."
"The Union Baptists."
"The United Christian
Church."
"Unitarian Baptists."
Unitarians.
United American Methodist
Episcopal.
"United Baptists."
"United Brethren."
United Brethren in Christ.
United Free Gospel
Methodists.
United Free Methodists.
United Presbyterian Church
of North America.
United Presbyterians.
Universalists.
Wesleyan Methodist
(Non-Episcopal).
Welsh Calvinistic
(Non-Episcopal).
"Wilburite Quakers."
Zion Union Apostolic.
Zwinglians.
       Etc.

To define the distinctive features of all these various sects, even if it were desirable, would be impossible within the limits of this volume; but from that fact it must not be supposed that such societies are mere shadows without substance. The history and peculiarities of each could be narrated and described, if necessary.

Thus the Protestant body known as the "Muggletonians" is not, as might be supposed, a Pickwickian invention, but a religious sect founded as long ago as the middle of the seventeenth century by a London tailor named Muggleton. He declared that he and another tailor named John Reeve were the "two witnesses" mentioned in the eleventh chapter of St. John's Revelation. He also taught that God left Elijah as vicegerent in Heaven when He descended to earth to die for mankind. He wrote a book, called *The Divine Looking-Glass,* and this was republished by members of his sect as late as 1846.

The "Glassites" also have played rather an important part in the religious life of England. The founder of this sect was a Scotchman by the name of John Glas, who, about two hundred years ago, formed a society, subsequently known as "Glassites" or "Sandemanians" (from Robert Sandeman, the son-in-law of Glas), as a kind of protest against the established Church of England. The present membership of the sect numbers about 2,000, and among their peculiarities are a love-feast eaten every Sunday, the "kiss of brotherhood," the washing of feet, abstention from "blood" and "things strangled," and a simple kind of communism. To pray with anyone who is not a Glassite is regarded by this sect as unlawful. It must not be supposed, however, that this peculiar society is composed of uneducated people, for one of its members was the distinguished scientist, Michael Faraday.

The sect of the "Jezreelites" still exists in London. It was founded by a certain James White, who, in the last century, published a book called *The Flying Roll,* under the name of James Jezreel. It is a message to the ten lost tribes of Israel.

The sect of the "Irvingites" was founded by the celebrated Edward Irving, the friend of Carlyle. They have a very handsome church in Gordon Square, London, and numerous chapels scattered through the city. This sect, which once had twelve apostles, appointed by Irving, calls itself the "Catholic Apostolic Church," and has an elaborate ritual. Each member is supposed to give one-tenth of his income to the Church. But enough: the state of Protestantism, revealed by such a list of heterogeneous and continually multiplying sects, is indeed appalling.

Granting that in many instances the differences between them relate for the most part to their various forms of ecclesiastical government, some of them nevertheless are mutually hostile and irreconcilable. But, whether their points of disagreement are important or not in the eyes of the disputants, *they prove beyond a doubt the lack of unity in Protestantism.* Every sect naturally owes its existence to the fact that it considers itself the correct type of the Christian Church, and therefore must regard the others as less perfect. We are sometimes told that this does not matter, since they all agree in the "essentials" of Christianity; but who is to decide what is essential? Each sect believes that at least one thing is essential—namely, that which *it alone* has, and which the others have not. Otherwise it would not have left the other sects, and begun a separate existence.

If it be true, however, that the divisions in Protestantism are *not* essential, then the scandal of this state of things is all the greater; for if God has given us a Revelation, He must have meant it to be received in its entirety. It is inconceivable that His message is of such small value, that we poor, finite creatures may select from it what pleases us, and reject the rest. One thing is certain—the idea of one divinely founded Church, possessing supernatural guidance, unity of doctrine and authority of discipline, is wholly lost among Protestant denominations, and the term "Unity," as applied to Protestantism, has no significance. There is at work in Protestantism a process of disintegration, which apparently nothing can check; for all these humanly created sects originate from the notion that dissatisfied members of a Church have a perfect right to leave it and found another, which they call "reformed." By consulting the list of sects, it will indeed be seen that there are "Reformed" Presbyterians, Methodists, Lutherans, Episcopalians, and the like, all of which churches are, of course, "reformations" of other "reformations" of the original Luther's "Reformation"!

Nor is there any reason why this process should not, like an endless chain, go on indefinitely, for that would be the natural result of the Reformation. It is the logical consequence of Luther's theory of the individual's right to interpret Scripture as he likes, and to "protest" against every interpretation which he does not like. No Protestant, therefore, can consistently refuse to others the right to "protest," since this it is which forms the very *raison d'être* of his own Church.

Now, in the midst of this chaotic state of things, we recognize the incontrovertible fact, that *Christ Himself founded one Church, and only one, and laid upon it certain commands and Sacraments.* This being so, how have His followers dared to leave that Church, and on their own responsibility set up another, or many others, deciding which of the original Sacraments they will retain and which they will discard, and which of Christ's commands they will obey? That they have done so is only too evident; but, having thus begun to pick and choose among Sacraments and customs, old as the Church itself, and having invoked the "right of private judgment" in matters of doctrine, where is the process to end? All of those sects agree in saying that the Bible is the one and only infallible source of truth, and all of them find in it some self-interpreted texts, on which to found *their special idiosyncrasy!*

But surely a Church, which was established by the Son of God, and which is still controlled and guided by the Holy Spirit, ought to deliver *the same message, with authority, everywhere.* Does any Protestant sect do that? Certainly not. Year

after year the Protestant schismatic spirit continues its ero-
sive work. It is like a river, which, having broken loose from
its appointed course, cuts for itself a multitude of new and
devious channels. Nor is this all; for, in proportion as these
channels multiply, so do Indifferentism and Agnosticism also
grow, until the world is threatened either with religious anarchy
or absolute irreligion. The well-known free-thinker and philosopher, Dr. von Hartmann, in comparing the Catholic
Church with Protestantism, says: "If it is a *Church* that is
to bring me to salvation. . .then I will look about me for
a firmly established, powerful Church, and I prefer to cling
to the Rock of Peter, rather than to any one of the numberless
Protestant sectarian Churches."

Deeply significant are the words of Cardinal Manning on
the religious condition of England after more than three hundred years of Protestantism: "Never before were the masses
of our people so without God in the world, never was spiritual
famine so widespread and blank. Millions in our towns and
cities have no consciousness of the supernatural. The life of
this world is their all. Never before were the schisms and
heresies, which have been generated by the first great heresy
and schism, so manifold and dominant. The Church of the
Anglican Reformation has given up well-nigh one-half of the
people to endless separations, which have exhausted its vitality." The contrast between Catholicism and Protestantism is
that between the solidity of a mighty mountain and the in-
stability of shifting sand. It is the difference between the weak
and the strong, the separate and the coherent, the passing
and the permanent.

None of the many sects of Protestantism is either large
enough, old enough, or strong enough to be likened seriously to the universal, ancient Apostolic Church of Rome,
and even a collection of such sects forms only an incoherent
group of mutually repellent particles. On the one hand, therefore, stands *discordant Protestantism*—wanting in discipline, lacking doctrinal unity, repudiating most of the original Sacraments

of Mother Church, and tending fatally to dissolve either into continually augmenting subdivisions or into ever-increasing Rationalism. On the other hand stands *united Catholicism*—immovable amid the ebb and flow of human innovations, impregnable to the attacks of heresies, indifferent to the rise and fall of empires, surviving spoliation, superior to schism, steadfast in persecution, and calmly watching the disintegration of its enemies! Thus does the changeless Church of Rome endure, and thus she WILL endure, till Christ who founded it shall come again.

Wonderful Body of the Living Christ! In faith, in Sacraments, in doctrine, in ceremonial, in language [Latin remains the official language of the Church, and the Mass is still offered in Latin in a growing number of places, notwithstanding the introduction of the vernacular into the liturgy in the mid 1960's.—*Editor,* 1990.], in discipline, in its identical catechism, and in its one obedience to a single Head—in chapel, in cathedral, in hamlet, in metropolis, in Europe, Asia, Africa, America and on the islands of all seas—everywhere and at all times IT IS THE SAME! Surely if the testimony of 1,900 years does not effectively prove the Church of Rome to be the institution founded by our Saviour on the Rock of Peter, then has the world no Church of Christ at all. How true are Cardinal Newman's eloquent words: "O long-sought-after, tardily found desire of the heart—the truth after many shadows, the fullness after many foretastes, the home after many storms! Come to her, poor wanderers, for *she* it is, and she alone, who can unfold the secret of your being and the meaning of your destiny!"

Chapter 10

LUTHER

Men should be changed by Religion, not Religion by men.
—BISHOP OF VITERBO.

The Church of Christ may be compared to His seamless robe. Luther and his followers tore a large piece from it.

All the waters of the Elbe would not yield me tears sufficient to weep for the miseries caused by the Reformation.
—MELANCTHON: Epistles, Book 4, ep. 100.

I NOW SAW that, if I were to enter any Christian Church at all, it could not be one of the numerous discordant sects of Protestantism, the oldest of which came into existence only four hundred years ago, but rather a Church, possessing universality of extent, unity of doctrine, historic continuity from the beginning, and authority in matters of faith and morals. Such—and such only—is the Roman Catholic Church, which represents the teachings and traditions of nearly two millenniums.

Still I felt bound to examine the question more minutely. Why had the Protestants left this Mother Church? Who was at fault?

The reason given by Luther and his followers for their apostasy was the necessity of "Church Reformation," especially because of certain abuses connected with the giving of Indulgences. But Reformation does not necessarily mean secession. All Catholics admit that some abuses then existed in the Church, but they believe that an ecclesiastical house-cleaning could have been effected without a definite rupture, which, as a matter of fact, convulsed all Christendom, caused rivers of blood to flow, and made a chasm in Christ's Church, which time may never close.

Did the mere fact that grave abuses had crept into the ancient Church create so hopeless a situation as to justify disruption? Did not Christ prophesy such a state of things in His parables of the tares and the wheat, and of the net filled with good and bad fishes? Was not one of His twelve disciples the traitor Judas? Did not another deny Him, and did not all of them desert Him?

All true Christians—Protestants as well as Catholics—believe that the original Church was an institution founded by the Son of God, and that its Founder promised to endow it with the Holy Spirit, and to defend it with complete success against the gates of Hell. Now that original Church can have been none other than the Catholic; and if, in 1517, this had become so irretrievably corrupt that it was necessary to replace it with another, it is evident that the gates of Hell HAD prevailed against it, and that Christ's solemn promise to preserve His Church had not been kept. But if such a hopeless state of things did not exist, then violent withdrawal from it was equivalent to rending it sacrilegiously, casting discredit on Christ's word, and claiming that the Protestant seceders were more competent to guide and teach the Church than was the Holy Spirit! If the faults in the Church at that time were those of individual conduct, rather than of doctrine (as was undoubtedly the case), then it was certainly the duty of the would-be reformers to remain in the Church and reform its wayward members.

But this they did not do. Their fault consisted in passing from an attack on the *abuses* of the Church to an assault upon its *Faith*. If, in previous centuries, whenever internal reforms had been required, the earlier Christians had thus acted, the Church would soon have crumbled into ruin. Because some individual members of a crew are behaving badly, it is not necessary to scuttle the ship.

In this respect an imperfect comparison might be made between the Catholic Church in the sixteenth century and the United States in 1861. Some reformation in regard to State rights and slavery was no doubt needful then in the great republic; but it is now generally admitted that such reforms could have been carried out without a war. As the secession of the South in 1861 was treason to the Union, so in 1517 the secession of Luther and his associates was treason to the Mother Church.

In studying this question, I found that I had hitherto read only the Protestant side of it, and had not fully appreciated the prominent part which politics played in the origin of the Reformation, or, as it might be better called, the *Revolution;* for the "squabble among monks," as Pope Leo X at first called the outbreak, was quickly seized upon by avaricious German princes, as a pretext to plunder the monasteries and churches of their subjects, and gradually entire nations made the movement an excuse to ravage one another's territories in the hope of spoils. The following words from the Protestant writer Lord Macaulay are significant: "The new theology spread with a rapidity never known before. All ranks, all varieties of characters joined the innovators. Sovereigns impatient to appropriate to themselves the prerogatives of the Pope, nobles desirous to share the plunder of the abbeys, good men scandalized by the corruptions in the Church, bad men desirous of the license inseparable from great moral revolutions, wise men eager in pursuit of truth, weak men lured by the glitter of novelty—all were found on one side."

That the revolt against Catholicism and the Papacy began with Martin Luther has given to his personality an exaggerated importance. He indeed started the conflagration, but many others spread the flames. It is, in fact, very doubtful whether, at the outset, Luther ever intended to go as far as his own violent passions and the patronage of princes ultimately led him. It is probable that the monk, who until the age of thirty-five had been a Catholic, initiated the Reformation much as a reckless individual fires a train which, later on, to his dismay ignites a powder magazine.

When Luther nailed his theses to the church of Wittenberg,

he attacked merely the *abuses* connected with Indulgences, not the doctrine of Indulgence itself. Indeed, at that time, he pronounced anathema on all who spoke against their efficacy. Moreover, before the heat of controversy had carried him beyond the possibility of a return, he wrote to Pope Leo X: "Most Holy Father, I cast myself at thy feet with all I have and am. Give life, or take it; call, recall, approve, reprove; your voice is that of Christ, who presides and speaks in you." But when he had committed himself irretrievably to the revolutionary movement, and found himself the mouthpiece of a powerful political party, with several princely supporters behind it, he could find no words vile enough to use in his denunciation of the Holy Father whom he had once revered, and of the Church whose altars he had reverently served.

So prominent, however, was the part which this man played in the Reformation, that it is well to pay special attention to his character and writings; endeavoring, however, to see him, not as the "Luther legend" represents him, but as he really was. Naturally, since I had never made an impartial examination of the subject, I had considered Luther only as the national hero of the German Protestants, the author of the hymn, *"Ein feste Burg ist unser Gott"* ["A Mighty Fortress Is Our God"], and the "brave monk" who conscientiously defied the Pope at Worms. But I discovered presently the reverse of the medal.

In the first place, commencing with externals, the face of Luther seemed to me nothing less than repulsive. Sensuality and brutality are stamped upon it more than on almost any countenance I ever looked upon in life or portraiture. If it may be compared to any creature of the animal kingdom, that animal would be a bull. There certainly is nothing in his expression indicative of spirituality. Let anyone contemplate it, and ask himself if any man, with such a head, mouth, neck and joul, can be considered as a deeply religious, spiritual leader and shepherd of souls, or as the founder of the religion of the "pure Gospel." It is rather the face of a sensual, self-willed fanatic; and such I soon perceived was really Luther's character.

Eating and drinking formed two very prominent features of his daily life. His biographical record, especially his letters to his "Katie," abound in proofs of this. One or two will be sufficient.

On the 29th of July, 1534, for example, he wrote to his wife that he had had nothing good to drink, and adds: "Thou wouldst do well to send me the whole cellar full of my wine, and a flagon of thy beer as often as thou canst." During his last weeks at Eisleben he wrote to his wife again (February 6, 1546): "We have plenty on which to eat and swill." (See also Grisar, Vol. 2, p. 305.) Among his utterances in the *Table Talk* are also the following: "If the Lord God holds me excused for having plagued Him for quite twenty years by celebrating Mass, He will assuredly excuse me for sometimes indulging in a drink to His honor. God grant it, and let the world take it as it will."

We all know that the Catholic practice of occasional fasting is strongly recommended in the Bible, even by Christ Himself. Thus Paul exhorts the Corinthian Christians (*1 Cor.* 7:5) to give themselves to fasting and prayer; and Jesus in His Sermon on the Mount bade His disciples, when they fasted, not to do so ostentatiously, but to their Father, who seeth in secret. We are told also that Christ Himself fasted forty days and forty nights in the wilderness; and, in praising those who had great faith, He said: "This kind can come forth by nothing but by prayer and fasting." (*Mark* 9:28). Luther, however, thus condemned a custom evidently very distasteful to him: "This doctrine is so wicked and shameful before God, that no carousing or gluttony, no intemperance or drunkenness could be so bad, and it would be better to be completely fuddled day and night, than thus to fast." (*Luther's Works,* Vol. 2, p. 730).

We shall find, later, other striking proofs of the importance given by Luther to man's animal propensities and of his alleged inability to control them.

One of the most significant acts of Luther's life was his marriage, under peculiar circumstances, with an ex-nun, who, like himself, thus violated a solemn vow to God. The circumstances were as follows. On the night before Easter, April 5, 1523, a certain Leonhard Koppe and two associates, according to a previous arrangement, abducted twelve nuns from the Cistercian cloister of Nimptsch in Silesia, and with the connivance of Luther brought them to Wittenberg. Soon after their arrival, Luther wrote a letter in which he called Koppe a "blessed robber," and compared him impiously to the resurrected Saviour! "As Christ," he writes, "at Easter had redeemed the world by His resurrection, so Koppe by his bold deed on Easter night had redeemed these nuns"! (*Luther's Works,* Vol. 2, p. 40).

Among these voluntary fugitives was Katharine Bora, whom Luther subsequently married, after the lapse of two years, at the age of forty-two, Katharine being sixteen years his junior. The marriage was celebrated by another apostate priest, by the name of Bugenhagen, who had recently taken a similar marital step.

There had evidently been much talk about Luther's attentions to this nun of former days, for the pastor Bugenhagen subsequently wrote: "Evil tales were the cause of Dr. Martin's becoming a married man so unexpectedly." (Grisar, Vol. 2, p. 175). There is no doubt that the reformer's friends were greatly shocked by this procedure on his part, and felt that he had done himself much harm.

The eminent scholar Erasmus wrote of this matrimonial venture: "It has been thought that Luther was the hero of a tragedy; but I regard him as playing the chief part in a comedy, that has ended, like all comedies, in a marriage." In another place he remarks, in reference to the number of monkish imitators of Luther in this respect: "The Reformation seems to have had no other purpose than to turn monks and nuns into bridegrooms and brides." Melancthon was much severer in his judgment of the affair. In a confidential letter to Camerarius, written June 16, 1525, he puts the chief blame for the marriage on the escaped nun.

"Luther," he says, "is light-headed and frivolous to the last degree; the nuns pursued him with great cunning, and drew him on. Perhaps all this intercourse with them has rendered him effeminate, or has inflamed his passions, noble and high-minded though he is." (See Grisar's *Luther,* Vol. 2, p. 145). He adds that he believes that Luther has fallen into an "inopportune change of life," and hopes that marriage will make him more moral. When we remember that Melancthon was the intimate friend of Luther, as well as his greatest theological supporter, we cannot question the truth of his observations and conclusions.

But the effect of his immoralities and of his marriage with a nun was trifling compared with the widespread evil wrought among the masses by his intemperate preaching and writing on such subjects. It was not enought that he himself had sinned; he was lashed on by an accusing conscience to defend his conduct, and to induce as many others as possible to do as he had done. If "misery loves company," so does sin. Indulging in the coarsest language, he denounced celibacy, ridiculed the vows of chastity, and urged both monks and nuns to follow his example, break their vows, and leave the cloisters! (*Luther's Works,* edition Walch, Vol. 12, pp. 1,797, etc.). The result of this was naturally deplorable. Eberlin of Günzberg, among others, writes: "Scarcely has a monk or nun been three days out of the convent, than they make haste to marry some woman or knave from the streets." (Grisar, *Luther,* Vol. 2, p. 124). Multitudes of hitherto virtuous monks and nuns considered themselves, on the authority of Luther, released from any obligation to fulfill their vows, and an appalling amount of harm was done both to their individual souls and to the public.

Even in pagan Rome respect for the vestals was maintained, as one of the bulwarks of society, after belief in the gods had largely disappeared. But Luther's teachings threw such safeguards to the winds, and emphasized man's animal nature as dominant and decisive. Chastity, he declared, was unnatural; celibacy was a sin; Sacraments were profitless; the Mass was idolatrous; there was no longer any need of examining one's conscience or of going to confession; and the Pope was Antichrist! Faith alone was essential to salvation; good works were superfluous. How startling is the contrast which Luther's life and teachings offer to the life and admonitions of St. Paul! The great Apostle wrote: "I see another law in my members, warring against the law of my mind and bringing me into captivity to the law of sin, which is in my members. O wretched man that I am! who shall deliver me from the body of this death? I thank God, through Jesus Christ, Our Lord." And again: "They that are Christ's have crucified the flesh with the affections and lusts." "If ye live after the flesh, ye shall die; but if ye through the Spirit do mortify the deeds of the body, ye shall live."

What added to the evil influence which Luther exerted was his denial of free will in man. "The human will," he said, "is like a beast of burden. If God mounts it, it wishes and goes as God wills; if Satan mounts it, it wishes and goes as Satan wills. *Nor can it choose the rider it would prefer, or betake itself to him;* but it is the riders who contend for its possession!" *(De Servo Arbitrio).* This was, however, tantamount to saying that whatever a man did, whether good or bad, was the work of either God or Satan, not of the man himself. Melancthon also wrote that "like the calling of Paul, so also the adultery of David and the betrayal of Christ by Judas, was the work of God." (See Alzog's *Church History,* ninth edition, Vol. 2, p. 154).

Luther's exact words in reference to man's inability to resist temptation are not fit to be quoted, but it is sufficient to say that he asserted that one could as easily remove mountains, create new stars, or bite one's own nose off as to keep the sixth (in the Protestant reckoning the seventh) Commandment! In his letter to Wolfgang Reissenbusch, a fellow monk, whom he was urging to renounce his vows and marry, Luther wrote (March 27, 1525) that his religious vow was worthless, because "chastity is as little within our power as the working of miracles." (*Luther's Works,* Weimar edition, Vol. 17, pp. 270-279).

It was Luther's idea, however, that so long as one had faith, conduct was not of great importance. Thus he wrote to Melancthon: "Be a sinner, and sin boldly, but believe more boldly still. Sin shall not drag us away from Him, even should we commit fornication or murder thousands and thousands of times a day." (Letter of August 1, 1521). So annoying to him were the Ten Commandments, that he wrote of them: "We must put the whole decalogue entirely out of our sight and out of our hearts. If Moses scares you with his stupid Ten Commandments, say to him at once: 'Take yourself off to your Jews! To the gallows with Moses!'"

Of course, to the multitude such revolutionary ideas as these were equivalent to the abolition of all moral and religious restraints, and the alluring doctrine of irresponsibility for sin was the natural consequence. Benedict Morgenstern, the Pastor of Graudenz, complained that if the Bohemians wished to live according to their own lusts, they did not hesitate to say: "Today we will live in the Lutheran fashion!"

Nor was this all. Luther directly incited people to deeds of violence against Catholic prelates. Thus (*Wider das Papsthum zu Rom,* 1545, 130) he wrote: "The Pope and the cardinals...ought to be taken; and, since they are blasphemers, their tongues ought to be torn out through the back of their necks, and nailed to the gallows!"

He also recklessly advocated the confiscation of Church property by the authorities. To the Elector Frederick and to Duke Johann of Saxony he wrote (July, 1524): "When they [the Catholics] are gone, and the churches and convents lie desolate and forsaken, then the rulers of the land may do with them what they please."

Such utterances produced, of course, among the populace

deplorable results. Soon nothing pertaining to the ancient Catholic Faith was any longer respected by millions of ignorant peasants, and they at last rose to act on Luther's suggestions.

In 1522 a rabble forced its way into the church at Wittenberg, on the doors of which Luther had nailed his theses, destroyed all its altars and statues, and having thrown their fragments into the street, drove out the clergy after them. In Rottenburg also, in 1525, the figure of Christ was decapitated and its arms were knocked off. On the 9th of February, 1529, everything previously revered in the fine old cathedral of Bâle, Switzerland, was destroyed. An old chronicler thus described the scene: "They fastened a long rope to a large crucifix, and many boys of eight, ten and twelve years dragged it to the marketplace, and sang: 'Oh, you poor old Jesus. . . if you are God, defend Yourself; but if you are man, so die!' " The Reformer Oecolampadius rejoiced at this sacrilege, and wrote to Capito: "That was a sight for the superstitious! They would have liked to weep tears of blood." (Janssen, 3.96).

Such instances of brutality and fanaticism could be cited by scores. No longer restrained by faith and reverence for all that they had held sacred, the peasants burned down numerous convents, plundered churches, smashed stained glass windows, hacked to pieces sacred crucifixes, and mutilated altars. Growing more daring, they stormed and sacked the castles of the nobles, and murdered many of their inmates in a barbarous manner. The bells, which had for centuries summoned them to prayer, now called them to the work of rapine.

It is impossible to dissociate these horrors from the teachings of Luther. Erasmus told him so plainly, as the hideous Peasants' War progressed. "We are," he said, "reaping the fruits *that you have sown.*" In fact, the peasants justified their conduct by texts of Scripture, which Luther had told them was their only and sufficient guide. "If we are mistaken," they said, "let Luther correct us from the Bible." Whether they would have let themselves be convinced by him is doubtful, if his opinion had run counter to theirs, for they were now infected with doctrine of "private judgment." Relying on this, they chose such texts as suited them, and found some, to their great delight, which gave them, as they thought, authority to rob the rich, and to "hold all things in common." So popular was this idea that one of the sects thus formed drove out from the city of Münster all its wealthy citizens, and established Communism there. The churches were despoiled of their pictures, images and sacred vessels. Simultaneously the most brutal and licentious passions also burst forth, and proved for a time ungovernable. In the name of "Christian liberty" each man claimed a right to marry several wives, and their belief in "Communism" led, in this respect, to frequent difficulties.

Their chief, John of Leyden, married three wives at once! Twenty-eight apostles were sent forth to preach this forerunner of Mormonism to a willing world! Why not? Luther had said: "I confess, I cannot forbit it, when someone wants to take several wives. It does not contradict the Scriptures. Only among Christians I would not like to see such an example introduced, because one, for the sake of avoiding scandal, should avoid *even what is allowable!*" These ideas did not long remain theoretical.

Protestants generally do not know, for naturally it has not been told them, that in order to retain for the "Reformation" the influence of Philip, Landgrave of Hesse—a man of notoriously loose morals, but of much political power—*Luther gave him permission to commit bigamy* by marrying, while his first wife, undivorced, was still living, the sixteen-year-old Marghereta of Sale. This marriage Luther authorized with the excuse that "their poor Church had need of pious lords and regents," and stated that it was done "in order to provide for the welfare of his [Philip's] soul and body, and to bring greater glory to God." This precious document was signed, not only by Luther himself, but also by Melancthon and several other Protestant theologians. Melancthon, it is true, at first felt scruples in regard to the proceeding, but subsequently overcame them with the ignoble excuse: "Philip threatened to apostatize unless we helped him!" (Ellinger, *Melancthon* p. 377). The bigamous union, thus approved, took place on the 4th of March, 1540, at Rotenburg, and several Reformers, including Melancthon, were present at the ceremony, which was performed by Melander, the Court preacher, who himself had three wives living!

How different from this disgraceful concession to a petty landgrave was the noble conduct of Bishop John Fisher and the great English statesman, Sir Thomas More, in regard to the divorce demanded by their powerful sovereign, Henry VIII! Both these Catholic heroes suffered death for their resistance to Henry's policy of the divorce and all that it entailed.

Luther himself became at last alarmed at the results of his "Reforms," but showed no pity for his poor, misguided dupes, who had provoked the Peasants' War. On the contrary, he turned upon them mercilessly, and urged the nobles to kill these "children of the devil," and to hunt them down like mad dogs ("tolle Hunde"). His advice was followed, and the revolt of the people was put down with atrocious cruelties. The loss of life among these poor fanatics, who, led astray by Luther's doctrines, wished to carry out their own ideas of what the Bible taught, is variously estimated at from fifty thousand souls to double that number. In one of the letters of Erasmus (Epis. 803), it is said that 100,000 perished. Professor Maurenbrecher, in his *History of the Catholic Reformation*, says that Luther and his associates had, previous to the popular rebellion, used such passionate, revolutionary language against all authority, that the result could easily have been foreseen. (Vol. 2, p. 312). Luther, however, expressed no regrets, but actually said: "I, Martin Luther, slew all the peasants in the rebellion, for I said that they should be slain; all their blood is upon my head. But I cast it on the Lord God, who commanded me to speak in this way!" (*Werke,* Erl. edition, lix., p. 284, *Table Talk;* see also Grisar, Vol. 3, p. 213).

Erasmus also wrote to him: "We are now reaping the fruit of your spirit. You do not acknowledge the rebels, but *they acknowledge you!*" (*Hyperaspistes,* Opp., 1, p. 1,032).

What wonder that Luther was often subject to attacks of profound melancholy? (See *Luther's Works,* ed. Walch, Vol. 14, p. 1,914). On one such occasion he wrote: "Since our doctrines have been preached, the world has grown steadily worse, always more godless and shameless, and men more avaricious and unchaste than under the Papacy. Everywhere are only greed, immoderate desires, lewdness, shameful disorder and hideous passions." (Döllinger, *Reformation,* Vol. 1, p. 289, etc.). Wittenberg, once the cradle of the Reformation, he said had become "a Sodom!" (*Luther's Letters,* Vol. 4, p. 753).

This opinion was shared by many of the leading men of the time. Melancthon declared: "The morals of the people become worse. Luxury, licentiousness and boldness are steadily increasing" (*Epistolae,* 1, 4, 100, 219). Erasmus also wrote: "What can be more ruinous than to let such words as the following come to the people's ears? 'The Pope is Antichrist; Bishops and priests are mere grubs; man-made laws are heretical; confession is pernicious; works, merits and endeavors are heretical words; there is no free will; everything happens by necessity'. . .I see, under the pretext of the Gospel, a new, bold, shameless and ungovernable race growing up—in a word, such a one as will be unendurable to Luther himself." (*Epistolae,* book 19, p. 601, and book 18, p. 593).

Again he writes (*Works,* Vol. 9, p. 1,026): "Sound human reason teaches me that a man cannot honestly further the cause of God, who excites so great an uproar in the world, and finds delight in abuse and sarcasm, and cannot have enough of them: Such an amount of arrogance, as we have never seen surpassed, cannot possibly be without some folly, and such a boisterous individual is not at all in harmony with the apostolic spirit."

These words of Erasmus remind us that still other characteristics of Luther remain to be considered. No impartial student—even if he gains his information largely from Protestant sources—can fail to recognize that Luther's nature was essentially despotic. He insisted that his will in theological and ecclesiastical matters *must be supreme.* Everyone who differed from him in regard to dogmas he pronounced a heretic, if not worse, and this in words which frequently were far too low and vulgar to be reproduced. Among the mildest of his utterances is: "Whoever teaches otherwise than I teach, condemns God, and must remain a child of Hell" (*Sämtliche Werke,* 28, 346). After such words he hardly needed to say: "I can hear and endure nothing which is against my teaching." (*Works,* ed. Walch, 8, 1974).

At one time, it is true, he appealed to the universities of Europe to pronounce upon his doctrines; but when their answer was a condemnation of his dogmas, Luther became wild with rage. On this account he denounced the University of Paris as "the mother of errors, the daughter of Antichrist, and the gate of Hell!" The "right of private judgement" was evidently intended by Luther to belong to him exclusively.

It is commonly said that Luther inaugurated the right of free investigation. Nothing is less true. He *talked* of it, as a reason for abandoning the traditions of the Church, but he did his utmost to bring about complete subjection to an unassailable Bible. . . *as he interpreted it!*

He instituted thus a pope of printed paper, instead of a pope of flesh and blood. Moreover, *since he constituted himself the authoritative interpreter of the Bible, he practically claimed for himself infallibility.* One of Luther's contemporaries, Sebastian Frank, wrote despondently: "Even under the Papacy one had more freedom than now."

This despotic attitude was, however, not confined to Luther. It lay in the system itself. Calvin also claimed for himself infallibility, and wrote to Aubeterre (*Lettres françaises,* Vol. 1, p. 389): *"Dieu m'a fait la grâce de me déclarer ce qui est bon et mauvais."* ["God has given me the grace to declare what is good and evil."—*Editor,* 1990.] Hence he demanded the death penalty by fire or sword for heretics—that is, for those who differed from him; and, as all the world knows, he had his theological opponent, Servetus, after long imprisonment, burned to death over a slow fire.

It was not long, however, before conflicts over "heresy" broke out between the Reformers themselves, for the fatal tendency of Protestantism to disintegrate began at once to show itself. Sometimes the result of this was almost ludicrous; for the rulers of even the smallest German principalities claimed the same right that powerful potentates had, and forced upon their subjects the particular brand of Protestantism which they had chosen to adopt! Accordingly, the Protestants of certain duchies were obliged to change repeatedly their faith from one Confession to another, to suit the different "private judgments" of successive sovereigns!

In 1556 the Pfalsgraf, Otto Heinrich, declared the doctrine of Luther to be the exclusive religion of the land. But his successor, Frederick III, only three years later, established Calvinism as the State religion. His son, Ludwig, however, in 1576 brought Lutheranism in again, and banished from the country all Calvinist ministers, teachers and officials. In 1583 the pendulum swung back once more, and Ludwig's brother Johann re-established Calvinism. Thus the unhappy people, in the space of less than forty years, were compelled to change their religious faith four times, to say nothing of the original change from Catholicism to Protestantism!

Some men, as they grow older, become gentler and more tolerant. This was not the case with Luther. Vituperative to the last, he died as he had lived. Shortly before his death, he wrote two horribly abusive pamphlets, one against the Jews, the other "Against the Papacy, founded by the devil at Rome." The title page of the latter exhibited a disgusting picture, which proved again the essential coarseness of the author's nature, and the contents of the book are what one might expect from such a frontispiece. It seems to exhaust the entire vocabulary of German vituperation. Döllinger calls it "a document, whose origin can scarcely be explained otherwise than by supposing that Luther wrote the most of it when under the influence of intoxicating drink." (Döllinger, *Luther,* p. 48). In his pamphlet against the Jews, among the epithets which Luther gives to those particular objects of his hatred are "Young devils damned to Hell," and he called upon all Christians in Germany *to burn down Jewish schools and synagogues, and to throw pitch and sulphur into the flames; to destroy their houses; to confiscate their ready money in gold and silver; to take from them their sacred books, even the whole Bible; to forbid their holding any religious services under penalty of death; and, if that did not help matters, to hunt them of the country like mad dogs!"* (*Luther's Works,* Vol. 20, pp. 2230-2632). These two fanatical productions were Luther's latest works; and thus it can be truly said that he died with the wish in his heart to persecute the Jews most cruelly, and with a curse on his lips against the Papacy.

Such being Luther's character, I was not much surprised to find him a most relentless and cruel hunter of "witches." Lecky, in his *History of Rationalism* (Vol. 1, p. 32), remarks of him: "The credulity which Luther manifested on all matters connected with diabolical intervention was amazing, even for his age; and when speaking of witchcraft his language was emphatic and unhesitating. 'I would have no compassion on these witches,' he exclaimed; 'I would burn them all.'"

The devil played a great role in the life of Luther, and no writer ever wrote of him half so frequently. In one small pamphlet he mentions him 146 times. Everyone knows the story of his throwing his inkstand at the devil in the Wartburg, but that was only one of thousands of instances when he believed that Satan appeared to him. He says repeatedly that the devil argued with him, ate with him, slept with him, and visited him in the form of a dog, a sow, a snake and other beasts. Such ideas may be perhaps attributed to a disordered brain; but the language which he uses in describing some of these experiences is unpardonably vulgar.

I do not wish to lay an undue emphasis on this side of

his character, but it cannot be with fairness left unmentioned in any study of the man, for "out of the abundance of the heart the mouth speaketh."

Nothing is more unpleasant in the *unexpurgated "Table Talk"* and *"Letters"* of Luther than the filthy and abusive expressions they contain. Of his merely vituperative language we find a specimen in a dispute over the significance of the Lord's Supper, in which Luther declared that Zwingli was a genuine heathen, and had a "blasphemous, in-bedevilled, through-bedevilled, and over-bedevilled heart, together with a lying jaw!"—*ein eingeteufeltes, durchteufeltes und überteufeltes, lästerliches Herz und Lügenmaul.* He proclaimed also that no Christian should pray for Zwingli, and that he would be damned to the brink of Hell, if he had any fellowship with him and his followers! (See Döllinger, *Luther,* p. 31).

It seems incredible that these "Reformers" could fling such low epithets at one another in reference to their views of the Blessed Sacrament, and no less extraordinary does it seem that Luther, whose privilege it had once been to celebrate the Sacrifice of the Mass, could write of it: "No sin of immorality, nay, not even manslaughter, theft, murder and adultery is so harmful as this abomination of the Popish Mass!" (*Luther's Works,* Erl. edition, vol. 9, p. 106).

Luther also spoke of ecclesiastics in an incredibly vulgar way, and sanctioned vile caricatures of them, which the illiterate mob could readily understand. A specimen of his language regarding religious orders is the following: "Barefooted friars are lice, placed by the devil on God Almighty's fur coat, and friar preachers are the fleas on His shirt!" He also adjured the authorities to take steps against the "blind priests, who run to the altar, like hogs to a trough!"

What wonder, therefore, that Erasmus wrote to this blasphemer: "Scarcely one of your books have I been able to read to the end, so great and insatiable is the tendency to libel which they display. . .Your books swarm with abuse on every page." (Grisar's *Luther,* p. 154).

The Swiss Reformer, Bullinger, the successor of Zwingli at Zurich, complains of Luther's "beastly and obscene facility of speech," and adds: "It is perfectly evident and unfortunately undeniable that, in the treatment of the Faith and of great and serious matters, no one has written more wildly, coarsely and indecently, and in greater opposition to all Christian propriety and modesty than Luther."

An excuse is sometimes found for him by such few Protestants as are acquainted with his works by saying that the age itself permitted such indecencies. But this is no excuse for Luther; for, while professing to reform that age, he actually surpassed in filthy language most, if not all, of his contemporaries. (For a few of his most objectionable expressions, see Grisar, Vol. 2, p. 229, and the authorities he quotes.)

How, then, can Protestants designate Luther as "more than a Saint, and the greatest of Germans, the strongest, deepest, richest spirit of the Christian Church"? (Hans Preuss, *Unser Luther,* 1917). It is to be explained only by the fact that in the hundreds of Protestant books, pamphlets and articles, published, in 1917, in honor of the four-hundredth anniversary of Luther's inauguration of the Reformation, the average reader learns only of the *legendary* Luther, whose carefully expurgated words and writings are alone quoted.

As an offset to all this, however, the Protestant world has always claimed that Luther, by his translation of the Holy Scriptures into his native tongue, first gave the Bible to the German people.

But even this assertion is not based on fact. All who care to investigate the matter can satisfy themselves that between the date of the invention of printing, about 1450, and the year 1522, when Luther published his version of the New Testament, *no less than fourteen complete editions of the Bible had already appeared in the German language*—1. that of Faust and Schöffer, about 1462, Mainz; 2. that of Johann Mentelin, about 1466, Strassburg; 3. that of Pflanzmann, 1475, Augsburg; 4. that of Andreas Frisner, 1470-1473, Nürnberg; 5.

that of Günther Zainer, 1470, Augsburg; 6. that of Günther Zainer (?), 1477, Augsburg; 7. that of Anton Sorg, 1477, Augsburg; 8. the same, 1480, Augsburg; 9. that of Anton Koburger, 1483, Nürnberg; 10. that published in Strassburg, 1485; 11. that of Hans Schönsperger, 1487, Augsgburg; 12. the same, 1490, Ausgburg; 13. that of Hans Otmar, 1507, Augsburg; 14. that of Silvan Otmar, 1518, Augsburg. Four more editions of the Bible had also during this time—that is to say, before the publication of Luther's version—appeared in Low German; so that in reality *eighteen editions of a German Bible preceded that of Luther!* Moreover, in addition to these complete translations, many separate portions of the Scriptures, such as the Psalms and selections from the Gospels, had been printed and freely circulated. (See Panzer's report of these editions to be found in the public library of Nürnberg, and Kehrein's *Zur Geschichte der deutschen Bibelübersetzungen vor Luther,* pp. 34–49 and 53–56).

This certainly does not justify the legend, dear to Protestants, that before Luther's time there was no German translation of the Bible, and that he dragged the Scriptures out from centuries of obscurity. All these editions of the Bible in German were printed to be sold, and were sold at a profit; and, *if sold, they were doubtless read.* Moreover, in addition to these, during the fifty years which elapsed between the invention of printing and the year 1500, there were printed about one hundred editions of the Bible in Latin—on the average two a year! This meant, of course, at that time much more than it would now, since then all educated men read and wrote Latin.

As a proof of the arbitrary spirit which Luther showed in making his translation of the Bible, we have the fact that he confessed to have added, for dogmatic reasons, the word "alone" to the text of St. Paul: "Therefore we conclude that a man is justified by faith without the deeds of the law." (*Rom.* 3:28). Luther rendered the passage "by faith *alone*"; and when reproached for this, he wrote: "You tell me what a great fuss the Papists are making because the word 'alone'

is not in the text of Paul. If your Papist makes such an unnecessary row about the word 'alone,' say right out to him:
'Dr. Martin Luther *will have it so,*' and say: 'Papists and asses
are one and the same thing.' *I will have it so, and I order it
to be so, and my will is reason enough.* I know very well that
the word 'alone' is not in the Latin and Greek text, and it
was not necessary for the Papists to teach me that. It is true,
those letters are not in it, which letters the jackasses look
at, as a cow stares at a new gate. . . It ['alone'] shall remain
in my New Testament, and if all the Popish donkeys were
to get mad and beside themselves, they will not get it out."
There, therefore, it remains to the present time. [The King
James Bible currently in use no longer has the added word
"alone" in this verse.—*Editor,* 1990.]

This was not, however, the only liberty which Luther took
with the Sacred Volume. He made contemptuous allusions
to several Books, not only of the Old Testament, but also
of the New. Among these were the Epistle to the Hebrews,
the second and third Epistles of St. John, the Epistle of St.
Jude, the second Epistle of St. Peter, the Epistle of St. James,
and the Book of Revelation. The latter he did not consider
as either Apostolic or prophetic, but put it on about the same
level as the apocryphal Fourth Book of Esdras, which he spoke
of "tossing into the Elbe"! On the Epistle of St. James, Luther
was especially severe. He called it an "epistle of straw," because this Book, in particular, contradicted his doctrine of
"Justification by faith alone," which, popularly interpreted,
had wrought such havoc with public morals. It is not strange
that he discarded the Epistle of St. James, when he encoun-
tered there such words as these: "What doth it profit, my
brethren, though a man say he hath faith, and have not works?
Can faith save him? Even so faith, if it have not works, is
dead, being alone. Wilt thou know, O vain man, that faith
without works is dead?" (*James* 2:14, 17, 20)

It is sometimes said that Catholics prize the Bible less than
Protestants. It is indeed true that, in the sense of allowing

everyone to interpret it to suit himself, and to found innumerable sects upon it, the Catholics are more careful in their use of the Bible than are Protestants; but the best proof of the wisdom of such care of the Scriptures is the result which often follows an unguided interpretation of their texts. The Catholic Church has stipulated, as a requisite for an *absolutely unrestricted* reading of the entire Bible, a certain degree of education. Thus to the reading of the Scriptures in Hebrew, Greek and Latin no objection has been made; but for those editions which have appeared in the language of the people, and which would be read, of course, by many Christians who possessed no special education, she has required that beneath the sacred text there should be printed a brief explanation of its meaning, as interpreted by the Fathers of the Church. We know that every heresy which has arisen out of the Christian Church has based its claims, however extravagant, upon some verses from the Bible; and all the sects of Protestantism are confirmations of the danger of a reckless reading of the Scriptures, *with no authority or tradition to give an ultimate decision as to the meaning of disputed passages.*

What greater proof of the Church's veneration of the Bible can be found than in the unexampled care and devotion with which many thousand copies of the Scriptures were made, for centuries, in Catholic monasteries and abbeys? These were often adorned with the most beautiful illustrations and marginal decorations and initials. How literally splendid and beyond all price are some of those old manuscripts! Many of them are decorated with intricate patterns that should be studied under a magnifying glass, and are illuminated in five or six different colors. It is evident that the most loving care was lavished on their embellishment, and some of their pages look like gold plates jewelled and enamelled.

To dissociate the Catholic Church from the Bible is impossible in the past and equally so in the present. In every Mass that is celebrated daily round the globe, when the time for the reading of the Gospel comes, Catholics always rise and remain standing till the Gospel has been solemnly sung or read; and before the celebrant begins to read the selection for the day, he utters this prayer: "Cleanse my heart and lips, O Almighty God, who didst cleanse the lips of the Prophet Isaias with a burning coal; and vouchsafe, through Thy gracious mercy, so to purify me that I may worthily proclaim Thy holy Gospel..."

This is merely one proof out of many that the entire code of the Church, her dogmas, her liturgy, her catechism, the sermons of her clergy, her Sacraments—in fact, her whole constitution and continuous life are grounded on the Bible. Indeed the bitterest reproaches have been heaped upon the Catholic Church by Rationalists precisely because, as they aver, she *clings too closely* to the Bible, and interprets it too literally; and it is from *Protestantism, not from Catholicism,* that the most injurious attacks upon the Bible have been made. In this connection it is well to recall the following words, which Pope Benedict XV wrote in a recent letter to the Catholic Truth Society in England: "It was with no little gladness of heart that the Holy Father learned of the work of the Society and of its diligence in spreading far and wide copies of the Holy Gospels, as well as of the other books of the Holy Scriptures, and in multiplying them so as to reach all men of good will...Most lovingly, therefore, His Holiness blesses all who have put their hand to this very excellent work; and he earnestly exhorts them to persevere with ardor in so holy an enterprise."

What, then, had I found at the end of my investigation of the history of Luther? Unquestionably a man of remarkable energy and great ability—qualities which he had used, however, not to reform and unify Christ's Church, but to assail, insult and rend it; and furthermore, a man, whose record shows

> *a grossly animal nature,*
> *immoral conduct,*

> *the assertion that man is wholly unable to resist sensual temp-*
> *tations,*
> *broken vows to God,*
> *a dangerous doctrine of salvation, without regard to a moral life,*
> *a violent, reckless style of preaching, which produced terrible*
> *results to human life and property,*
> *a condoning of bigamy, in order to retain a Prince in Prot-*
> *estantism,*
> *an astounding amount of vile and vituperative language,*
> *fierce intolerance of criticism,*
> *domineering arrogance in his treatment and translation of the*
> *Bible,*
> *scurrilous abuse of priests, the Pope and the Holy Mass,*
> *a belief in witchcraft and the advocacy of burning witches, and*
> *a direct incitement to burn and plunder Jewish houses, property*
> *and synagogues.*

What the results of Luther's revolutionary system in general have been, remains to be considered; but at this point I asked myself—What is there in this man's personality, character, or moral code, which of itself would induce me to espouse his doctrines?

To this I could only answer: Nothing.

Moreover, I felt that if it came to a question of individual leadership, I much preferred the saintly and heroic figures of Ignatius Loyola, Francis Xavier and Carlo Borromeo to the mutually reviling, dictatorial triumvirate—Luther, Calvin and Zwingli. Nevertheless, before making a final decision, I wished to study some of the results of Luther's "Reformation" in Germany, America and England.

Chapter 11

PROTESTANTISM IN GERMANY

Germany the Fatherland of Luther, presents a sad picture of religious life. . .and it is the Protestant theology itself which sows unbelief and undermines Christianity.
— PROFESSOR MASARYK, Protestant.

The Land which was the cradle of the Reformation has become the grave of the Reformed Faith. The Protestant Church in Germany is moribund.—Edinburgh Review, Oct., 1880.

I T IS claimed by most Protestants that whatever Luther may have been as a man, his system, which announces that the Bible is our only and sufficient guide and gives to all the liberty to interpret it as they like, has proved a wonderful blessing to mankind.

How can that be the case, however, when the essential principle of Luther's Reformation destroyed the unity of the Church of Christ, and has steadily driven Protestants ever since toward discord, sectarianism and infidelity? This tendency also seems to be inevitable, and hence, if Protestantism bears within itself the seeds of dissolution, it must at last disintegrate entirely as a religious entity.

This has already partly come to pass, and precisely in the country of its birth, *the land of Luther,* has Protestantism especially drifted into Rationalism. The influence of German skepticism, which has so thoroughly rationalized German Protestantism, spread, of course, long since also into England and America, but its effect, particularly in the United States, was very different. In America, where there is no State religion, those who adopt heretical opinions in theology usually leave the Protestant denominations, either for the half-way house of Unitarianism, or for avowed Indifferentism or

141

Agnosticism. In Germany, however, where the support of an established, national Church is more or less identified with patriotism and official patronage, a multitude of nominal members, though disbelieving its doctrines, still linger in the fold, and even occupy at times its highest offices! The same is true, as we shall presently see, in England.

The best that can be said of Lutheranism in Germany today [It should be borne in mind that the author wrote this in 1920.—*Editor,* 1990.] is that it contains undoubtedly many pious and sincere Christians, but that it has become only one out of many Protestant varieties, produced by the Lutheran theory of "Private Judgment." In fact, were it not for the ecclesiastical appointments at the State's disposal, and for the stipends given to the clergy and officials for Church maintenance, the centrifugal force in Protestantism would probably soon shatter it to fragments. So slight is now the cohesive power of Lutheranism, that within its limits the widest differences in doctrine are allowed. Liberal Lutherans can hardly be distinguished from Unitarians. Many of the laity, and many even of the clergy also, no longer believe the dogmas of the Holy Trinity, the Divinity of Christ, the Virgin Birth, and other features of the Apostles' Creed. If parents still have their children confirmed, it is not always because either they or their offspring really possess decided religious convictions, but because in Germany it has long been legally necessary for every citizen to declare his position in regard to the religious "Confessions" of the country; that is, to state in which of them he wishes to be officially classed—whether as Protestant, Catholic, Jew, or *Confessionslos.*

Yet, after all, the language of the Lutheran catechism is so explicit, and the words of the confirmation service so impressive, that one is shocked to find that it is now to such an extent an empty form. For a goodly number of the children thus confirmed rarely, if ever, go to church again; largely because their parents do not care to force them to attend a service which they themselves neglect. Hence among German Lutherans church attendance is estimated at only from 2 percent to 14 percent of the population, while the number of communicants often falls below *one-tenth* of those entitled to partake of the Holy Sacrament! [Of course, the Lutheran "Holy Eucharist" is invalid; the Lutheran denomination does not have the Sacrament of Holy Orders by which men receive the power to offer the Holy Sacrifice and change bread and wine into the Body and Blood of Christ.—*Editor*, 1990.]

A few quotations from some Protestant authorities will establish the correctness of these statements. The celebrated Court chaplain at Berlin, Dr. Stöcker, wrote, some years ago, as follows: "We have provincial churches, in which every degree of infidelity to the Faith, and every hostility to the Creed, is allowed, even in the pulpits. We have just now had the case of a diocesan superintendent and clergyman, who has, in an article, characterised the Divinity of Christ as a false doctrine; yet he still remains in his twofold office!" In a Protestant paper of Berlin (*Kreus Zeitung*, No. 193, 1902) occurs the following: "The Church, then, is expected to give up absolutely the dogma of the Resurrection of Jesus Christ, with which it stands or falls, and to let Easter sermons be preached on the subject of the decaying corpse of Jesus! And the persons who see in these things true Christianity either hold ecclesiastical offices and dignities, or are teachers and professors of distinction and influence!"

The renowned Protestant theologian, Professor Adolf Harnack, some of whose words in praise of "Jesus as man" have been quoted in a previous chapter, is looked upon by many Protestants in Germany as the latest and highest exponent of modern Protestant theology. His book entitled *The Essence of Christianity* has passed through several editions, in the preface to one of which he states that he has received expressions of the liveliest satisfaction with his work, *Not only at home, but "from many other countries, from all denominations, and from all theological and ecclesiastical centres."* What he has to say, therefore, on the subject of modern Protestantism is certainly of the greatest importance. Among other things, Professor Harnack rejects the Fourth Gospel as a trustworthy historical source, and denies that it was written by St. John. The Gospel ascribed to St. Luke he also considers to have been written, not by Luke, but by someone contemporaneous with the Emperor Domitian, A.D. 81–96. From the first three Gospels also he would eliminate the miraculous. Jesus, in his opinion, called Himself the Son of God merely in the sense that He knew God better than anyone who had preceded Him. In fact, Professor Harnack says distinctly: *"Jesus Christ does not belong in the Gospel!" "Jesus Christus gehört nicht in das Evangelium."*

These ideas are not, of course, original with Professor Harnack, and I had been familiar with them in rationalistic circles for forty years; but what is remarkable is the fact that they are, according to his own statement, now *accepted and applauded by Protestants all over the world.* In the *Evangelical Church Paper of Berlin,* Dr. Stöcker remarks: "If Dr. Harnack is right, then Christianity has lived for nearly nineteen hundred years in the greatest errors, which offend against the majesty of God; for this erudite man denies the Divinity of Christ, His actual Resurrection, the miracles of Scripture, and therewith all the supernatural in Christianity. Accordingly, Christ has really nothing to do with the Gospel! . . . Whoever agrees with Dr. Harnack cannot believe in the Redeemer. This modern theology has a different religion from ours. Let us understand clearly, in merely this one point, the difference between the new and the old faith, and ask ourselves: May we pray to Christ or not? May we in hours of distress of soul call to Christ, 'Lord have mercy on us?' The Church of all the centuries *has* prayed to Jesus Christ. But if we do not consider Him as God, we cannot any longer pray to Him. To pray to man is blasphemy. Either one thing, or the other!" (No. I, 1902).

In the *Hengstenberg Evangelical Church Paper* appeared the following: "In Bremen everyone can preach what he will."

(No. 49, 1901). At a confirmation service in that city, a clergyman recently said: "There never was a sinless Saviour; we believe in no miracles. Jesus is not the Lamb that taketh away the sins of the world"!

This spirit of rationalism in the Protestant Churches is, however, not confined to Germany. It is very widespread in Protestant Scandinavia, and in Switzerland also, the home of Zwingli and Calvin.[1]

In 1901, in Berne, at a memorial service in honor of Pestalozzi, the high school Professor, Dr. Vetter, delivered an address in which he said: "Religious instruction, as it is now given in the schools, must be done away with, *because it rests on the belief in a personal God!*" In reply to a criticism of this address, Professor Vetter, among other things, wrote: "In the eyes of the present generation a God is nothing else than a creation of our thought, an emanation of the human intellect. This God was never born in a supernatural way, as God; He has never risen from the dead. These things were useful as realities only for humanity in its childhood. Your colleague in Neuchâtel, who preached against my speech, because I treated the Resurrection as a fable, belongs also to that childish generation. Otherwise he would know that *many pastors and the most of our contemporaries consider a personal God,*

---

1. The strongly Protestant *Berner Tageblatt* in Switzerland recently printed a leading article on "Victorious Catholicism," in which it mournfully confessed that "Protestant North Germany is tearing itself in pieces. The Lutheran Church there is silent and dismembered. Every pastor preaches his own catechism, and many pastors in blind folly are helping to establish the supremacy of the proletariat. What wonder if German Catholics entertain the hope that, in the universal misery and despair now prevalent, many Protestants of all classes will find their way back to the bosom of that Church which by her changeless faith and tranquilizing institutions promises to their restless souls abundant peace and satisfaction? We must look for these expectations to be fully realized, not only in Germany, but also in England, America and Switzerland." The article closes with the prediction that, if Germany is to be saved from chaos and ruin, this will in all probability be accomplished principally by Catholic South Germany. It expresses also the hope that the limitless Individualism which is so characteristic of German Protestantism today can be counteracted, for otherwise German Protestantism will lose its vitality.

the Trinity, the Redemption, the Resurrection, the Last Judgment, and all miraculous stories which one tells to children, as fables!"[2]

What wonder that the *Allgemeine Evangel-Lutheran Kirchzeitung* exclaims: "It is enough to make humanity mourn to see how our youth are being ruined." Yet these professors and pastors who believe nothing, or almost nothing, of the fundamentals of Christianity, if they desire a position in the Church, must state under oath that they do believe in the Incarnation of the Son of God, in His work of Redemption, in the Inspiration of the Bible by the Holy Ghost, and other essentials of the Creed! I prefer not to characterize this conduct, but will let Friedrich Perthes speak of it in his autobiography: "Infidels go into positions in the Church, and stand there as pastors, who before God and man are perjurers and hypocrites."

The University of Halle has given to the majority of North Germans their theological education. For years the favorite lecturer there on the subject of Church history was the celebrated Professor Gesenius. F. W. Krummacher, in his autobiography, relates the following: "I cannot think of Gesenius otherwise than having on his lips a sarcastic smile, whenever he alluded to any of the specifically Christian truths, or to any of the Biblical miracles. It was especially in his lectures on Church history that his incredulity often exhibited the

---

2. Friends of the author have been recently residing in a Swiss village, the Protestant pastor of which they describe as a thorough unbeliever in the doctrines of Christianity. Nevertheless, though many regard him as an atheist, he preaches on Sunday and even prepares the children for their first Communion! The servant of my friends once boasted to them that their pastor was a free-thinker. In response to their indignant inquiry how the villagers could tolerate for their spiritual guide a man who denied the existence of God, the young girl shrugged her shoulders and replied: "Oh, we are all free-thinkers here!" Certainly the morals of the village justified the assertion. This pastor was obliged by law to hold occasionally a kind of Sunday school for a brief period, but the young girl assured my friends that he soon became so bored with his task that he sent the children out to play, while he himself went to the nearest inn, where he played cards all the Sunday afternoon. It is only fair to state, however, that the Swiss Cantons have a great amount of autonomy in such matters, and hence may vary somewhat in their religious status.

most unlimited frivolity. We frequently felt that we were being led by him through an immense lunatic asylum, where nothing was to be seen except material for pitiful sympathy or Homeric laughter. The Professor's witticisms were liberally rewarded with the latter. The whole Olympus of his auditorium, always crowded to the furthest limit, resounded with shouts of merriment. Woe to him who learned the history of God's Church on earth in no other way than through the treatment given to it by that caricaturist in a doctor's robes." (p. 39).

The *Edinburgh Review* (October, 1880) contained an article on "Germany in the Present and the Past," which stated that the land which was the cradle of the Reformation had become the grave of the Reformed Faith. "The Protestant Church of Germany," it declared, "is moribund. All comparatively recent works on Germany, as well as all personal observations, tell the same tale. Denial of every tenet of the Protestant Faith among the thinking classes, and indifference in the masses, are the positive and negative agencies to which the Church of Luther and Melancthon has succumbed."

In the correspondence of the distinguished philosopher Ludwig Feuerbach we read: "An unbelieving Protestant of South Germany wrote, in 1870, to his friend Feuerbach as follows: 'I have until now, out of consideration for certain people, always gone to Communion every year on Good Friday, and must frankly confess that I have been ashamed of myself for doing so. My better self revolted at such hypocrisy. Yet, what else can I do, since I must live, as a small tradesman, in dependence on those people? I am now too old to emigrate, and it would be hard to tear myself away from my beautiful mountains. I ask you for your advice in this matter, which is so important to me.'" Feuerbach replied: "Religion is so dead and devoid of credit, that it is a matter of perfect indifference whether one conforms to its usages or not"! (Vol. ii., p. 231, 1874).

In regard to this state of things, Hohoff, in his "Revolution," says: "Hypocrites are always to be found, more or less, but *such a widespread religious deception, as is practiced now inside of modern Protestantism,* is seen nowhere in world history, not even at the time of the dying out of ancient heathenism." The historian Menzl in his *Kritik des modernen Zeitbewussteins* (pp. 245–247) says: "In the name of Education it is claimed that *all that is specifically Christian, even in Protestantism, must be rejected*. . .With the open or secret approval of the educated public, infidelity is spreading more and more widely among the lower strata of society. . .The number of those who no longer believe anything is growing appallingly among the people, especially among our youths, whose unbelief expresses itself in the only way possible, the crudest and most brutal forms." (pp. 245–247).

The Prussian General Superintendent, Dr. C. Büchsel, a pious and believing Lutheran, wrote in his Memoirs (*Erinnerungen aus dem Leben eines Landgeistlichen,* 1883) the following: "A preacher in the neighbourhood had preached at Easter against the doctrine of the resurrection of the body. A man went to him and asked whether he had understood him correctly. The pastor, whom he found playing cards, took a groschen from the table, and said: 'Go and buy a rope, and hang yourself, and then you will find out how it is with the resurrection. When you can, come and tell me about it.' The man came to me, and requested me to report the matter to the King. When I refused to do so, he was silent at first, but said, as he took his leave: 'I see plainly that one crow does not pick out the eyes of the rest of the flock.' Another man was in the habit of going from one church to another, and heard a great variety of doctrines. He often came to hear me also. When I met him, one day, he said to me: 'I do not go to church any more, for I become absolutely confused, and no longer know what I ought to believe.' I referred him to the Bible, and told him to examine the question for himself, but he replied: 'Oh, they all appeal to that; but which of them is right?' "

The Protestant philosopher Masaryk says: "Germany, the Fatherland of Luther, presents a sad picture of religious life. . .and *it is the Protestant theology itself which sows unbelief, and undermines Christianity.*"

It is needless to multiply instances of this kind further. If these are not sufficient to reveal the state of the Protestant Church in Continental Europe, and the tendency among its leaders to go into Indifferentism, Rationalism and Deism, then evidence is worthless. Protestantism in Germany has become, for the most part, a labyrinth of contradictory private doctrinal opinions, and is *little more than Rationalism in the garb of Christianity.*

The wonder is that those who disbelieve in a personal God, in the Divinity of Christ, in His Resurrection, Ascension and Redemption—in fact, in all the supernatural characteristics of Christianity, wish to remain, and *are allowed to remain,* within an institution in whose catechism all these doctrines are explicitly taught!

Protestantism, we are often told, is the very core and pith of German progress and character; but what *is* Protestantism? The Protestant Dr. Stöcker calls the views of the Protestant Dr. Harnack heretical, while the latter regards the views of Dr. Stöcker as childish. Who shall decide when Doctors disagree? Where is there among Protestants any authority to put an end to the existence in the same Church of absolutely irreconcilable dogmas, and to eliminate from the Church those who deny its very *raison d'être,* the Divinity of its Founder, and who teach the youth of Europe to disbelieve the existence of God?

To such a rationalistic Protestantism as this I was unwilling to return. Amid the notions which its leaders advocated I had wandered as a Unitarian and Agnostic for nearly half a century, and wished to have no more of them. Why should I seek to save myself from spiritual shipwreck on a raft whose dissolution appeared imminent?

"But have you some more *personal* proof of this condition

of Protestantism in Germany?" the reader may perhaps inquire. "Abundant proof from personal experience," I at once reply.

Out of several instances let me cite a conversation which I had recently with a distinguished German scientist and his wife. I had related to them something which had transpired in a "Reformed Lutheran" church, in a town where I had once resided, and which had seemed to me a striking illustration of religious apathy. At Pentecost I had attended the Protestant service there, and at its close had been surprised to see almost the entire congregation leave the ediface without communicating, to do which they had been especially invited. I paused to note how many members actually lingered for that purpose. In the whole church, left empty save for themselves and me, were only *five* communicants kneeling at the chancel rail, and they were waiting there for the return of the pastor, who, according to his usual custom, had stepped out into the churchyard through the sacristy door, and was shaking hands with some of his parishioners. Yet when I spoke of the painful impression made upon me by that scene, neither the Professor nor his wife could understand my feelings. "Many Protestants," they assured me, "no longer care to partake of the Lord's Supper. *We,* for example, never do. The rite has no significance for us."

"But surely," I replied, "Protestants hold that Jesus instituted that most solemn Sacrament, as a symbol of His death for the remission of sins?"

"All Protestants do not hold that doctrine," was the answer; *"we* feel no need of Christ to stand between ourselves and God. We do not pray to Him, and do not wish to go to the Communion service."

"But the Divinity of the Son of God...?" I faltered.

"We think of Jesus merely as a man," remarked the Professor's wife; "wonderfully gifted spiritually, like the Hebrew prophets, it is true; but we do not consider Him as God."

"You are, then, Unitarians or Deists," I said; "and that is

an attitude which I understand, and once agreed with. But what astonishes me is the fact that you—holding such views—*still class yourselves with Protestants,* and are so regarded by the Evangelical pastor of this city."

"My dear sir," explained the Professor, "we are Protestants because Protestantism means freedom; and because liberty of private judgment in matters of doctrine is our rule of life. As Protestants, *we are all free to believe what we like to believe.* I do not want anyone to form my creed for me, or to compel me to go to church. Some of us Protestants go to church; others do not; *we* do not. Some of us believe in the Divinity of Christ and in His miracles; others do not; *we* do not. Many of us believe in a future life; *we do not.* For us death means annihilation, a dreamless sleep. Nevertheless we class ourselves as Protestants, because Protestantism signifies the spirit of free inquiry, which is the spirit now prevailing at our modern universities."

"You may well be proud of your modern universities," I answered, "and no doubt they are thoroughly imbued with the spirit of Rationalism; but you, Professor, know as well as I do, that Europe does not owe her oldest, and hitherto most famous, institutions of learning to Protestantism. These antedated the Reformation, and were all founded by Catholics, most of.them by Popes. What a list they make when linked together! I cannot now recall them all, but among them certainly are the Universities of Rome, Bologna, Perugia, Pisa, Padua, Florence, Ferrara, Naples, Paris, Toulouse, Orleans, Montpellier, Poitiers, Avignon, Grenoble and Louvain; Valladolid, Salamanca, Lisbon, Prague, Cracow, Vienna, Oxford, Cambridge, Heidelberg, Cologne, Erfurt, Leipzig, Rostock, Trier, Freiburg, Basel, Ingolstadt, Mainz, Tübingen, Wittenberg, and Frankfurt on the Oder. Even the University of Marburg, the first to be founded after the Reformation, as a bulwark of Lutheranism, was mainly constructed out of the confiscation of Catholic monasteries."

"I know, I know," replied the Professor; "but Protestantism is at all events the principle of progress; it is the secret of Germany's national efficiency today."

"Is it fair," I answered, "for you to attribute all the progress and efficiency of Germany to Protestantism, when *nearly half of Germany's population is Catholic?* If the Berlin Court is Protestant (that is to say, largely rationalistic), the Saxon Court is Catholic; if Prussia is largely Lutheran, Bavaria, Baden and the Rhinelands are conspicuously loyal to the Holy See."

"It is the Protestant part of Germany," he answered, "which has made it great, and surely you will allow that all Protestant lands are much more prosperous, enterprising and powerful than Catholic ones?"

"If that be true at present," I replied, "it is due to reasons which have little or nothing to do with Protestantism, *as a religious system.* Catholic countries also have been prosperous, enterprising and powerful in the past, *when commercial and political conditions were more favorable for them than they are today.* Was not Catholic Spain, before England began her well-known career on the seas, the foremost nation of the world? Did not her flag then flutter over half the globe? Was not Catholic France powerful under Louis XIV? Was not Catholic Florence enterprising under the Medici? Was not the Catholic Republic of Venice marvellously prosperous in its unexampled history of a thousand years of conquest, glory and magnificence? Nations have lives, like individuals, and pass through periods of childhood, youth, maturity, old age and even senility; but among the causes of their growth and their decay the principal factor has not been the *form* of their religion, but the lack of any real religious faith and character whatever. Facilities for commerce, a large accumulation of capital, conveniences for inland traffic by lakes and rivers, natural mineral resources, the discovery of new trade routes, and the quicker utilisation of mechanical inventions—these are a few of the causes which have determined the rise and long supremacy of nations; just as a lack of such advantages, excessive luxury, political corruption, the use of slave labor, and repeated wars have led to their decline. Some of these causes certainly have, in modern times, contributed to the material prosperity of the so-called Protestant nations; but what shall we say of the *methods* which those lands have used, and are still using, to acquire and retain their wealth and power? Materially they have prospered; but in the sphere of *ethics and religion* a sterility and blight have fallen on them which are fatal to their *spiritual* progress. It is true that this sterility and blight have tainted Catholic countries also, but insofar as this has been the case, it has been owing to the fact that *these were not genuinely religious or really Catholic,* but practically as godless and immoral as the others in respect to the policy of their Governments. For, after all, what is the standard by which the present world's 'prosperity' is measured? It certainly is not God's standard, but rather that of the average hedonist. This means, financially, the making of large fortunes by any means; socially, indulgence in sensuous enjoyments; commercially, seizing by force or intrigue the markets of the world, as 'spheres of influence'; and politically, the crippling or destruction of commercial rivals, combined with a cunning manipulation of the masses under the pretence of a 'free press' and of that chimerical panacea for all social ills—Universal Suffrage. History often shows a startling disproportion between a nation's inward virtue and its outward 'prosperity.' It has been largely a record of

'Truth forever on the scaffold,
Wrong forever on the throne.'

In any event, I do not think it fair to identify the Catholic Church with what are loosely called 'Catholic' countries. Strictly speaking, there are no 'Catholic' countries. There are peoples, most of whose inhabitants practice, or at least profess, the Catholic religion; but *there is not a single one of them whose politics is based upon the principles of the Catholic Church, or which is governed by men who really conform to them.* And yet these so-called 'Catholic' countries, although their Governments may be practically atheistic, are often accused of deeds and characteristics which have nothing whatever to do with the doctrines of the Church of Rome, or with Christianity in any form. Do not forget that thirty years ago Père Hyacinthe said: 'Atheists are now masters of the French Republic.'"

"But," said the scientist's wife emphatically, "you must concede that in the countries where the Catholic religion prevails, there is much more social immorality than in Protestant lands."

"Are you acquainted with social conditions in this respect prevailing in England, Scotland and Sweden?" I replied. "I do not like, however, this arbitrary separation of nations into categories of virtuous sheep and vicious goats, for it may well be doubted whether the total sum of moral depravity in any one race or country is really so much greater than in others. We judge of them too superficially. Some races, like some individuals, display their vices openly; while others hide beneath a gloss of hypocritical piety or prudery far greater depths of evil. In any event, may I remind you that there are weightier sins than those of the flesh, if we may judge from Christ's own words. For since such sins are often temperamental rather than essentially vicious, they may be, relatively, more excusable than such cold-blooded crimes as deliberate cruelty, intentional calumny, the impoverishment of countless widows and orphans through the wrecking of railroads or illegitimate speculation, the pitiless exploitation of the helpless poor, the hideous system of child labor, and the helping of criminals to escape justice through the use of perjured witnesses or legal technicalities. Now all these sins are peculiarly characteristic of certain Protestant lands, which consider themselves much more virtuous than their Catholic neighbors, because such crimes, forsooth, may be unaccompanied by *visible* carnal weakness. What the respective balance of guilt may be in the sight of God, is not for us to say; but it is remarkable that Christ—Man's future Judge—said to the woman taken in adultery: 'Neither do I condemn thee; go and sin no more,' though He repeatedly exclaimed to certain highly placed and sanctimonious persons: 'Woe unto you, Scribes and Pharisees, hypocrites! for ye are like unto whited sepulchres, which indeed appear beautiful outwardly, but are within full of dead men's bones and of all uncleanliness. Even so ye also outwardly appear righteous unto men, but within ye are full of hypocrisy and iniquity' (*Matt.* 23:14, 27, 28). There is an immense deal of hypocrisy in this respect in so-called Protestant lands, and, in regard to 'immorality,' as you define it, it is well to remember that in no country in the world are women so chaste and above reproach as in Ireland, although no land is more devoutly loyal to the Catholic Church than is the 'Island of the Saints.'"

The old Profesor smiled. "I quite agree with you," he said, "that so-called 'Protestant' countries have no right to accuse the so-called 'Catholic' lands of sin of any sort. They have enough of their own. But this is going far afield. Let us return to our original theme—that of the present condition of Protestantism. In Germany, I must admit, although there still remains much genuine faith and piety among her Protestants, their Protestantism, as a whole, bears little resemblance to Lutheranism, and is honey-combed with Rationalism. But how is it in America?"

My answer to that question is contained in the next chapter.

Chapter 12

PROTESTANTISM IN AMERICA

The American cleric—I refer to the non-Roman parson—is the poorest paid minister of religion in the world, so far as I know, and I know a good deal about this matter...This mean, this low treatment of the clergy goes hand in hand with the most wasteful extravagance in all other church affairs. I know a church that gives four thousand dollars a year for its music, and twelve hundred to its pastor...I know a country church, made up almost of millionaires, that gives one thousand dollars to its rector. Such cases could be multiplied many times over throughout the United States.—THE REV. MUNROE ROYCE: The Passing of the American, pp. 105, 111.

Dr. J. B. Hingeley stated at Atlantic City, January 8, 1920, that 51 percent of the Protestant ministers in America averaged less than one thousand dollars a year, and that less than 1 percent of the entire number received as much as three thousand dollars a year.

THAT THERE are hundreds of thousands of sincere and deeply religious Protestants in America there can be no doubt.

Many of their churches are flourishing, many of their pastors are men of piety and eminent ability, many of their benevolent societies are noted for their charities, and all contribute liberally to the cause of Foreign Missions. Some even show considerable misplaced zeal in trying to make Protestants out of the Catholics of other Christian lands. All this is conceded at the start. But, when American Protestantism is looked at *as a religious system,* and is compared, as such, with Catholicism, it certainly does not correspond to the one, Apostolic, undivided Church which Jesus founded, and for

156

the unity of which He prayed so tenderly. On the contrary, there is no country in the world where Protestantism has become so fragmentary as in the United States.

At the first glance it presents an appearance of unity, but it is like the rings of Saturn, which, seen from afar, seem to be solid masses, but in reality are only congeries of individual aerolites, loosely held together. Protestantism in America is a conglomeration of more or less antagonistic sects, whose rivalry in country towns and villages is frequently intense, so keen is their desire to secure the greatest number of members, the most attractive preacher or the best music.

In many towns of the United States whose Protestant Church-goers are hardly numerous enough to fill a single meeting house, three or church four buildings stand within short distance of one another, all owned by different Protestant denominations, yet all of them half empty. The Rev. Dr. Robert Westly Peach of Newark, in a minority report which he submitted to the Interchurch Council on Organic Union, which met in Philadelphia in 1919, stated that Protestants in America had built perhaps 100,000 superfluous churches at a cost of $500,000,000. "The Roman churches," he says, "are crowded; ours, on an average, less than one-quarter filled."

From *The Passing of the American,* whose author, the Rev. Munroe Royce, is a Protestant clergyman, I cite the following: "I heard the Bishop of Montana, a short time ago, speaking as the representative of the Episcopal Church, say that the rivalry among the different churches in his diocese was most disgraceful. No sooner is a new town started in that State, than a wild rush begins by the representatives of the various religious bodies to secure the most desirable corner lots for church sites. Business rivalry is not more keen than this church struggle to get there first. The Bishop spoke of two little towns of only a few hundred inhabitants, where there were actually two Methodist Episcopal Churches—one north, the other south—confronting each other from opposite sides of the same street, when one of these churches could accommodate nearly all the inhabitants of the place! Of course there were, I suppose, Baptist, Presbyterian, Episcopal and others, besides these two Methodist ones." The story is told of a visitor to one of these towns, who, greatly impressed by the number of church edifices there, exclaimed: "How very religious your townspeople are!" "Not at all, stranger," was the reply, "it only shows how cussed mean they be!"

Many Protestants, of course, see the absurdity of such sectarianism, and deeply lament it; but many do not. Some years ago, a real estate agent, who was "booming" a western town, issued a circular in which the fact was mentioned, *as an inducement to settle there,* that in its population of six thousand there were seventeen different kinds of religion to choose from! That agent lacked a sense of humor.

A Methodist minister reported recently that he had discovered nine different Protestant sects in a town of Illinois, containing a population of only eight hundred souls! Another declared that in the same State he had found in seventeen families *sixteen* different forms of religious belief. (*Christian Unity,* by the Rev. M. M. Sheedy, 1895, p. 50). What wonder that a prominent Protestant American minister recently exclaimed: "We have magnificent church machinery in this country; we have costly music and great Sunday schools; and yet, within the last twenty-five years, the Churches of God in this land have averaged less than two conversions a year each!" (*idem,* p. 46). It is needless to say that the speaker of these words did not include among the "Churches of God" the Apostolic Church of Rome, but referred to Protestant organizations only.

This statement is not surprising when we consider the effect that must be produced by the sight of so many little struggling and frequently hostile denominations, all claiming to be Christians. Such a spectacle does not tend to make thoughtful people wish to join any of them. It affords perhaps a striking illustration of individual Christian "liberty," but does not correspond to the idea of the Church founded and outlined by Our Saviour.

It is religious individualism run mad.

But if the quantity of these Protestant divisions is unedifying, still more so is the quality of some of them. For in their number, one discovers these extraordinary specimens of the result of "private judgment" included in the list of Protestant sects given in Chapter 9 of this volume. Many Protestants, it is true, regard such varieties of Christianity as the Mormons, the Dowieites, Dunkards and Muggletonians with disapproval or abhorrence, and say that they should not be looked upon as "Protestants" at all; yet *Protestants they really are,* as distinguished from Roman Catholics, in that they all profess to believe at least some of the doctrines of Christianity, but justify their own peculiar idiosyncrasies by the principle of the right of private judgment, which Luther and his colleagues advocated in the sixteenth century, and which has been defended by all Protestant denominations ever since.

Protestantism is defined in the *Standard Dictionary* as a term "generally applied to and accepted by *all Western Christians who are not Roman Catholics,* embracing the various Lutheran, Reformed and other ecclesiastical bodies, though it is discarded by some High Church Anglicans." That some of these "ecclesiastical bodies" do not approve of others is nothing new in Protestantism, as we have seen in the study of the life of Luther, but no one can deny that *all of them are Protestant, and none of them is Catholic.* Whatever opprobrium, therefore, attaches to them belongs to *Protestantism, not to Catholicism,* for they are the direct and logical consequence of a principle which justifies the individual interpretation of the Bible, and the right to form independent sects and churches, based on such interpretation.

Among the most zealous advocates of Protestantism in America is a class known as "Evangelists" or "Revivalists." These find upon American soil a fertile field for their operations. The most conspicuous of their number at the present time is a former baseball player, known as "Billy Sunday." It is a lamentable fact that such great numbers of American

Protestants patronize and aid financially this pulpit clown. Were this not so, he would not be referred to here, for his language is that of the race track and the prize ring, and his blasphemous irreverence should be revolting to everyone who desires the name of Christianity to be respected. That he draws crowds to listen to his ribaldry is not surprising, but any "conversions" made by such appeals as his must have a questionable value.

In the center of the huge, barrack-like buildings which are reared for his auditoriums there is a broad aisle, strewn with sawdust, on which his "converts" are invited to present themselves, to shake hands with the speaker at the conclusion of his harangue. This, in the parlance of Billy Sunday, is called "hitting the sawdust trail"! Many of his expressions, like those of Luther, are too coarse and indecent to be quoted, but some idea of his vulgarity can be gained from the following extract from one of his sermons. He thus describes the chosen friends of the Saviour of Mankind at Bethany: "Mary was one of those sort of Uneeda-biscuit, peanut-butter, gelatin-and-pimiento women. Martha was beefsteak, baked-potato, apple-sauce-with-lemon-and-nutmeg, coffee-and-whipped-cream, apple-pie-and-cheese sort of a woman! So you can have your pick, but I speak for Martha. Hurray for Martha!" (*Literary Digest,* April 24, 1915).

This is his way of speaking when in good humor; but when enraged by opposition, his language is almost unprintable. One of the most respectable Congregational clergymen in America is Rev. Washington Gladden, a gentleman of learning, reputation and advanced years. To this gentleman, who had criticized some of Sunday's utterances about "Evolution," the revivalist yelled, while he at the same time shook his fist in his face, "Stand up, you bastard evolutionist! Stand up with the infidels and atheists, the whoremongers and adulterers, and go to Hell! Stand up on your hind legs, you stinking polecat!" In regard to this treatment Mr. Gladden remarks: "One must not think that these vulgar words were uttered in a corner; they were heard by an audience numbering many thousands. The evangelists who use such language carry with them, unfortunately, from city to city *the unqualified recommendation of a number of Protestant ministers!* It is a phase of modern religious life that deserves the serious consideration of intelligent Christians."

It certainly does deserve their consideration, if Protestant ministers and the members of their churches do openly approve of such disgraceful travesties of Bible characters, such virulent abuse, and such low ridicule of sacred themes. Wellnigh incomprehensible, therefore, is the fact that this man was allowed to speak, presumably by invitation, at the University of Pennsylvania on March 30, 1914, in presence of the professors and some four thousand students. In the course of his remarks before this supposedly educated assembly, he described Pontius Pilate as a "stand-pat, free-lunch, pie-counter, lick-spittle, tin-horn, nut-cracker politician"! What must be the effect of such gutter dialect as this on youthful students? Can it leave in their minds—especially in this age of irreverence—the slightest veneration for the Gospel of Christ? How is it possible that Christian people do not see that such performances as these degrade the Protestant Church and even religion itself? How deplorable must the condition of some Protestant churches in America be, when advocates like Billy Sunday have to be resorted to, to keep them from dissolving!

Such mournful eccentricities as these in the Christian life betray a state of spiritual desolation. A church replete with Christian faith and true religious zeal would never tolerate them. Certainly such a man would never be allowed to speak in a Catholic church, or anywhere else under Catholic auspices. What shocks one most in the performance of Billy Sunday is not alone the irreverence which he himself exhibits, but the lack of reverence for sacred things existing in the crowds who flock to hear him.

Perhaps it is this which causes many Protestants to use their churches for secular purposes on other days than Sundays.

This is not true of Episcopalian churches, so far as I am aware, nor is it by any means a universal custom among other Protestant denominations. Nevertheless, it is a fact that a very large number of Baptist, Methodist and Congregational church edifices in America are used on weekdays as places of entertainment; for, in order to raise money for their expenses, churches are frequently leased for concerts, lectures, stereopticon exhibitions, "bell ringers" and travelling companies. The first play ever witnessed by my wife was given by a strolling troop of actors in a Methodist Episcopal church, in which an improvised stage had been erected where the pulpit usually stood.

This play was called "Taming a Tartar"! What sentiment of "Holiness to the Lord" could survive such a desecration? True, we are told, as an excuse, that these religious societies must adopt "business methods" in order to exist; and no doubt life is hard for them, as separate entities, when competition is so fierce, and congregations are so small; but it is questionable whether they do not lose thus more than they gain.

It is characteristic of most Protestant churches in America (as everywhere else in the world), that they are open only for an hour or two on Sundays, and once a week for an hour in the evening, whereas Catholic churches remain open all day long and every day, so that one may enter them at any time, if not to attend some service, at least to pray. But Protestant exclusiveness is not confined to hours of worship.

To every observer it is evident that most of those who assemble in the prominent Protestant churches of American cities are well-dressed, prosperous members of the community. Poor, plainly clad people are less often seen there. It is not likely that such people would be turned away, should they present themselves, but they would probably receive the impression that their proper place was in the mission chapel, where they would "feel more at home, don't you know." It is possible that humble working people would be admitted to the pews of a few of the wealthy church-goers, but *any such equality before God, as is continually seen in Catholic churches, is never observed in Protestant congregations.*

It is also evident that in America the great majority of worshippers in Catholic churches are from the poorer classes. This fact reminds me of a story told me by a dear Catholic friend. Once, when a young girl, she was visiting at a palatial residence on the Hudson, and asked her hostess where she could find a Catholic church in the neighborhood. "There is a wretched little Catholic chapel three miles away," was her reply; "but you can't go *there*. Only poor Irish servants and Italians attend service there." "Well," answered my friend with spirit, "that is where I *shall* go; for the religion I belong to began in a stable, and I don't care if it ends in a stable!" I have been told that this reply of the ardent young Catholic was never forgotten by those who heard it. In fact, is it not amazing that any genuine Christian can condemn a Church for being the one great Christian body that welcomes and retains the poor! To do so is to show a spiritual snobbishness, surpassing that of the Pharisees.

How perfectly does the admonition of St. James apply to such a case: "My brethren, have not the faith of Our Lord Jesus Christ, the Lord of glory, with respect of persons. For if there come unto your assembly a man with a gold ring, in goodly apparel, and there come in also a poor man in vile raiment, and ye have respect to him that weareth the gay clothing, and say unto him, Sit thou here in a good place; and say to the poor, stand thou there, or sit here under my footstool; are ye not then partial in yourselves, and are become judges of evil thoughts? Hearken, my beloved brethren, hath not God chosen the poor of this world rich in faith and heirs of the Kingdom which He hath promised to them that love Him? But ye have despised the poor."

In Catholic churches rich and poor, poet and peasant, kneel, worship and partake of Holy Communion together, side by side, without distinction. *Before their altars all are equal.* The Catholic Church is, in fact, pre-eminently the Church of the poor, and thus fulfills one of the principal conditions laid down by our Saviour, to convince St. John the Baptist of His Messiahship: "The poor have the Gospel preached to them."

But is not the United States the vaunted paradise of democracy, the reader may inquire? In theory certainly, but not in practice, at least in many departments of the nation's life. It is to be feared that in American towns populous enough to have any social distinctions, Protestant churches are too often *social institutions with religious names,* whose members are to a great extent composed of the rich and "respectable" people of the place.

The relative grades of social "standing" of the different denominations, *and even of particular churches in the same denomination,* are carefully defined and keenly felt; and so well is this understood, that persons coming to reside there frequently choose their special sect of Protestantism, and even a particular church within that sect, with a view to the social advantages to be gained from them. Hence the most serious accusation against American Protestant churches in general is that their distinguishing features are social rather than religious. The beauty of the edifice, the quality of the music, the eloquence of the preacher and his personal popularity, together with the social and financial prominence of the members—these are the principal causes that determine their sectarian success. If one asks an American whether he is a Methodist, a Baptist, or a Presbyterian, he will probably answer (unless he be a regular communicant in "good and regular standing")—"I attend Rev. Mr. Smith's church," or "I go to hear Mr. Brown." In other words, the personality of the preacher is the paramount factor.

To gain and to retain the needed poularity is, therefore, a matter of great importance to a Protestant minister. Of course the poorer pastors, settled in the country, know little of these conditions. They struggle on amid a number of contending sects, as poverty-stricken as their own, and often have great difficulty in feeding, clothing and properly educating their children. If the statements quoted on the title page of this chapter are true—and I have no reason to doubt them—the average Protestant minister in the United States must possess much devotion and self-denial, for most of them are married men with families. But what kind of appreciation of the Protestant clerical profession and of its value to the community do such meager salaries show?

In the larger towns, exalted positions and high salaries are given to exceptionally gifted preachers and social favorites, but their incomes must be well earned. The lives of popular city clergymen are often a kind of social slavery. In the majority of cases such ministers are dependent for their office on the good will of wealthy and influential parishioners, who often are not actual members of the church, yet virtually control its policy. Hence they not only fear to preach as boldly as they otherwise would do, but have to toil like galley slaves in making themselves popular with their congregations; for, whatever else a Protestant minister in America may be, he *must* be a social favorite in order to become a "success." The keen competition between rival denominations makes it, in fact, essential that their ministers should be "up to date." One way of acquiring this popularity consists in making numberless social calls, which leave the minister little time for study, reading and the cultivation of spirituality. I have known clergymen and their wives who, for months at a time, never had a single evening at home! They were continually making calls. If such visits were of any spiritual benefit to the parishioners, or indeed had anything to do with religion, the practice would be praiseworthy; but they are almost invariably of a social character only, and cultivate in those who make them little else than superficiality of conversation and worldliness of manners, which weaken genuine respect for the clerical vocation. I have known ministers who felt obliged to keep a list of the birthdays of the prominent members of their flock, that they might never forget to send or bring to them flowers or other gifts on those occasions!

The truth is that prosperous, well-paid Protestant ministers have become, like similarly situated Anglican clergymen, men of society. As married men, mingling in social functions, they find it difficult to lead a sober, Christian, spiritual life, particularly if they have extravagant, worldly sons and pretty daughters, who must "go into society." A certain standard of dressing is then demanded for both mother and daughters, and the preoccupation necessary for the preparation of their toilettes, together with the inevitable conversations and "table-talk" upon such subjects, morning, noon and night, including discussions about the prices of gowns and hats, and the permissible line of the corsage—have a disastrous effect upon the religious life of the paterfamilias, if not on that of the entire household. Hence worldly standards and methods of life are inevitably more and more adopted by them. Even the kind of recompense given for faithful church work is affected by this state of things.

To my personal knowledge the wife of a clergyman in the United States has long been in the habit of giving her Sunday school class and members of the choir a treat by taking them in a body once or twice a year to the theater or opera. Should someone ask who those finely dressed ladies and gentlemen are who are seated together at some popular play, he may be told that they are the "Church of St. Blank's theater party"! I am far from condemning the hearing of good operas and decent dramas, but I recognize the existence of a subtle, indefinable law of the *fitness of things;* and there is something sadly incongruous in the fact that *such* means are resorted to in order to attract young people to the church and to reward them for attendance. Something is wrong here, but whether the fault lies chiefly with the Protestant churches themselves, or with the clergy, or with the parents, is beyond my power to decide.

Still more objectionable are the sensational and frequently

vulgar announcements, made on Saturday in American newspapers, of the special attractions offered on the following day in Protestant churches. These form a mournful commentary on the condition of those churches, if they are obliged to use such methods to allure the public. I quote the following notices, taken quite at random from a Boston newspaper—

DUDLEY STREET BAPTIST CHURCH: Rev. George R. Stair, pastor. Rev. George H. Thompson, the Harp Evangelist, will preach. 10:30, "Railroading to the Devil's Vineyard"; 7:30, "Why I Changed from Ballroom Harpist to the Ministry." Harvard male quartet. Sunday-school, 12 p.m.

TREMONT TEMPLE BAPTIST CHURCH: The largest church in New England. "Strangers' Sabbath Home." Pastor, Dr. Cortland Myers; music by Lotus male quartet; Mrs. Lamson, soprano; Mr. Fairbanks, organist; Temple chorus. Morning subject, "The Devil's Poison for Our Religious Life and Its Antidote"; the second sermon in the series of "Love Stories of the Bible in the Matrimonial Wreckage of Boston" will be given in the evening; subject, "Isaac and Rebecca—The Most Romantic Meeting and Engagement of Them All. 'Before and After' in Marriage at Once the Greatest Comedy and Tragedy." Doors open at 10:00 and 6:30; Bible school at 12.

CHAPEL OF THE VEDANTA CENTRE, I, Queensberry Street, Fenway. Service with address by Sister Devamata, Sunday, 11 a.m. Subject, "Practical Value of Yoga."

WARREN AVENUE BAPTIST CHURCH, corner West Canton Street. Herbert S. Johnson, D.D., and Rev. Frank B. Haggard, pastors. Pastor Haggard preaches at 10:30, subject, "Love First and First Love"; 7:30, subject, "For Such a Worm as I"; mixed quartet, a.m.; chorus choir, p.m.; Mr. Erskine A. Gay, director. Welcome to all.

BAPTIST CHURCH IN BROOKLINE, 1375, Beacon Street. Rev. Walter M. Walker, D.D., acting pastor. 10:45, "Over the Wall"; 12:10, Bible school, men's Bible class, Mr.

William E. Perry, teacher; 7:30, chapel service, "Grit and Glue." You are invited.

FENWAY THEATER: Services of the Universalist Church of Boston. Morning worship, 10:45. Dr. Roblin's theme, "Jesus and the People's Plaudits," the fourth of a series of sermons on the "Life of Christ." Musical selections from "The Seven Last Words," by Dubois; the choir will be assisted by Mr. Daniel Kuntz, violinist; prelude, "Arioso," by Bach, violin and organ soprano solo, "All Ye Who Travel"; bass solo and chorus, "Father, Forgive Them"; tenor and bass duet and chorus. "Verily Today Thou Shalt Be with Me in Paradise"; "Andante," by Giraud, violin solo; tenor solo and chorus, "Father, Into Thy Hands I Commend My Spirit"; "It Is Finished." Afternoon, at 3:30, community singing of international songs, with pictures, short addresses by Dr. Roblin and Jan Hornicek, Instructor of Romance Languages at Dartmouth College; choir selection, soprano and also duet, "Recordare," from Verdi's "Requiem."

I quote the following also from *America* (a Catholic weekly in New York), published on January 17, 1920, p. 287:

"Pictures with a moral punch," that is the description of his new "movie service" given by the pastor of the First Unitarian Church, Louisville, KY, the Rev. Mr. Akin. It is the latest device to fill the empty pews of non-Catholic Churches. Members of his congregation recorded that the average attendance for the "fifteen leading churches" of Louisville was less than seventy. Catholic churches were clearly not considered, since their normal problem is to find space for all those who come to worship. To attract "fully 600 persons" Mr. Akin advertised a free movie-picture show, "Passing of the Third Floor Back," in six reels, with the famous actor, Forbes-Robertson, in the stellar role. Services began with the singing of the "Long, Long Trail," after which the women sang and the men applauded, and then the men sang and the women applauded. With this beautiful harmony and mutual admiration established, "the substitution of a picture sermon for a spoken sermon" began. In the full flush of his first success the Rev. Mr. Akin advises all pastors to follow his example. A far simpler method might be suggested, and that is to rent a moving-picture theater and put up the sign: "Everybody Welcome, Everything Free." There will then be no longer any need of erecting churches.

Still more unedifying are the announcements of a "popular" Protestant minister in Brooklyn, as quoted by the above paper in its issue of February 14, 1920, p. 377. The titles of this preacher's sermons for the month of January, 1920, were: "Wild Horses" (Swanee River Quartet); "The Lion Tamer" (Joseph Martell, baritone); "The Snake Charmer" (Evangel Trumpeters' Quartet); and "Pigs is Pigs" (Evangel Trumpeters' Quartet).

To one who has the least conception of the dignity and holiness of Christ's Church, such cheap, sensational methods of attraction are nauseating. In striking contrast to all this, the Catholic Church, strong in her unity of faith and in her splendid discipline, is not compelled to degrade herself by these means, any more than to dishonor her sanctuaries by letting them for popular amusements during the week.

She has a hold upon the people, which Protestantism does not and cannot have, for among the latter's countless sects the rigid discipline, unity of faith and ultimate authority of the Catholic Church are wanting. This is the more remarkable when one thinks of the self-denial which that Church demands of her members. What would most Protestants say, if they were required to attend Divine service *every Sunday and Holy Day,* and if this rule compelled them sometimes to go to church at five, six, or seven o'clock of a winter morning? All Catholics do not do this, it is true, but literally millions of them do, and even regard it as no hardship. Their sentiment is expressed in the lines:

The night is past, the dawn is breaking,
I rise, dear Lord, to go to Thee,
My slothful ease with joy forsaking
For what Thy love prepares for me.

Swift through the starlit, sleeping city
I hasten to the House of Prayer;
Dear friends, regard me not with pity—
The Bread of Life awaits me there.

A hunger for that Bread impels me,
A craving for celestial food,
A whisper in my soul, that tells me
To seek and find the Son of God.

These are no careless statements. I have frequently tested their accuracy, and have repeatedly seen priests and communicants going faithfully through cold, storm, and darkness at those early hours. In the small European city where I lived for years, Masses are said in many churches *every half-hour on Sunday from five o'clock in the morning to half-past eight.* Then follows High Mass in the principal church at nine, and there is a concluding Mass at ten. During the week also Masses begin *every day* equally early, but are not so numerous. The most remarkable thing about these services is the fact that even the very earliest are well attended, and most of the others crowded. Nor is this state of things peculiar to that community. It is practically universal. I know a priest who, in a large city, says Mass every morning at half-past five, and he tells me that he *always* has, both on Sundays and weekdays, a large attendance, consisting chiefly of working men and mothers of families, seeking God's blessing before going to their daily toil.

It is certainly easier, in America, as everywhere else, to be a Protestant than a Catholic, supposing both are sincere and desirous of doing their duty. A Protestant keeps his spiritual books without an auditor. He can attend church or not, much as he pleases, so far as any reprimand from his minister is concerned; he may hold extremely rationalistic views, need not go to Holy Communion, and is not obliged to make any individual confession to which humiliation and penance are attached. So long as Protestants preserve an outward form of unity and make good contributions to the church's treasury, few questions ever will be addressed to them in reference to faith, still fewer in regard to morals. The subject of religion is, as a rule, ignored in conversations between Protestant pastors and parishioners, and the latter might well conclude that their minister cared very little about their spiritual condition; for when does he ever question them, unasked, upon such subjects?

In the Catholic Church, however, there are very solemn checks and balances in the accounts of all. The Mass, Confession, Penance, Holy Communion—these are awful Sacraments, involving duties the neglect of which in the Catholic Church leads to momentous consequences, and by these solemn Sacraments she holds the members of her fold as no other Church can do.

In view of all these considerations, I think that an unprejudiced observer must conclude that united Catholicism, with its *devoted, celibate clergy,* is better able to stimulate and retain the religious life of the people than disintegrated Protestantism, with its married, and therefore more or less socially fettered, ministers. Certainly Catholic priests, who are free from all domestic ties, can devote themselves unreservedly to their duties, wherever these may lead them, as Protestant ministers cannot do. Not only are the former unhampered by the claims of a social life, which often cool a pastor's fervor with the chill of worldliness, but they are not restrained from duty through the fear of bringing contagion to their families should they expose themselves to malignant diseases, as Catholic priests invariably do, when cholera, yellow fever, or other pestilences desolate the land. What an appalling storm of protest and entreaty would be raised by the wife and daughters of a Protestant minister, should he propose to run the risks which every Catholic priest assumes as a matter of course!

As time went on, therefore, and I observed the doors of Protestant churches closed on weekdays and the greater part of Sunday also, yet found the Catholic churches always open, and services going on, or confessions being heard, or individual worshippers kneeling in devotion, at every hour of the day; when I further perceived how many burdened souls were always seeking aid or consolation at their hallowed shrines; and in particular when I assisted at the solemn celebration of the Mass, whose wonderful old prayers have accompanied it down the ages, a thousand years before a Protestant was born—I realized more and more the enormous difference between the two confessions.

"But," it may be objected, "Protestants have once a week a sermon, and that is sufficient for them." Is it? I have known many Protestants whom the sermon alone did *not* satisfy, and who were painfully aware that, while Catholics regard their churches primarily as sanctuaries for prayer and worship, Protestants often look on theirs chiefly as places for pulpit oratory and pleasing music. Serious Protestants are, therefore, frequently conscious of a spiritual hunger that is not appeased by a "good sermon," however eloquent it may be. They are also haunted by the thought that the reason why the principal feature of their service has thus become the sermon, is that—through their rejection of the Mass—the role of Protestant ministers has been reduced from that of priests to that of preachers. In any case, *hearing sermons about God is a very different thing from praying to Him and adoring Him.* The latter is what God requires from His children; the former is what man prefers to do, as something easier and more agreeable.

Anglican and Episcopalian Protestants, it is true, give less importance to the sermon than do Non-Conformists [Non-Conformists are Protestants other than Anglicans or Episcopalians.—*Editor, 1990.*]; for, having borrowed almost wholly from the Catholic Missal, the former have composed a liturgy, which is—so far as it goes—a noble vehicle of devotional expression.[1]

With Non-Conformists, however, who possess little or no liturgy, the sermon is the all-important factor; although too often, being more of an ethical or literary production than a spiritual appeal, it is of little value as an aid to religion. Non-Conformist services are, of course, characterized by prayers, but these are individually improvised efforts which do not seem to represent the sentiments and aspirations of the auditors, since they elicit from them no responses. They have the appearance rather of detached, personal performances on the part of the minister, who stands while praying, during which time the members of the congregation also do not kneel, and sometimes do not even close their eyes. Moreover, such is the liberty of speech accorded to every Non-Conformist minister, that his public prayers frequently resemble orations, or political addresses, in which he seems not to be speaking to Almighty God, but to be trying to impress his more or less critical and indifferent audience. Such prayers are often reproduced in print as having literary or political significance!

In Catholic churches, on the contrary, the stately prayers and collects of its ancient liturgy are usually closely followed by the worshippers in their prayerbooks; and in the litanies and Rosary the responses are fervently made. By Catholics

---

1. Most of the beautiful words used in the Anglican and Episcopalian prayers and collects are merely translations or adaptations from the Missal of the Catholic Church. Thus in the Anglican service the Psalm "O come, let us sing unto the Lord" is the opening psalm in the Catholic Matins—the *Venite adoremus.* The Psalms appointed by the Anglicans for every day in the year, as well as the Lessons, correspond almost exactly to those in the Breviary, read by every Catholic priest daily. The noble *Te Deum,* "We praise Thee, O God," comes from the earliest Catholic offices; and the "O be joyful" is the *Jubilate* of the Breviary. The Apostles' Creed and Nicene Creed are, of course, of Catholic origin; and the "Lord be with you, and with thy spirit" is the literal translation of the *Dominus vobiscum, et cum spiritu tuo* of the Mass. Most of the Anglican collects and prayers are also simple English versions of the Catholic Latin; while "Glory to God in the highest" is, of course, an English rendering of the time-honored *Gloria in excelsis* of the Mother Church.

the sermon is regarded as of vastly less importance than the Sacrifice of the Mass, in which the morning service always centers. Then, though there should not be within the church, besides the officiating priest, one solitary person—a most improbable occurrence—the sacrifice of Christ would still be celebrated just the same. The blessing is for those who join in its intention; the loss is for the absent.

I cannot close this chapter more effectively than by quoting here the words of the late Dr. Crosby of New York, a Protestant who understood his country and its characteristics as well as any man of his time. He says: "The great bulk of the Protestant Church is identified with the world. It has a name to live, while it is dead. It has turned its doctrines into nationalism, or rationalism, and its life into selfishness. The old landmarks are gone. Family prayer is given up. Prayer meetings are ignored, worldly partnerships are formed, social sins are connived at and even excused, the pulpit is made a stage on which to strut and pose before a gaping world, and religion is made one of the instruments of fashion."

NOTES—(1) A recent report of the Federal Council of Churches in the United States declares: "The Roman Catholics still have more priests than churches, but in the Protestant churches there are about *forty percent* more parishes than there are ministers to serve them. In the South, for example, there are said to be *three thousand* Baptist Churches with no pastor. In the same section there are eighteen hundred Methodist churches with no preachers, and about one thousand Episcopal and one thousand Presbyterian churches in a like condition."

The report further states that the number of young men in America who enter theological seminaries with the intention of becoming ministers has greatly decreased. Referring to this, *America,* in its issue of January 8, 1921, remarks:

"There are forty thousand Protestant churches without pastors. . .What is the matter? This is the question asked. To a Catholic the answer is clear. Protestantism is no longer a religion, but a nebulous form of sociology that shifts with the wind of popular opinion. But young Americans are not sufficiently interested in such a cult to give their lives for its preservation and advancement."

(2) Statements rather uncomplimentary to American Protestants, but taken out of their own mouths, have recently been printed in the *Religious Digest*. Thus Dr. S. Parkes Cadman is quoted as writing in the *Western Christian Advocate:*

"The Church of Rome takes care of its priorities. We throw them away to the winds, and where are we? For example, in New York today there are a million so-called Protestants. They are not even decent pagans. They go nowhere to church and make no contribution to any part of the church. They come into New York from every part of this country, and if they had church letters they are never presented. On Sundays the sons of class leaders and deacons and elders are among the automobile riders, and if they ever come out at all you have to dig them out from under a pile of filthy Sunday newspapers. When they come to church they walk in as though they were bestowing a compliment on Almighty God by being there. We cannot have a church that way even though you raise ten million times ten million. There has got to be a new church consciousness."

Again, a writer in the *Christian Century* says in this same connection:

"The metropolitan cities have thousands of Protestants on the road to paganism. They are the new rich, who by 'climbing' processes, have outgrown the village and small town and gotten into metropolitan cities. The career of these has been marked by intense individualism. They may drop in once in a while on the church that represents the faith of their fathers, but it is to sample things superciliously and without a sense of responsibility."

Chapter 13

THE CHURCH OF ENGLAND

The differences within the Church of England are far greater than those which sever Non-Conformist bodies from the Established Church, and from one another.—LORD AVEBURY.

The schism which rent England from the Divine Tradition of Faith, rent it also from the source of certainty.
—CARDINAL MANNING.

THE HISTORY of the Church of England presents another proof of the disintegrating force forever prevalent in Protestantism. That history should, therefore, be recalled by everyone who is confronted by the question: "Why should I not become an Anglican, or a Protestant Episcopalian?" What, then, was the origin of Anglicanism?

Of all the sovereigns who espoused the cause of the Reformation, the one who naturally most concerns the English-speaking race is Henry VIII of England. Until self-interest had induced this monarch to change his attitude toward the Reformation, he had opposed both Luther and his doctrines. In fact, in 1521, as a reward for a treatise issued by him against the monk of Wittenberg, Henry received from Pope Leo X the title of "Defender of the Faith." This title, however, though gained by him as an *opponent* of the Reformation, was not renounced by him when he turned against its Papal giver. On the contrary, he not only retained it, but actually caused it to be made by Act of Parliament, in 1543, a permanent acquisition of the Crown, and as such it has ever since remained the title of all British *Protestant* Sovereigns! Does it never occur to them that the "Faith" which Henry was rewarded for defending was that of the Catholic Church they now repudiate?

Luther replied to Henry's treatise in his usual style, and called its royal author a "crowned ass," a "fool," a "liar," a "blasphemer" and a "hog." When, therefore, we find Henry, some years later, eagerly following the example of many German princes in declaring himself independent of the Church of Rome, and joining those whose doctrines he had once condemned, we naturally seek the motives of his *volte-face*. We find them in his love for women and desire for loot.

As for the first, it is well to recall the fact that for several years previous to his assumption of the role of a Reformer he had been trying to prevail upon Pope Clement VII to annul his marriage with Queen Catherine, that he might marry Anne Boleyn. The Queen appealed to the Pontiff to defend her, as she was certainly Henry's true and lawful wife and had been so for twenty years. Nor did she appeal in vain. The Pope, although by yielding could probably have kept England Catholic, resisted every blandishment, and bade the profligate King recall his wife, and send away her rival, threatening him with excommunication if he should refuse to do so. Henry, however, determined at all hazards to install his mistress in the place of Catherine, dismissed the Papal representative, Cardinal Wolsey, and soon appointed as his successor in the Archbishopric of Canterbury his pliant tool Thomas Cranmer, one of whose earliest acts was to declare the King's divorce legitimate. Working through him, Henry soon took the law into his own hands, and acted with astonishing celerity. On June 1, 1533 Anne Boleyn was crowned; in the following month the breach between the King and Pope became complete; and in 1534 Henry caused Parliament to proclaim him the "Supreme Head on earth of the Church of England."

We need not linger long upon the record of this Head of the English Church. On the day following the execution of Anne Boleyn, to whom he had been married only four years, he married Jane Seymour; a year later, he espoused Anne of Cleves; and to her succeeded the gentle Catharine Howard, who also was beheaded after fifteen months of matrimony, thus making room for Catharine Parr, who herself narrowly escaped the scaffold.

Yet it was on this cruel and disreputable Prince that a Protestant Parliament conferred the legal right to define what was orthodoxy and what was heresy, to regulate the ritual of worship, to decide on the interpretation of Scripture, and to appoint or to dismiss every clergyman in his dominions!

When one investigates, therefore, the origin of the Anglican Church, one finds that its founder was the murderer of two wives, the repudiator of others, and the executioner of many of the noblest Englishmen of the time, who had the conscience and the courage to oppose him. Among these were the venerable Bishop Fisher, more than eighty years of age, and Sir Thomas More, one of the most distinguished men of his century. These martyrs could not bring themselves to acknowledge the supremacy of Henry in things spiritual, and therefore were beheaded with the axe. The Abbots of Glastonbury, Reading and Colcheter, who also bravely resisted Henry's sacrilegious demands, were likewise accused of treason, and the contents of their abbeys were confiscated. So easy is it to find excuses to plunder defenseless wealth!

The first of these illustrious victims was eighty years of age and a great invalid. He was, however, dragged on a hurdle to the top of a hill, overlooking his once beautiful abbey, which had been partially laid in ruins, and when "he would confess no more gold and silver," was hanged and quartered! Soon many other less distinguished monks and priests, who would not take the required oath to Henry as the Head of the Church, and had refused to preach to their parishioners that the Pope was Antichrist, were either hanged, beheaded, quartered or disembowelled. Nor were these deeds of cruelty confined to England.

When Henry began his persecution, there were about 1,000 Dominican monks in Ireland, only four of whom survived when Elizabeth came to the throne thirty years later.

What is important to remember is that Henry VIII *did not*

commit these crimes as an ordinary man or for ordinary motives. He did them that he might make more secure his authority as the Supreme Head of the Reformed Church of England, and it was by these acts of persecution and spoliation that he did make himself and successors rulers of that Church.

His plundering of the Christian shrines and consecrated cloisters in his realm has rarely been surpassed in any land. Protestants themselves admit this. An Episcopalian clergyman concedes that Henry's "character was about as bad as it could be, while his confiscation of our Church property makes him the greatest church robber that ever lived." (Little's *Reasons for Being a Churchman,* p. 142). We can form some idea of what an opportunity for spoliation that Head of the Church of England had, when we remember that there are now in England several thousand churches which were originally Catholic sanctuaries. Many of these still stand upon the same foundations which supported them five centuries ago, and some of them have not essentially changed since they were built, four hundred years before Henry VIII was born. The treasures contained in these and other churches were of marvelous richness, beauty and historical value. Hundreds of lists of "Church goods," still extant in England, prove this fact; for they describe minutely marble altars, sculptured tombs, massive silver railings, frescoes, statues, paintings, gorgeous vestments, chalices, monstrances, croziers, beautifully illuminated books, rare manuscripts, elaborate crucifixes in wood and silver, processional crosses and banners of the most elaborate workmanship. On all these Church possessions the spoilers of the "Reformation" were let loose, and the result was fatal. The priceless objects disappeared, like leaves before a swarm of locusts. The chalices of gold and silver which had for centuries held the Holy Eucharist, illuminated missals of great value, bells, statues, crucifixes; all were seized and sold, if not destroyed. Incited by the lust for plunder, a wanton passion for destruction burst forth also in extreme ferocity.

From a depraved desire to defile what once had been held sacred, mobs stalled their horses in the nobly decorated cloisters, melted the consecrated bells, broke stained glass windows, and sold the spoils of precious libraries to tradesmen, to serve as fuel for their stoves! Surplices, vestments and altar linen were turned into tablecloths and curtains, or else sold as curios. (*The Reformation of the Church of England,* Vol. 2, p. 68). Many of the most beautiful ruins in Great Britain, such as the once exquisitely sculptured Melrose Abbey, are eloquent reminders of Protestant iconoclasts and pillagers.

Remarkable also is the fact that the Reformers turned away thousands of poor people from the monasteries, where they had been fed for years; and drove out nuns by thousands into a derisive world, with no support, and yet forbidden to marry, under penalty of being arrested as common felons! (*Historians' History of the World,* Vol. 19, p. 185). The monasteries had, it is true, in the course of time, accumulated much wealth; but this may truthfully be said to have been the *patrimony of the poor,* for the doors of those institutions were always open to the suffering and needy. Together, these institutions owned perhaps a third of the land; but they cultivated it, were proverbially lenient landlords, and their charities were boundless. James E. Rogers, Professor of Political Economy in Oxford, says in his *Six Centuries of Work and Wages,* Vol. 2, p. 358: "The Church of the Middle Ages conferred inestimable benefits on mankind, and especially on England...England was planted full of monasteries and capitular bodies. They had, to be sure, the fatal gift of wealth, but they seem to have used it well. They were founders of schools, authors of chronicles, teachers of agriculture, fairly indulgent landlords and advocates of generous dealing toward the peasantry."

In other words, in England, as elsewhere, the relief of destitution was the fundamental religious duty of medieval Christianity, a duty faithfully performed by English monasteries. Today a few rich men possess still more of England's land,

and much of this lies idle, or is used for hunting, the peasants being frequently forbidden to occupy it on any terms! How have the people profited by the exchange? The English writer on political economy, Dr. Percy Withers, recently said: "In England and Wales 77 percent of our people, that is about 30,000,000, live herded on little more than *one-tenth* of the land!. . .The results are physical unfitness, disease, squalor, drunkenness, thriftlessness, moral depravity, needless suffering and criminal waste."

What makes the crimes of Henry VIII and Elizabeth peculiarly atrocious is the fact that the Church which they discarded, plundered and persecuted, was *the Church which had been for a millennium the Church of all the English.* It was Pope Gregory the Great who in A.D. 590 dispatched St. Augustine and other monks to convert the inhabitants of the British Isles from heathenism to Christianity, and for nearly a thousand years the people of England, priests and laity alike, had been in close communion with the Papal See. Up to the time of Henry VIII the spiritual supremacy of the Pope had never been denied in England, and the primates of the Church had never been installed there, till their appointments had been ratified by the Successor of St. Peter. British bishops were present also at the important Councils of the Catholic Church, and Pope Hadrian IV was an Englishman, the son of a simple farmer.

Yet in the face of these facts, the Church of England in its "Homily of Idolatry" distinctly states that "for 800 years and more, laity and clergy, learned and unlearned, all ages, sects and degrees of men, women and children of *the whole of Christendom have been at once drowned in abominable idolatry, of all vices most detested of God and most damnable to man!"* If this horrible indictment be true, where is the verification of the Saviour's promise that the gates of Hell should not prevail against His Church? Did He not keep His word through all those centuries? Can we believe that the vast majority of Christians were allowed to live and die for ages in the grossest error? Can we suppose that the divinely founded Catholic Church, which was already old before the first of Britain's heathens was baptized, was, during all that time, left unprotected by the Holy Ghost, and governed by a line of Antichrists?

Yet if this ancient Faith was so beloved and deeply rooted in the English people, how was it possible so quickly to destroy it, and to supplant it with another? The means employed for such a task must have been powerful indeed. One thing which made it easier was the political situation of England, caused by the rupture with the Vatican; for, through the Pope's refusal to sanction Henry's divorce, Elizabeth, the daughter of Anne Boleyn, was held by Catholics to be illegitimate. Her cousin, therefore, Mary Queen of Scots, a Catholic and wedded to the young King of France, became thereby the rightful heiress to the English throne. Her coronation would, however, have meant the transfer of England to the dominion of France, and the fear of such an event formed one of the principal reasons why so many Englishmen sacrificed their religious convictions, and recognized Elizabeth as head of the Church which she had forced upon them, however much they personally disliked her.

A still more potent cause of the rapid apostasy of England from Catholicism was the terrible persecution inflicted on all nonconformists. To realize what this was, it is necessary only to refer to the Acts of Parliament, passed in the reigns of Henry's successors, Edward VI and Elizabeth.

In 1548, Edward VI, as supreme head of the Church, caused it to be ordained that any clergyman not using the Book of Common Prayer, or *using any other form of prayer,* should suffer imprisonment for life! Three years later, this was extended to the laity, and the law read: "If *any person be present* at any form of prayer or ecclesiastical rites, other than those set forth in the Book of Common Prayer, he shall suffer imprisonment for life." In fact, both priests and many of the laity were forced to adopt Anglicanism, or suffer death in ways of which the axe was the most merciful.

All Catholics were placed under the harrow of oppressive laws. To become a Catholic was to commit an act of high treason. No Catholic might be the master of a school; if he sent his child abroad for education, all his estates could be forfeited, and he became a civil outlaw. If a Catholic did not attend Protestant worship, he was not allowed to come within ten miles of London, to travel more than five miles away from his home, and could not bring an action at law. Moreover, no christenings, marriages or burials could take place among them except according to the rites of the Church of England. Espionage and treachery wcrc well rewarded. A statute of Parliament, passed in 1605, reads: "Any person discovering where Mass was said, shall have his own pardon and *one-third of the goods forfeited by the attainder."* Executions speedily began. Sir James Stephens reckons them, at one time, at about 800 a year. (See Cardinal Newman's *Present Position of Catholics in England,* pp. 215–217).

Hallam, in his *Constitutional History of England* (Vol. 1, p. 146), says that the revolting tortures and executions of Jesuit priests in the reign of Elizabeth were characterized by a "savageness and bigotry, which I am sure no scribe of the Inquisition could have surpassed." If the details of these atrocities were here narrated, they would form very unpleasant reading for Protestants, accustomed as they are to think that all religious persecution has been done by Catholics. As Newman says: "It is pleasanter (for them) to declaim against persecution, and to call the Inquisition a hell, than to consider their own devices and the work of their own hands." It was, however, a veritable reign of terror.

"No man could enjoy security in the privacy of his own house, where he was liable at all hours, but generally in the night, to be visited by a magistrate at the head of an armed mob. At a signal given, the doors were burst open and the pursuivants in separate divisions hastened to the different apartments, examined the beds, tore the tapestry and wainscoting from the walls, forced open the closets, drawers and coffers, and made every search which their ingenuity could suggest, to discover either a priest or books, chalices and vestments appropriated to the Catholic worship. To resist or remonstrate was only to provoke additional aggression. All the inmates were interrogated; their persons were searched, under the pretext that superstitious articles might be concealed among their clothes; and there are instances on record of females of rank whose reason and lives were endangered from the brutality of the officers." (Lingard, *History of England*, Vol. 6, pp. 166-167).

All these and many other equally cruel measures for dragooning the Catholic inhabitants of England into the new State Church, of which the English Sovereign was the head, may be read in the Acts of Parliament passed in 1568, 1581, 1587, 1605, 1627, 1670, 1700 and 1714; and as a proof that these atrocious laws were pitilessly carried out, we may recall the fact that, in 1626, Lord Scroop was accused of being too lenient, because he had convicted only 1,670 Catholics in the limited area of East Riding in Yorkshire.

Established by such methods, and deliberately severed by is founders from the Mother Church, the Church of England must, therefore, be regarded by an unprejudiced student as merely a human institution, most of whose excellences are derived from the Church which it abandoned. It was made by Henry and his Parliament a State creation, and such it still remains. Under the supremacy of the British Sovereign and Parliament, it really forms a department of the government, "the ecclesiastical section of the Civil Service."

Moreover, being divided by internal dissensions, its dogmas cannot be defined with certainty. Although all Anglican clergymen are obliged to sign, and even to take an oath to accept and teach its famous "Thirty-Nine Articles," in their *"literal and grammatical sense," in the "plain meaning thereof,"* many of them repudiate that "plain meaning," and hold and preach doctrines which are explicitly denied in the Thirty-Nine Articles, and condemned by most of their bishops. Such cler-

gymen, however, say quite frankly: "The Thirty-Nine Articles and the Prayer-Book do not mean what you think they
mean. It is true, most of our bishops think as you do, and
say that we are wrong, *but it is they who are mistaken.*"

It is evident, therefore, that the differences in the Church
of England are not limited to trivialities, or to questions of
"Church millinery," as many suppose. On the contrary, they
are often very serious, and affect the conduct of the soul and
its obedience to God's commands.

Lord Avebury declares that "the differences within the
Church of England are far greater than those which sever
nonconformist bodies from the Established Church, and from
one another!" "Low" members of that Church sometimes
invade the congregations of their "High Church" brethren,
and interrupt the services with shouts and threats! Some towns
of England are notorious for such demonstrations, which are
known as "surplice riots." The Anglicans who thus protest
against the High Church ceremonies are unquestionably sincere, and claim that they are acting in defense of the Prayer-
Book; but *who possesses the authority to interpret the Prayer-Book?*
The High Church finds in it one thing, the Low Church
another, the Broad Church a third, and the Rationalistic, or
"No Church," still another! It is of no use to appeal to the
bishops, for they are themselves divided. Each party boasts
of having some of them as patrons. What wonder, therefore,
that the skeptic says: "I will hear you, when you can agree
on what you wish to teach me." The reproof is well-deserved.

The "Broad Church," for example, does not wish to use
the Athanasian Creed, while the "Low Church" finds it very
edifying. "High Church" and "Broad Church" also look upon
the Sacrament of Holy Communion from entirely different
standpoints. One holds that it involves the miracle of Transubstantiation; the other claims that it is merely a memorial
service. Both, it is true, repeat the same liturgy, but each gives
to the words of the Prayer-Book a special interpretation, which
would create a great sensation if expounded in an interchange

of pulpits. Moreover, while some Anglicans regard the Church of Rome as the "Scarlet Woman" and the very embodiment of idolatry and blasphemy, others in the same Church believe in the Divine Presence in the sanctuary, adopt auricular confession, and in their altar decorations, incense and the use of candles approach as nearly as possible to the ceremonies of the Roman Catholic Church.

Still more remarkable is the fact that, while some members of the Anglican communion call themselves Protestants, and are proud of it, many of the High Church clergymen and laity *repudiate the name,* and even declare that Protestantism is a heresy!

History proves, however, that the founders of Anglicanism were really Protestants of the deepest dye, that they were actuated by the same fierce hatred of Catholicism which the Lutherans possessed, and that they even surpassed these in the cruelty of their persecutions and in their plundering and destruction of Catholic property.

Nor must we forget that still another section of the Church of England practically discards the leading doctrines of Christian theology, including the Incarnation, Resurrection, Ascension and Divinity of Christ, as well as the personality of the Holy Ghost!

Already, some fifty years ago, there was published in England a volume entitled *Essays and Reviews,* which was the work of six prominent professors and clergymen of the Anglican Church. The doctrines advocated in this book were in such open defiance of the generally accepted Christian dogmas, that other eminent members of that Church at once declared that they were *"essentially and completely at variance with the doctrinal teaching of the Church of England, and cannot, even under the shelter of any names, be advisedly maintained by honest men who hold her ministry!"* Could language be more unequivocal than this, or condemnation stronger? Yet the authors of the volume, though presumably "honest men," neither retracted their statements nor resigned their clerical positions!

An American free-thinker wrote from England in reference to this book (*National Reformer,* November 24, 1860): "This is a work of the greatest importance. *It sets aside the old theology entirely,* and propounds the rational views of Paine and Voltaire with just that mixture of cloudiness which you might expect from persons who, while they see the folly of the old superstitions, yet remember that they are clergymen, and feel that they are but partially independent and free. . .We are on the eve of a great religious revolution. . .Many of our great writers cling to the doctrines of God and a future state, but *they have no more faith in the Divine authority of the Bible, or in the supernatural origin of Christianity, than you or I.* . .The works of Professor Baden-Powell,. . .Professor Jowett (two of the compilers of the *Essays and Reviews*), etc., are doing a world of good!"

Now who is to decide, and to enforce decisions, in a church like this? Theoretically, a King or Queen is supposed to do so, but really, in any test case, the decision rests, not with the Sovereign, or the bishops, but with Parliament. And what is Parliament? A legislative assembly, mostly composed of laymen, many of whom are atheists, agnostics or Israelites, in other words, a transitory congress of the representatives of all religions and of no religion! Moreover, since the royal head of the English Church has now been shorn of many of his kingly prerogatives, the actual Head of the Church of England is the chief of that particular political party which happens to be temporarily in power.

Today this chief is Mr. Lloyd George,[1] a Welsh dissenter; and not long ago the world beheld the still more remarkable

---

1. The following is from the *Church Times* (an Anglo-Catholic weekly) of November 5, 1920:

"At last we know who is the bishop maker. *Y Cymro* reports the proceedings at the breakfast with the Prime Minister of a deputation of Welsh Calvinistic Methodists, drawn to Downing Street to discuss the questions of temperance legislation and chapel sites. A correspondent furnishes us with this translation of the Welsh report: 'The Prime Minister said that already he had nominated over half the bishops of the Established Church, "or rather," he said with a roguish

spectacle of a Jew, Benjamin Disraeli, appointing the Archbishop of Canterbury and other prelates of the Established
Church!

In forming an estimate of the Church of England, it must
be also borne in mind that, although it holds so prominent
a position in social and political life *at home,* it is, abroad,
comparatively insignificant. The late Father Hugh Benson,
a convert to Catholicism, although his father had been the
highest prelate in the Anglican Church, the Archbishop of
Canterbury, gives this striking picture of the isolation and
provincial character of that Church outside of England: "My
contentment with the Church of England suffered a certain
shock by my perceiving what a very small and unimportant
affair the Anglican communion really was. There we were,
travelling through France and Italy down to Venice, seeing,
in passing, church after church, whose worshippers knew nothing of us or of our claims. I had often been abroad before,
but never since I had formally identified myself with the official side of the Church of England. Now I looked at things
through more professional eyes and behold, we were nowhere.
Here was this vast continent apparently ignorant of our existence! I believed myself a priest, yet I could not say so to
strangers without qualifying clauses... As I came back alone
through Jerusalem and the Holy Land, my discomfort increased. Here again, in the birthplace of Christendom, we
were less than nothing... In all the churches it was the same.
Every Eastern heretical and schismatical sect imaginable took
its turn at the altar of the Holy Sepulchre, for each had at
least the respectability of some centuries behind it—some sort

---

look in his eye, "Mr. Ernest Evans chooses them and I appoint them. He now
and then goes to hear them preach, and when he returns he sometimes says about
some of them, 'That one has ability, he'll do.' " ' We had supposed that the King
appointed, on the advice of the Prime Minister; it appears that the Prime Minister
now appoints, on the advice of Mr. Ernest Evans, and another prerogative of the
Crown has quietly fallen into abeyance. What else Mr. Ernest Evans may be we
have been unable to discover; that he is the power behind the Throne Mr. Lloyd
George assures us."

of historical continuity. But the Anglican Church, which I had been accustomed to think of as the sound core of a rotten tree, had no privileges anywhere; it was as if it did not exist; or rather it was recognized and treated by the rest of Christendom purely as a *Protestant sect of recent origin*."

The confusion which prevails in the Anglican Church is well illustrated in a conversation given in Lady Georgiana Fullerton's admirable story, entitled "Mrs. Gerald's Niece." Was it true, the Abate asked, that her husband was an English clergyman? Yes, she answered, he was an Anglican clergyman. The Abate sighed. She hastened to say: "But he is not a *Protestant;* he is a Catholic, an *Anglo*-Catholic." "Not a minister of the Church of England, then?" "Yes of the *Catholic* Church of England." "But that is impossible, Signora. If he was an English Catholic priest, he could not be married." "He is not an English *Roman* Catholic priest, but a Catholic priest of the Anglican Church." "But the Anglican Church is Protestant." "No," Ita eagerly rejoined, "that is the mistake. It has been *thought* to be Protestant, but it is really Catholic." "We cannot be talking of the same Church, Signora; I mean the Church of England, to which the Rev. Nilson belongs." "Oh, yes, it is the same Church; but my husband thinks *quite* differently from Mr. Nilson. Nothing can be more different. Edgar believes in the Real Presence, in Confession and Absolution." "Bravo," exclaimed the Abate; "but then how can he be of the same religion as the Rev. Nilson, who tells our people that the Blessed Sacrament is nothing but a piece of bread, etc?" "Well, it is not the same *religion,* but the same *Church.*" "Are there, then, two religions in the same Church?" "Edgar," she answered, "says that what Mr. Nilson teaches is heresy." "Then why does your Church let him teach it?" "It cannot help it; *some of our bishops think as he does!*"

A singular theory has of late found favor among certain Anglicans, who desire recognition from the older forms of Christianity. This "Branch Theory," as it is called, claims that the Roman Catholic, Greek and Anglican Churches are "branches" of the one Church of Christ. This idea may be pleasant to those Anglicans who know themselves to be in schism from the Mother Church, and would like to be readopted, *without making any essential concessions;* but it is utterly rejected both by the Eastern Church and the Church of Rome, each of which is very much larger than the Church of England. Neither of these will accept the Anglican, with his mutilated Sacraments and his repudiation of several fundamental doctrines, common to both; and both refuse to recognize as Apostolic, Anglican orders, dating from the Reformation only, or to consider Anglican clergymen as genuine priests; a fact which becomes all the more striking, when one perceives that Anglican orders are repudiated, not only thus by the greater part of Christendom, but even by millions of Englishmen themselves.

But, even supposing that there are ecclesiastical "branches" of this sort, where is the *trunk,* of which they form a part?

Surely there must be somewhere an ancestral trunk, from which they all derive their origin. But, if so, can there be any doubt that this must be the first and oldest of all Churches, the one founded by Christ and His Apostles, the Roman Catholic? Yet in that case, the Greek and Anglican "branches" are no longer attached to the parent stem, but have fallen away from it.

In England the only *living* branch is the Catholic Church, for this has never separated itself from that parent stem, but is still vitally connected with it. Cardinal Merry del Val says of this scheme: "A Branch Theory has been devised as a compromise, with which to satisfy the yearnings of many an aching heart. But, alas! without avail. We, too, hold a 'branch' theory, but it is the one of which our blessed Saviour spoke. Branches there are, and must be, in the One Church, but not branches which have no stem, and are cut off from the Vine, with their leaves scattered 'High,' and 'Low' and 'Broad.' Our Lord spoke of such branches, and said: 'If anyone abide not in Me, he shall be cast forth, as a branch, and shall wither.'" (*Papal Claims,* p. 127).

It is not strange, however, that many Anglicans endeavor thus to effect a reconciliation with the Mother Church, and that the members of the High Church party are especially dissatisfied. What are their lighted and incensed altars, without the sacrifice of the Mass, which gives to them their *raison d'être?* What is their stately ritual without the doctrine of the Real Presence, which alone can justify it? How stirring are the eloquent words of Cardinal Manning in reference to the removal of the Holy Eucharist from England's old cathedrals, a deed which robbed them of the Sacred Host, which had for centuries been guarded in the tabernacle, as the token of Christ's presence! "Does anyone know the name of the man who removed the Blessed Sacrament from the Cathedral of Canterbury or York Minster? Was it in the morning, or in the evening? Can we hope that some holy priest, in sorrow, out of love for his Master, removed His eucharistical Presence to save it from profanation? Or was it some sacrilegious hand that dragged Him from His throne, as of old He was dragged from Gethsemane to Calvary? Canterbury and York went on, the day after, as the day before; but the Light of Life had gone out of them. There was no holy sacrifice offered morning and evening. The Scriptures were read there, but there was no Divine Teacher to interpret them. The Magnificat was still chanted, but it rolled along empty roofs, for Jesus was no longer on the altar. So is it to this day. There is no light, no tabernacle, no altar; nor can there be, till Jesus shall return thither. They stand like the open sepulchre; and we may believe that angels are there, ever saying: 'He is not here. Come and see the place where the Lord was laid.'"

If anything more were needed to reveal the confusion and antagonistic differences in the Church of England, it could be found in the recent scandal in its ranks, occasioned by the appointment of a rationalistic bishop. This nomination, though, of course, agreeable to some Anglicans, was exceedingly offensive to others, who considered it a proof that unbelief at present is not only taught by many of the clergy unrebuked, but that such teaching is officially encouraged. Many Anglican bishops, therefore, protested against the appointment, and declined to take part in the consecration. Ten distinguished Anglican clergymen have, in fact, on this account, gone over to the Church of Rome. This is, however, no unusual circumstance. The Cardinal Archbishop of Westminster stated recently that there are, on the average, about 9,000 conversions from the Church of England to Catholicism annually. In 1901 in Liverpool alone 1,000 such converts were received, almost all of whom were from the educated classes (Jacob Scherer, *Why I Love My Church,* p. 106). Among these were Lord Brampton, the artist Aubrey Beardsley, and many Anglican ministers. The Rev. Mr. Scrolls, formerly of the Church of England, writes: "Almost one-fourth of the Catholic clergy in England are converts, and were once Anglican preachers."

Is it probable that this movement will become so general that the greater part of the English State Church will go over to Catholicism? Surely every Catholic must hope and pray for such an event, and there are many who believe that this will soon take place, especially in view of the recent "Anglo-Catholic Congress," held in London in June, 1920, where the High Church Anglican party made a remarkable demonstration of piety and fervor, and of a desire for reconciliation with the Mother Church and all ecclesiastical bodies in Christendom. On that occasion twelve Anglican bishops recited the "Hail Mary" in unison on the platform of Albert Hall, and many were the "concessions" which the representatives of that party were willing to make to all who differed from them.

Yet not on mere *external similarities* to the ceremonies, liturgy and practices of the Catholic Church can hopes be based for a union between Anglicanism and Catholicism. The increasing number of individual converts to the Church of Rome might, it is true, make such a reconciliation seem at first quite probable; but even though the "Anglo-Catholics" do adopt

large portions of the Catholic liturgy, and freely use consti-
tuents of the Roman service such as candles, incense and vestments; nay, even though they willingly avail themselves of
the Sacrament of Penance and pay due reverence to the Blessed
Virgin, all this remains inadequate.

The desired reunion never can take place, *so long as the Church
of England refuses to acknowledge the spiritual authority of the Successor of St. Peter at the Vatican,* and on that point the vast
majority of Anglicans are as yet inflexible. Nothing is plainer,
however, than the fact that the final test of true Catholicism
is the recognition of the Pope, as the Head of the Church
of Christ on earth, infallibly preserved by the Holy Ghost
from proclaiming erroneous doctrines in his *ex cathedra* utterances on matters of faith and morals. The most ardent ad-
mirer and imitator of things Catholic, *if he does not accept that
spiritual authority of the Pope, has no legitimate place in the Roman
Catholic Church.* It must be one thing or the other. If the essence of Protestantism is the right of individual private judgment, its *quintessence* is the rejection of the Papacy. The lines
of the High Church Anglicans and Catholics are undoubtedly parallel, but merely parallel lines can never meet.

The only remedy for the numerous denominational divisions which Anglicans and Dissenters alike lament is union
under the divinely appointed, central authority of the Pastor
of Christ's Church on earth. So long as they reject this, their
only unity will be that of protestation against Catholicism.

In view of all these facts, does it seem credible that there
are actually Anglicans who firmly believe that theirs is the
one, true, visible, Catholic Church of God and that *the Church
of Rome is in schism from it, not it from the Church of Rome?*

In regard to the latter assertion, an able writer has well said:
"When there are two bodies, one of which is great, the other
small, one ancient, the other modern . . . it is evidently not the
great or the ancient which becomes responsible for a separation, but the smaller, modern body. A small portion, detached
from a mountain, can never with propriety be called the

mountain itself." (Keenan, *Controversial Catechism,* p. 93).

Such Anglicans as those above mentioned apparently ignore the following facts:

1. That they form a small minority of the Christian believers living on their island, and but a fraction of its inhabitants;

2. That their claims are not allowed or even seriously considered outside of Great Britain and her Colonies;

3. That their Church was established by a king and Parliament only about four centuries ago;

4. That its area of efficiency is chiefly limited to the narrow space between the cliffs of Dover and the Scottish frontier;

5. That it is painfully unreliable as to doctrine and severed into sections by internal differences; and

Finally, that it is objected to by nearly forty millions of British and Colonial Dissenters!

★   ★   ★

What is to be the future of the Church of England, as a corporate institution? Undoubtedly it has within its fold thousands of genuinely pious souls and fervent votaries; yet if the present social and political movements toward democracy should cause its disestablishment, depriving it of State support and national prestige, it would in all probability not long survive. The immanent centrifugal force, which it derives from Protestantism, and which is working constantly for its dissolution, would then act still more rapidly, disintegrating it, first, into its various sections, and then dividing it into two great streams, one moving toward the Church of Rome, the other toward the ranks of the Dissenters and the Rationalists.

One of the latest judgments pronounced upon the Anglican Church is that of Mr. Robert Keable in a book entitled, *Standing By; War-Time Reflections in France and Flanders* (E. P. Dutton and Co., 1919). The author was a missionary of the Church of England in Africa, and acted as war chaplain in France. In this book we find the following statement: "One cannot help feeling that nine Protestant chapels out of ten have ceased to have any religion at all. Protestantism seems to be largely sermons, organized relief works, and temperance legislation. In the Church of England one is slowly suffocated...There must be hundreds of priests and laymen who see, in the searchlight of this war, that *of all religious failures in history it would be hard to find one more tragic and complete than the failure of the Established Church of England.* That for the hundreds who see it, there are thousands who do not, and that for the thousands who do not, there are tens of thousands who do not take enough interest in a palpably worn out institution to think about the matter at all, only emphasizes the tragedy."

★   ★   ★

Hence, much as I admired many things in the Church of England, as it exists today I could not bring myself to enter it. To me it lacked the seal of the Supernatural. It does not acknowledge the authority of the Chief Bishop of the Church, unquestionably founded by Christ. It does not go back to the age of the Apostles, or indeed, within fifteen hundred years of it, but sprang into existence in comparatively recent times, under very questionable circumstances, and through the use of cruel and obnoxious methods. Moreover, it has not the first essential of the Church of Christ, *Unity of Faith.* It is, on the contrary, a House of Confusion. It has not even the right to call itself "Catholic," if we employ that term in its legitimate meaning of "universal," for it is national in its establishment and limited in area. The Roman Catholic Church, on the other hand, is fettered by no confines of nationality or geography. It enters every country in the world, preaching the Gospel to every creature, and uniting men of every race in a religion whose doctrines, discipline, language and ritual are everywhere the same.

Is there any other body of Christians which is thus One and Universal? None. All other Christian Churches are local or national; but the Church of Peter, though "Roman in its center, is Catholic in its circumference." The Church of England is consoling, beautiful and inspiring precisely in those features which it borrows or inherits from Catholicism, yet it reminds me of a costly lamp, hung in a small side-chapel of a vast cathedral. It certainly emits a mellow radiance, but its pale light illumines only a restricted area, falls on comparatively few, and grows continually fainter with advancing years.

Chapter 14

DIFFICULTIES SURMOUNTED—
PAPAL INFALLIBILITY

*Either Christianity is divinely preserved, or it is not. If it
be divinely preserved, we have a divine certainty of faith. If
it be not divinely preserved, its custody and its certainty now
are alike human, and we have no divine certainty that what
we believe was divinely revealed.*—CARDINAL MANNING.

*I never could understand how the Church could be infallible,
and its head liable to be mistaken.*—REV. ROBERT SUFFIELD,
Unitarian Minister.

*What binds me to the Catholic Church is the continuous
line of Bishops down to the present Pope.*—ST. AUGUSTINE.

HAVING COME thus far, and having satisfied myself
that neither in rationalized Lutheranism, nor in discordant Sectarianism, nor even in divided Anglicanism could I find that Authority, Unity and Catholicity which
I desired, why did I not at once become a Catholic?

Alas! those seekers after Truth who, like myself, have stood
upon the threshold of the Church of Rome, heirs to the
prejudices of their youth, and shrinking from offending relatives and friends, well know how every social, scientific and
theological objection is laid hold of by the trembling soul,
as an excuse for further hesitation and delay. Nor are these
various objections figments of the fancy. They are real, and
must be resolutely faced and overcome. How these were met
and vanquished in my own case naturally forms a further
portion of this narrative.

Fearing to make the all-important decision until these problems had been solved, I turned to grapple with them. They

principally grouped themselves round certain dogmas of the Church, which constitute essential articles of Catholic Faith. It is the custom now among some varieties of Protestants to look upon dogmas as unimportant. This has not always been the case. On the contrary, Luther's great doctrine was that men are saved and justified by faith alone, and that, provided suitable dogmas are believed, good works are quite superfluous. Now, however, his followers tend to the other extreme, and are fond of asserting that it does not matter what one believes, provided the life one leads is exemplary. As a matter of fact, however, in theological thought (as in all thought), accuracy of expression is as necessary as accuracy of reasoning. Clear, unequivocal statements of conclusions, mutually arrived at and accepted, are essential to any body of believers. Such clear and unequivocal statements are its dogmas, and are as necessary to the Church as bones are to the human frame to hold its flesh together.

Now it is conceded by all Christians that the Saviour sent His Apostles "into all the world" to teach mankind the truths of His Revelation. But *to teach is to define,* and there can be no definite teaching without something definite to teach. That "something definite" is dogma. Cardinal Manning states this truth admirably: "All knowledge must be definite...Is not this true in every kind of knowledge? What would a mathematician think of a diagram which is not definite?...What, again, is history which is not definite? History which is not the record of definite facts is mythology, fable and rhapsody...What are moral laws which are not definite? A law which is not definite carries with it no obligation. And as in human knowledge, so above all in Divine. If there be any knowledge, so above all in Divine. If there be any knowledge which is severely and precisely definite, it is the knowledge which God has revealed of Himself. Finite indeed it is, but definite always." (*The Grounds of Faith,* pp. 5, 6).

But if Christ's dogmas are to be defined and taught, the teachers authorized to teach and to define them must have been, and must still be, preserved from stating them errone-ously. To begin with, the Apostles whom Christ Himself sent into the world "to teach all nations" must, *in this respect*, have been infallible, and there is not the slightest doubt that those Apostles claimed for themselves such an infallibility.

St. Paul, for example, says: "Though we or an angel from heaven preach any other Gospel unto you than that which we have preached unto you, let him be accursed." (*Gal.* 1:8). To make sure that his words would be understood, he even repeats them thus: "As I said before, so say I now again: 'If any man preach any other Gospel unto you than that ye have received, let him be accursed.'" St. John also writes: "If there come any unto you, and bring not this doctrine, receive him not into your house, neither bid him God-speed." (*2 John* 10).

But the same Divine preservation from doctrinal error must have been also true of the successors of the Apostles. Can we suppose that Christ would give the *early* Christians infal-lible teachers, yet leave succeeding generations, century after century, to be instructed by fallible ones? On the contrary, Christ not only commissioned the original leaders of His Church to teach His Revelation, but *promised them the guidance of the Holy Spirit "all days even unto the end of the world."* It was natural, therefore, that the Apostles should make provi-sion for the work of their successors, when they themselves should have passed away, and this provision they certainly made. The form of Church government established by them, under God's guidance, was that of Bishops, or "Overseers" and their subordinates. Already in the earliest times we read: "Take heed, therefore, unto yourselves and to all the flock, *over which the Holy Ghost hath made you overseers,* to feed the Church of God." (*Acts* 20:28-30).

Somewhere, therefore, on this planet this Church of God must still be in existence, and must be the custodian of Chris-tian truth, as Christ delivered it and meant it to be taught, and as the Holy Spirit has preserved it. One Church alone has claimed from the beginning to be that custodian, and this is the Apostolic, Roman, Catholic Church, which dates from the days of the Apostles. None other claims the right to speak in matters of faith and morals, as with the voice of God. But the Catholic Church cannot do otherwise, for it holds that the faith of the Apostles was entrusted to it by Christ Himself and also by the Holy Ghost on the day of Pentecost, and that these fundamental dogmas have been protected ever since that time from error by the Holy Spirit, as Christ promised should be the case. These dogmas form a definite deposit of revealed facts, which were imparted once for all, and may be neither changed nor repudiated. If, then, the Catholic Church were to renounce by one jot or tittle its claim to be this visible and infallible custodian, whose privilege it is to preserve the truth and to teach it *with authority,* it would immediately sink to the level of the schismatic and heretical bodies, in which authoritative doctrine and discipline have disappeared.

I asked myself, therefore: "Do I believe that the Saviour has kept His promise, and that His Spirit has really remained in His Church, in order to guide it into all truth and to preserve it from error?"

My answer was: "I *must* believe it, or else hold either that Christ has not been truthful, or that the Holy Ghost has done His work imperfectly. Either of these hypotheses was untenable. How, then, could I escape the conclusion that, *in the sphere of faith and morals,* the Church—directed by the Holy Spirit—is preserved from error—in other words, *is infallible?* I could not escape it. It is logical and necessary that the Catholic Church should claim to be protected supernaturally from erroneous doctrine; for if it did not make that claim, it would deny or doubt the promises of Christ. *Belief in the infallibility of the Church is a belief that Christ has kept His word.*

The Protestant writer Mallock—the author of *Is Life Worth Living?* truly says: "Any supernatural religion which renounces its claim to absolute infallibility, can profess to be a semi-revelation only. Insofar as it professes to be *revealed,* it, of course, professes to be infallible. But if the revealed part be hard to distinguish and understand; if it may mean many things; and if many of those things are contradictory; it might just as well have never been made at all, *if it has no interpreter...*To make it an infallible revelation—or in other words, a true revelation at all to us—we need a power to interpret the testament itself."

In view of this need, God has given men that power of interpretation; for, on the day of Pentecost, the promised Holy Spirit came to the young Church for the special purpose of teaching it, guiding it into all truth, and abiding with it forever. Christ's words on this point are unmistakable: "I will ask the Father, and he shall give you another Paraclete, that he may abide with you for ever. The spirit of truth...shall abide with you, and be in you...The Paraclete, the Holy Ghost,...will teach you all things, and bring all things to your mind." (*John* 14:15).

Now what Church was this, to which the Holy Spirit was thus promised as Divine Teacher and Guide? Evidently the only Church existing at the time, the only one whose proofs are unassailable, the ancient, Apostolic Catholic Church, whose grand supremacy endured unchallenged for so many centuries, and from which the Protestants separated four hundred years ago. Whence come the countless subdivisions among these Protestants, except from their disbelief in the supernatural guidance of the Church by the Holy Spirit? If that belief had been maintained in Luther's time, there would have been no schism from the Mother Church.

Reduced to the last analysis, *the Reformation was a revolt against belief in that promise of Christ.* But to abandon thus the original Church, to which He had pledged the Holy Spirit's guidance and protection for all time, was to insult that Spirit by doubting either His presence or His efficacy!

How can those who deliberately separate themselves from the original Church be certain that they have not lost the sanctifying and illuminating Presence of the Holy Ghost? The

promise was not made to separate individuals, or to a congeries of differing sects, but to *one Church, for whose entire
unity its Founder prayed pleadingly, almost with His latest breath.*
Not independent, private judgment, but the Spirit of God,
was to guide the Church into all truth.

But in this Church of Christ, as in every government and
properly organized institution on earth, there must exist an
ultimate authority, which shall decide when bishops disagree.
As a nation has its responsible ruler, a judiciary its supreme
court, an army its commander-in-chief, and a ship its captain, so must the Catholic hierarchy have a responsible, recognized Head, who shall give a final decision in matters of faith
and morals. And this has always been the case.

Among the Apostles this place was held by Peter, to whom
Christ uttered the impressive words: "Thou art Peter, and
upon this Rock I will build My Church; and the gates of
Hell shall not prevail against it. And I will give unto thee
the keys of the kingdom of Heaven; and whatsoever thou
shalt bind on earth shall be bound in Heaven; and whatsoever thou shalt loose on earth, shall be loosed in Heaven."
These words of Christ are alone sufficient to prove that
Peter was designed by Him to be the leader of the Apostles;
but there are also many other indications that he was so
regarded, not only by his Master, but likewise by his associates. Significant is Christ's thrice-repeated question to him:
"Simon Peter, lovest thou Me?"—a question which was once
supplemented by the words "more than these?"—that is, more
than these other disciples love Me? On receiving Peter's
answer to this inquiry, Jesus immediately gave to him the
commission: "Feed My sheep; feed My lambs." The Saviour
apparently required greater love from Peter, precisely because He was about to raise him to an especially exalted
post—that of Chief Shepherd of His flock, His Church.

It is also worthy of notice that whenever the names of
the Apostles are enumerated in the Gospels or in the Acts,
Peter's name always heads the list. Thus in St. Matthew's

Gospel (10:2) the list begins with the words: *"The first,* Simon, who is called Peter." This qualification "first" must denote leadership, for in point of time Peter had not been the first of the disciples to come to Jesus. His brother Andrew had not only preceded him, but had actually brought him, later, to the Saviour *(John* 1:40-42). Even when there is no specific enumeration of the Apostles, Peter is always mentioned first, as if his precedence were a matter of course. Thus, in *Mark* 1:36 we read: *"Simon* and they who were with him followed Him." In *Luke* (9:32) also we find: "But *Peter* and they that were with him were heavy with sleep." Even if only the three most intimate disciples are spoken of, the order is *"Peter,* and John and James." So also in *Acts* 2:29 we find: *"Peter* standing up with the eleven," and (5:29): *"Peter* and the Apostles answered." In *Acts* 10 occurs the account of a direct, thrice-repeated revelation made from God *to Peter only.* In fact, in his first description of this vision Peter distinctly says: "God hath shown *me* that I should not call any man common or unclean"; while in his second allusion to the vision *(Acts* 15) it is stated that when the elders and Apostles had come together, Peter rose up and said: "Men and brethren, ye know how that a good while ago *God made choice among us,* that the Gentiles *by my mouth* should hear the word of the Gospel and believe." And, when Peter had finished his discourse on this occasion, "all the multitude kept silence." *Peter* also, as being the one who had authority to do so, passed judgment upon Ananias and Saphira, who had sworn falsely to the Apostles; and so great was the effect of their immediate death, and other deeds performed by Peter, that *(Acts* 5) the sick were brought into the streets and laid on couches there, that at least his shadow might fall upon them.

It was from *Peter's* boat that Jesus addressed the multitude *(Luke* 5:3); it was to *Peter,* as the evident leader of the little band, that the tax-gatherers came and asked: "Doth not your master pay tribute?"; and it was *Peter* whom Christ commis-

sioned to pay the tribute money. (*Matt.* 17:24–27). Of *Peter*
especially it is recorded: "The Lord is risen indeed, and hath
appeared unto *Simon*"; and the angel at the sepulchre bids
the women to go and tell the disciples *"and Peter"* that the
Lord goes before them into Galilee. The Saviour said also
that He had prayed particularly for *Peter,* that his faith should
not fail, and then commanded *him* to confirm the brethren.
This command in itself implies a certain superiority, but it
was intensified by the words of Christ, when Peter gave utterance to that article of faith which is the cornerstone of
the Christian Church: "Thou art Christ, the Son of the living God." Thereupon Jesus immediately called him "blessed,"
and added: "Flesh and blood hath not revealed it unto thee,
but My Father which is in Heaven." Christ Himself, therefore, declared that *God the Father had made this direct and special
revelation to Peter, and on the strength of this fact* Jesus at once
vouchsafed to him the wonderful declaration and prophecy
in reference to the building of His Church. We cannot, therefore, wonder that the supremacy of Peter, and naturally that
of his direct episcopal successors, has been the constant tradition of the Church.

St. Chrysostom, in his third homily on Penance, speaks
of Peter thus: "Peter himself, the chief of the Apostles, the
first in the Church"; and again: "When I name Peter, I name
that unbroken rock, that firm foundation, the great Apostle,
the first of the disciples." Again: "After so great an evil [the
denial], He again raised him to his former honor, and entrusted to his hand the primacy over the universal Church."
Eusebius also (A.D. 324), in his "Chronicle" (2:150), writes:
"The Apostle Peter, when he had first founded the Church
of Antioch, sets out for the city of Rome, and there preaches
the Gospel, and stays there as prelate of the Church for twenty
years. . . He, Peter, besides the Church of Antioch, also first
presided over that in Rome until his death."

St. Leo (Pope 440–461) is still more emphatic. He writes
("S. Leo ad Marc.," *Epis.* 78): "Peter was Prince of Our Lord's

Apostles. Peter's see was Rome. Peter's successor I am. Peter devolved upon his successors the universal care of all the churches. My solicitude has no bounds but the whole earth. There is no church under Heaven which is not committed to my paternal care. There is none that the jurisdiction of St. Peter does not govern."

All the Church Fathers who have given a list of the Bishops of Rome have mentioned Peter as the first. Thus, St. Augustine, when enumerating the Bishops who had governed the Church of Rome, begins with the words: "We reckon from Peter; and to Peter succeeded Linus; to Linus succeeded Clement, and so on." (*Epis.* 53, ad Generosum). The Apostolic succession from St. Peter is, in fact, recognized by millions of Protestants also, particularly by the Church of England, which attempts to derive her Apostolic orders solely through that succession in the Catholic Church for fifteen hundred years.

Nor is there any longer any reasonable ground for doubt that St. Peter was actually Bishop of Rome. The historical proof of his residence and death there is now admitted by practically all scholars, whether Protestant or Catholic. Lightfoot, Ellicott, Farrar, Westcott, Ramsay and Gore in England; and on the Continent, Renan, Wiesler, Harnack, Hilgenfeld, Thiersch and Ewald—accept it as unquestionable. The Roman archaeologist, Lanciani, says: "For the archaeologist the presence and execution of SS. Peter and Paul in Rome are *facts established beyond a shadow of doubt by purely monumental evidence.*

"There was a time when persons belonging to different creeds made it almost a case of conscience to affirm or to deny *a priori* those facts, according to their acceptance or rejection of the tradition of any particular church. This state of feeling is a matter of the past, at least for those who have followed the progress of recent discoveries and of critical literature. . .The fact was so generally known that nobody took the trouble to write a precise statement of it, because nobody dreamed that it could be denied. How is it possible to imagine that the primitive Church did not know the place of the death of its two leading Apostles?" (See much more on the subject in Lanciani's *Pagan and Christian Rome,* pp. 123–129, 140, 148).

In reference to this subject, Cardinal Manning spoke the following noble words: "It is said, 'Yes, but the primacy of Rome has been denied from the beginning.' *Then it has been asserted from the beginning.* Tell me that the waves have beaten upon the shore, and I tell you that the shore was there for the waves to beat upon." (*Grounds of Faith,* p. 53).

Today, after an historic Papacy of nearly two thousand years, there sits within the Vatican, as the Head of the Catholic, Apostolic Church and the Chief Pastor of the Christian world, the two hundred and sixty-first successor of St. Peter, Pope Benedict XV. [The current Supreme Pontiff is Pope John Paul II, the 266th Pope.—*Editor,* 1990.] If, therefore, we believe that Christ has kept His promise, and that the Holy Spirit has directed the decisions of His Church in matters of faith and morals through the centuries, can we suppose that, when this or any other Supreme Head and Pastor of that Church formally defines a doctrine to the world, he is not guarded by the grace of God from proclaiming error?

But if we do believe that he is thus guarded, then we believe the Church's much misunderstood and bitterly criticized dogma of Papal Infallibility, *for that is all it means.*

The Church does not require anyone to believe that the Pope is infallible as a man, an author, a statesman, a legislator, or a disciplinarian. In all such spheres of thought and action he is liable to error, like other mortals. On all such subjects different Popes may have diverse opinions. The essential point is that *they are protected from proclaiming error in their formal, ex cathedra, definition of faith and morals.*

If Popes were to contradict each other in matters of doctrine, as Anglican Bishops do, they certainly could not be considered infallible in such matters. But they do *not* thus contradict each other. Not one genuine instance can be given in which a Pope has condemned a doctrine which had ever really been taught, *ex cathedra,* by any of his predecessors.

One must also bear in mind that the infallibility of the Pope does not mean that he is sinless. The Pope is liable to commit sin, because, like every Catholic, he is a frail human being, who for this reason is obliged to confess to a priest and to submit himself to the Sacrament of Penance, as the lowliest of his flock must do. Every day, in celebrating Mass, he solemnly confesses at the steps of the altar in the presence of the people that he is a sinful man. He also begs those present to pray to God for him, and implores God's mercy through the Lord Jesus Christ. Later still, striking his breast, he utters the words: "Lord, I am not worthy that Thou shouldest enter under my roof, but say only the word, and my soul shall be healed." This is a part of the *daily confession* of the Head of the Catholic Church, who utters it while bending or kneeling before the figure of his crucified God, having already privately confessed his sins to some priest, inferior in rank and probably younger than himself. To say of any such aged successor of St. Peter, who daily utters such a confession and such prayers as these, that he is "the Man of Sin and Son of Perdition, who opposeth and exalteth himself above all that is called God" is both wicked and foolish.

Nevertheless, some Protestants use such language in regard to him, and the Presbyterian Westminster Confession describes the Pope as "Antichrist and the Son of Perdition"; and in Chapter 24 of that Confession there can be found the following: "Such as profess true and reformed religion should not marry with infidels, Papists, or *other idolaters."* Yet not so long ago the ancestors of the compilers of that Confession were devout believers in that very Apostolic Catholic Church which now they bitterly revile.

Why Protestants should call the Pope "Antichrist" is, so far as the term is explained in Scripture, somewhat difficult to see. The Apostle John gives in several places an exact definition of Antichrist. Thus he says (*1 John* 5:22): "He is Antichrist that denieth the Father and the Son." "Every spirit that confesseth not that Jesus is come in the flesh, is not of God; and *this is that spirit of Antichrist,* whereof ye have heard that it should come; and even now it is in the world." (*idem* 4:3). "Many deceivers are entered into the world, who confess not that Jesus Christ is come in the flesh. This is a deceiver and an Antichrist." (*2 John* 7). The heretics here denounced are evidently either the Arians, who denied the Divinity of Christ, or the Manichaeans and Gnostics, who denied His humanity, claiming that Christ took upon Himself only the *semblance* of man, and only seemed to die upon the Cross. But certainly, whatever else the Catholic Popes may be charged with, no one can truthfully say that they have ever denied either the Divinity or the humanity of Christ, or the fact that He came into the world. Such a charge would be preposterous. On the contrary, it is precisely they, and they alone (for there was then no other Christian Church), who have always authoritatively proclaimed the double nature of the Incarnate Son of God, and who condemned implacably such anti-Christian heresies. The application to them of the name "Antichrist" is, therefore, a senseless calumny.

The truth is, the conditions for salvation are the same for the Pope as for all other Christians. But his is a less easy task than theirs. His position as the earthly Head of the Church makes his responsibility almost overpowering. Even his life is insecure. Out of the first thirty Pontiffs in Rome, twenty-nine were martyrs, and whether Benedict XV will also meet a violent death cannot, in these appalling days of anarchy and malignant hatred of the Church of Christ, be certainly answered in the negative.

Comprehending, therefore, that "Infallibility" does not mean that the Pope is exempt from error in worldly things, but merely that, as the divinely appointed Pastor of Christ's Church, *he is protected from the formal enunciation of error in matters of faith and morals,* the dogma of Papal Infallibility presented to me no more difficulties. On the contrary, I accepted it with satisfaction and relief.

Chapter 15

PURGATORY AND INDULGENCES

Somewhere thou livest, and hast need of Him;
Somewhere thy soul sees higher heights to climb;
And somewhere still there may be valleys dim,
That thou must pass to reach the hills sublime!

Then all the more, because thou canst not hear
Poor human words of blessing, will I pray—
O true brave heart! God bless thee, whereso'er
In His great universe thou art today!

They pass beyond our touch, beyond our sight; never, thank
God, beyond our love and prayers.

PURGATORY

THE DIFFICULTY in regard to papal infallibility having been overcome, I turned to consider the Catholic doctrine of Purgatory and the Sacrament of Penance. My feelings in respect to this will best be shown by the following extract from a letter which I wrote about this time to a Catholic friend.

"MY DEAR FRANCIS:

"I find no special difficulty in the Catholic dogma of Purgatory. On the contrary, the idea of a state of purification, appointed for those souls, who, though redeemed by Christ, are nevertheless still unprepared to pass at once into God's presence, appears to me logical and even comforting. I think that every soul who feels his own unfitness for the Beatific Vision (and who does not feel this?) must *wish* for such a state of preparation, even though attended with a cleansing punishment. The lack of this idea in Protestantism leads, I think, to an objec-

tionable feature in their system, namely, the altogether improbable and presumptuous supposition that the soul of some
monster of depravity can straightway enter the society of
Heaven, provided only that he says, at the last moment of his
ill-spent life, that he repents and believes in Jesus as the Son
of God. Christ's Divine insight into the soul of the penitent
thief, who hung beside His Cross on Calvary, could justify,
of course, His promise to him of an immediate entrance into
Paradise; but that was a solitary instance, upon which one can
hardly build much hope. The statement, often loosely made,
that, since 'Jesus paid it all, all the debt I owe,' a hardened criminal is thereby rendered *instantaneously* fit for Heaven, is dangerously demoralizing. The Bible assures us that 'there shall
in no wise enter into the heavenly City of God anything that
defileth, or that is defiled,' and the acquisition of a pure character
is not the affair of a moment by means of a deathbed repentance. I never shall forget the description in a Chicago paper,
many years ago, of the hanging of a Negro, who, on the night
before his execution, was said to have repented of a peculiarly
atrocious crime, and 'knew that he was saved.' The report was
heralded by the flaring headline 'Jerked to Jesus'! This blasphemous alliteration probably did less harm, however, than the
sensational story which accompanied it, of the Negro's 'edifying remarks' which preceded his death. The idea of such a
wretch going at once to Heaven was revolting to a sense of
justice and even of decency. No Catholic would have supposed
such a translation probable, or, save for a miracle, possible.
We know, of course, nothing of what the purgatorial state may
be [At the time of writing this the author was obviously un-
aware of the many revelations to holy souls regarding the sufferings of those in Purgatory. Cf. *Purgatory Explained* by Fr. F.
X. Schouppe, S.J. (TAN, 1973, 1986).—*Editor,* 1990.], through
which the soul must pass, to reach the sphere to which God
calls it; but that *some* place of purification must exist for those
who pass into eternity with no sufficient spiritual preparation, appears to me just, necessary and consoling."

To this my friend replied as follows:

"I well remember the crudely blasphemous headline which you quote. It had a great success, and was accounted 'clever,' though I am sure its ribald, vulgar character shocked all in whom a consciousness of the dignity of life and of the majesty of death remained, even though they had no positive Christian faith. There is little, if any, analogy between the case of the wretched Negro and that of the penitent thief, for the latter was redeemed by his humility and faith. He did not 'know that he was saved.' He confessed his guilt in a supreme moment, and admitted the justice of his punishment. Whether or not the grace given him by Our Lord was the only one ever offered him, we are not told; but to this opportunity at least he did respond, and by a single aspiration expiated with his dying breath a life of crime. That the consoling doctrine of Purgatory should appeal to you does not surprise me. There is hardly a religious system of antiquity in which some similar provision is not found. It was left for the 'Reformers' of the sixteenth century to reject this immemorial dogma of the Church. When they denied the sanctity of the Mass and many other sacramental features of Catholicism, the doctrine of Purgatory went with the rest. If the souls of the dead pass instantly into an eternally fixed state, beyond the efficacy of our intercessions, then all our requiems, prayers and similar practices are vain. But if, on the contrary, we believe in the Communion of Saints—that is, in the intercommunion of the threefold Church, militant on earth, suffering in Purgatory, and triumphant in Heaven—then we on earth can influence, and be influenced by, the souls who have crossed the border. Few, indeed, quit this life in a state of purity and grace which warrants their immediate entrance into Heaven. Still fewer, let us hope, are those to whom the blessed refuge of Purgatory, that halfway house of our dead, is closed. I cannot conceive how Protestants can believe as they do on this point, nor is it astonishing that their rejection of Purgatory has been followed, in the case of many, by the elimination of a belief in Hell; for the latter doctrine, *taken alone,* is monstrous. In fact, all Catholic doctrines are interdependent; they stand or fall together. You cannot pick stones out of the arch, and expect it to stand, for it will not do so. Purgatory is one of the most humane and beautiful conceptions imaginable. How many mothers' aching hearts has it not soothed and comforted with hope for some dead, wayward son!"

Soon after receiving this letter, I read the following words from Mallock: "As to the doctrine of Purgatory, time goes on, and the view men take of it is changing. It is fast becoming recognized, that *it is the only doctrine that can bring a belief in future rewards and punishments into anything like accordance with our notions of what is just and reasonable;* and so far from its being a superfluous superstition, it will be seen to be just what is demanded at once by reason and morality." My attention was at this time also called to the fact that the idea of Purgatory is no longer confined exclusively to Roman Catholic Christians. At a recent General Convention of Episcopalians in America, resolutions looking toward prayer for the dead were defeated by only a very small majority.

The doctrine of the Catholic Church in reference to Purgatory states that there *is* such a place, in which souls suffer for a time, before they can be admitted to the joys of Heaven, because they still need to be cleansed from certain venial sins, infirmities and faults, or still have to discharge the *temporal* punishment due to mortal sins, which is as yet uncancelled, though the *lasting* punishment of those sins has been forgiven and removed through Christ's atonement. Furthermore, the Church declares that by our prayers and by the acceptable Sacrifice of the Mass we may still help those souls, through the merits of Christ. Beyond this statement the Church's formal doctrine does not go; but it is *not* an article of Catholic faith that there is in Purgatory any material fire. [Whereas this statement is perfectly true, Fr. F. X. Schouppe, S.J., in

Purgatory Explained says of the pain of Purgatory that "it is the common opinion of the Doctors that it consists in fire and other species of suffering," and he quotes among others St. Robert Bellarmine (1542-1621), a Doctor of the Church, as follows, "Almost all theologians teach that the reprobate and the souls in Purgatory suffer the action of the same fire." (P. 33, 1986 ed.).—*Editor,* 1990.] It is generally believed that souls in Purgatory suffer spiritual anguish from the fact that they then feel acutely, as they could not do on earth, the perfect happiness from which they are for a time excluded, while they must also understand the enormity of the sins which they committed against their Heavenly Father and their Saviour.

INDULGENCES

Unlike the doctrine of Purgatory, the subject of Indulgences possessed for me unusual difficulties, partly because it was associated in my mind with the abuses which had led to the revolt of Luther, partly because the modern English word "indulgence" creates in the non-Catholic the impression of a culpable relaxation of some needed discipline. The term "indulgent father," for example, is almost a reproach. Accordingly I resolved to talk the matter over with a Catholic theologian, who gladly placed himself at my disposal.

"Father," I said to him, as we approached the subject, "what *is* precisely an Indulgence?"

"Let me first tell you what it is *not*," was his reply; "*it is not in any sense whatever a remission of sin—past, present, or to come.* It has, in fact, nothing to do with the forgiveness of sin, and above all it does not mean, as is sometimes wickedly asserted, a permission to commit sin with impunity for any specified period of time."

"Not in any sense whatever a remission of sin—past, present, or to come," I repeated slowly; "how different that is from the definition which one usually hears! Still, it is a remission of something, is it not?"

"Yes, it is a remission of some portion of the *temporal* punishment due for sin."

"Father," I said, "I think I understand what is theologically meant by 'temporal punishment,' but make believe that I do not, and kindly tell me what the Church considers it to be."

He paused a moment, and then said: "God's punishment of sin chiefly concerns eternity; the Church's punishment is limited to time. Indulgences have nothing to do with eternal punishment. The Church believes that for all sins committed— even though they have been forgiven by God—*a certain amount of punishment is still due,* either in this life, or in Purgatory, or in both. In this respect she acts as men's tribunals do. A criminal may be sorry for his sin, yet he is not on that account discharged from earthly courts as guiltless. On the contrary, the law imprisons, fines, and sometimes even hangs him just the same, whether he is penitent, or not. If mere repentance could absolve from punishment in this world those who have committed arson, murder, theft, or perjury, it would be dangerous for society. The criminal could easily feign repentance, or think at least that his *regret* for sin was quite the same as true repentance for it. These sentiments are, however, not identical. One may feel deep regret for one's misconduct, yet be without repentance, which is a genuine sorrow for the act, *as sin against God,* combined with self-condemnation and a determination to commit the sin no more. In any case, society's laws of self-defense cannot be based upon subjective feeling; and neither could the Church maintain her discipline thus, for God alone can read the hearts of men. What the State does in this respect, the Catholic Church has always done. Sincere contrition is, of course, required for absolution; but, in addition to that, the Church says: '*Bring forth fruits worthy of your professed repentance;* give evidence of your sorrow by expiation of some sort.' The common sense of mankind approves of such a course.

"The fatal weakness of Luther's doctrine was that it taught justification by faith only. We say that good works also are necessary [In order to be of spiritual worth these good works must be done in the state of grace, that is, with one's soul united to Christ as a living branch is united to the Vine. Thus, these good works are not merely human works, but "divinized," so to speak.—*Editor,* 1990.], and that, although a man is saved through Christ alone, nevertheless that 'God will render to every man according to his works.' (*Rom.* 2:6). According to the Protestant theory, no proof of repentance (to be given through penance or reparation) is demanded. The doctrine, 'Jesus paid it all, all the debt I owe,' is thought to have absolved the penitent from every obligation to do penance for his sinful past. Now certainly that Christ alone could make atonement for us by His death is an unquestionable feature of the Catholic Faith; but to believe that our salvation from eternal punishment is everything, and that *no evidence of contrition is required here,* is demoralizing. How many Protestants I have known, who thought that their belief in certain dogmas sufficed to counterbalance sins, which they *continued to commit,* relieved by nothing save occasional spasms of regret! It seemed to them sufficient to have at times a strong subjective sentiment of sorrow.

"In order to make the doctrine of Indulgences still clearer," the Father continued, "let me remind you that every civilized government in the world takes into consideration, when dealing with criminals, that in most cases there exist extenuating circumstances. These sometimes warrant a mitigation of the usual penalty, and the State therefore often cancels months or even years of a convict's sentence on account of good behavior. Such mitigation on the part of the State corresponds to the Church's Indulgences."

"An Indulgence, then," I said tentatively, "is an abbreviation of the sinner's temporal sentence?"

"Precisely so," was the reply.

"And is that what is meant, for example, by an 'Indulgence of a hundred days?'" [The Church's new regulations on indulgences, published in 1967, stipulate that indulgences are to be designated only as "plenary" and "partial," with no designation of a time period for partial indulgences.—*Editor*, 1990.]

"Certainly."

"But now the Church inflicts no punishment of a hundred days."

"No; but she did so once," replied the priest. "In former times the Church's penances for mortal sins were very severe. They often included long periods of excommunication, as well as fasting on bread and water, lengthy pilgrimages, and the like. A murderer was sometimes condemned to penance for twenty years, an adulterer from five to fifteen years, a curser of his parents to fast on bread and water for forty days. But when, for example, a sentence of a hundred days had been inflicted, and the condemned man had made partial reparation for his evil conduct by works of charity or self-denial, his term of punishment could be shortened, at the discretion of the Bishop, to perhaps fifty days, *on the theory that he had done by his good works as much towards the payment of his temporal punishment as if he had undergone the penance of the other fifty days also.* You say quite rightly that the Church at present does not give such punishments as she formerly did. Today she limits herself to ordering prayers, fasts, alms-giving and similar satisfactions. Nevertheless *the principle is the same,* and an 'Indulgence for forty days' means that as much of the temporal punishment inflicted has been paid off by the good deeds of the penitent, *as would, in former times, have been expressed in the term 'forty days.'* "

"But why does the Church continue to employ that ancient mode of reckoning?" I asked.

"The Church is conservative," was the reply, "and she adheres to the old expression, because through many centuries the amounts of temporal punishment were always estimated in terms of days. Hence 'days' have come to be the Church's ' standard of reckoning the length of penances, just as the degrees on a thermometer are used for measurements of heat and cold."

"Is there any instance in Scripture," I asked, "of the infliction of temporal punishment on a sinner who had been already pardoned by God?"

"Do you remember," replied the Father, "what the prophet Nathan said to King David? David had repented of his heinous crime; but Nathan told him plainly that this was not sufficient. 'The Lord hath put away thy sin,' he said to him, 'and *thou* shalt not die. Howbeit, because by this deed thou hast given great occasion to the enemies of the Lord to blaspheme, the child that is born unto thee shall surely die'; and although David besought God to spare the child, and fasted, and lay all night upon the earth in supplication, nevertheless 'it came to pass on the seventh day that the child died.'"

"Why do not Protestants recognize the necessity of some temporal punishment for sin?" I asked.

"It is indeed remarkable that they will not do so," he replied; "and it is stranger still that, when they say no penitential deeds whatever are necessary, they do not see that they are practically giving to their flocks a plenary Indulgence for all time! What a hue and cry they would make if we did such a thing! The truth is, Protestants, by eliminating all need of penances, all belief in Purgatory, and (at present almost universally) all belief in Hell, have fashioned for themselves a very easy system of religion. They are not only their own confessors, but also their own judges as to whether God has pardoned them; moreover, they lay upon themselves no works of expiation, and keep discreetly silent about any punishment in the future life! Faith is considered all-sufficient. It is a demoralizing system. No wonder that many of them hate the Catholic Church, which stands before them, like their own accusing consciences."

"What are the requisites for obtaining an Indulgence?" I inquired.

"First of all," answered the priest, "the applicant for an Indulgence must have confessed his sins with genuine contrition, and received absolution. *An Indulgence always presupposes* pardon, and unless the applicant is in a state of grace—that is, unless he has been forgiven and restored to God's friendship and favor—he has no claim to an Indulgence."

"Whence does the Church derive her authority to remit temporal punishment?" I asked.

"From the same words of Christ, which justify the giving of absolution in God's name," was the reply; "they are 'Whatsoever ye shall bind on earth, shall be bound in Heaven; and whatsoever ye shall loose on earth, shall be loosed in Heaven.' Moreover, St. Paul, in the person of the Lord Jesus Christ, both imposed penance and relaxed it in the case of a sinful member of the Church of Corinth. He really granted him what we call an Indulgence, by shortening his punishment, and readmitting him to communion, precisely as the Church does now."

"But," I objected, "of what use are Indulgences to saintly Christians, whose sins are so exceedingly rare that their temporal punishments in this life must be trifling? Why do they also seek Indulgences?"

The Father smiled. "I am going," he said, "to reveal to you a very beautiful and consoling feature of the Catholic Church. All Catholics, and many Protestants also, repeat every Sunday in their Creed the words: "I believe in the Communion of Saints.' But what use do the Protestants make of this wonderful dogma? None whatever. *They never invoke the intercession of the Saints in their behalf,* nor supplicate their aid in the great battle of life with sin and sorrow. Some of them even doubt whether the blessed souls in Heaven know what is going on here! Hence, if one speaks of having been influenced or aided by a Saint, Protestants, as a rule, will tap their foreheads significantly, and hint that such a one is 'very erratic' or inclined to spiritualism! Catholics, on the contrary, make a great deal of this doctrine; and among the privileges connected with it in their minds is that of a spiritual treasury of saintly merits."

"A spiritual treasury!" I repeated in astonishment; "what

is its nature, and what are the merits which it contains?"

"Picture to yourself," he answered, "a fund, founded originally by Christ, but still increased by separate contributions, large and small, paid in by charitable souls. Imagine that this fund is used to ransom captives from detention, and to relieve the needy and the suffering." He paused. "Do you see where we are coming to?" he asked.

"Not yet," I answered; "please continue."

"You said just now," resumed the priest, "that there are pious souls, who do far more by deeds of mercy and self-sacrifice than is required to discharge the temporal punishment due for *their own* sins. But shall the superabundant merits gained by them remain unused? Not so; the Church believes that all such merits, credits, satisfactions—call them what you will—are gathered up by God into a fund of mercy, love and grace, which Christ can then apply, together with His own essential merits, to struggling, suffering souls either in this world, or in Purgatory."

"Was this a custom of the early Church?" I asked.

"It was her custom from the very earliest times. A striking illustration of it was given by the Christian martyrs, who often wrote from their prisons to the Church, entreating that, by reason of their own courage in confronting death, the time of penance inflicted on their less heroic brethren might be shortened. Gradually then, as these and other martyrs passed to their reward, the practice was extended, so that such superabundant merits might be gathered into the 'treasury of the Church,' to be applied either to those who are attempting to discharge their debt of temporal punishment here, or else to those still suffering in Purgatory."

"But what is the need of *our* superabundant merits," I asked, "when Christ's own merits are infinite and in themselves sufficient to accomplish everything?"

"God wishes us," replied the priest, "to pray for others, as well as for ourselves. The doctrine of the Church is that we can assist our friends both here and in Purgatory by our supplications, and that the merits which we earn beyond our own needs, may, through God's grace, be employed towards the completion of the temporal punishment which those who are dear to us may have to pay. 'Bear ye one another's burdens, and thus fulfill the law of Christ.' There is thus formed a tender bond of sympathy between ourselves and the Church suffering, as well as with the Church triumphant. What a blessed privilege it is," he continued, "to feel that by some act of self-denial, humiliation, penance, love, death, martyrdom—one is not merely helping on one's own poor soul, but may help those of others also!"

This was a presentation of the doctrine of the Communion of Saints that appealed to me very strongly, and I asked: "May not such merits, offered for the dead, serve as a kind of *expiation for the harm which we ourselves have done them while in life?*"

"Precisely," said the Father eagerly; "you anticipate what I was about to say. Which of us does not sometimes shudder at the thought of deeds in our own past, which may have swelled the list of sins our loved ones have committed? Which of us does not feel that, but for our neglect or evil influence, some soul now in eternity would have sinned less, or have attained a nobler character? Who does not often tremble under his responsibility for part at least of the unholy state in which some friend has passed into the future life to stand before his Judge? What can we do for them? Merciful God! are they for evermore beyond the efficacy of our prayers? May we not mitigate their penalty by doing something here, *since, if they are now suffering, the fault is partly ours?* What joy, what comfort, what alleviation of remorse shall we not feel, if such a possibility is realized! What a stupendous source of consolation, therefore, is this spiritual treasury, whose merits God may graciously apply to those whom we have led astray!"

"A beautiful and comforting belief indeed!" I said; "but can a Catholic be certain that the merits which he gains by an Indulgence will be applied to those particular souls for whose release he longs?"

"Over God's treatment of the souls in Purgatory," said the Father gently, "the Church has no control or knowledge. The living only are her subjects. The dead have passed beyond her jurisdiction. But if our love for souls is great, God's love for them is surely greater, and we can offer for their benefit the merits that we earn, believing that our Heavenly Father will apply them to the friends for whom we pray, if our request be in accordance with His infinite wisdom."

"The enemies of the Church have asserted," I ventured to say (and felt ashamed of doing so), "that Indulgences can be purchased."

"Never!" exclaimed the priest indignantly; "yet it is easy to see how this erroneous idea originated, for a release from temporal punishment is sometimes granted on condition that the *penance* shall be in the form of almsgiving. In that way enemies of the Church have sought to justify their hideous accusations that Indulgences are sold."

"But Tetzel?" I began, and hesitated.

"Well," said the Father, smiling, "I am not afraid to talk of Tetzel. His purpose was at least a good one. The glorious Church of St. Peter's at Rome—the pride of every Catholic heart, and the object of universal admiration—was then in need of funds for its completion. Hence, in accordance with the practice of sometimes substituting almsgiving for canonical penance (of course, after due repentance and confession), if a Catholic made then for that church a contribution which involved some sacrifice of self, he received release from a certain amount of the *temporal* penance still due him for sins already committed. Tetzel, as a Dominican monk, was authorized to make collections for this purpose, and to give Indulgences to those who deserved them. That he exceeded his powers, and allowed his zeal to lead him into imprudences, may have been true. If so, he had his reward. 'Woe unto the world,' said Christ, 'because of offences [scandals]! For it must needs be that offences [scandals] come; but woe to that man by whom the offence [scandal] cometh.' [*Matt.* 18:7]. But recollect that if abuses occurred in the dispensation of Indulgences in the sixteenth century, they were *abuses*—not a regular part of the Church's system. That many excellent things may be abused we know from every days' experience; and if we should condemn all means of benefitting poor humanity because abuses graft themselves upon them, charity itself would soon become impossible. The Council of Trent promptly repudiated such abuses, and declared that all Indulgences thus obtained were worthless. If Luther had merely protested against such practices, as was his right, and if, while remaining in the Church, he had worked with others to reform them, he could have done great good. But to seek to destroy a Church because it has some faulty members, and to attack a beneficial dogma because of some abuses which have gathered round it, is as unwise as to desert a ship because its keel is fouled with barnacles."

"What, then, is your last word to me, Father, on the subject of Indulgences?" I asked him, as I rose to go.

The theologian paused a moment, as if to choose the most appropriate terms, and then replied: "It is a precious doctrine of great value, but it is liable to be abused, and easily misunderstood by those outside the Church. Yet we should not, on that account, discard it. It is a dogma eminently fitted to incite men to good works—not only on their own account, but also for the sake of others. Make use, then, of this unique privilege," he added, as he pressed my hand, "and remember, 'Greater love hath no man than this, that he lay down his life for his friends!' "

Returning from this conversation, I read again the following stanzas, which I had had in my collection many years:

IN MEMORIAM

O'er land and sea love follows with fond prayers
Its dear ones in their troubles, grief and cares;
*   There is no spot*
On which it does not drop this tender dew,

Except the grave, and there it bids adieu,
   And prayeth not!

Why should that be the only place uncheered
By prayer, which to our hearts is most endeared,
   And sacred grown?
Living, we sought for blessings on their head;
Why should our lips be sealed when they are dead,
   And we alone?

Shall God be wroth because we love them still,
And call upon His love to shield from ill
   Our dearest, best,
And bring them home, and recompense their pain,
And cleanse their sin, if any sin remain,
   And give them rest?

Nay, I will not believe it. I will pray,
As for the living, for the dead each day.
   They will not grow
Less meet for Heaven, when followed with a prayer,
To speed them home, like summer-scented air
   From long ago.

Chapter 16

THE SACRAMENT OF PENANCE

Confess your faults one to another.—JAMES 5:16.

He that covereth his sins shall not prosper; but whoso confesseth and forsaketh them shall have mercy.—PROV. 28:13.

My son, give, I pray thee, glory to the Lord God of Israel, and make confession unto Him; and tell me now what thou hast done; hide it not from me.—JOSH. 7:19.

THE OBLIGATION to confess one's sins to a priest and to obtain from him, as God's appointed agent, absolution, is doubtless one of the hardest things for a non-Catholic to submit to.

My prejudices against the Confessional had been of many years' standing, and I did not know at first whether I could ever overcome them. I soon saw, however, that the question was not whether I liked the system or not, but *whether it was founded on Christ's teaching and the command of the Church.*

First, did Christ establish it? I had to acknowledge that He did. His words are unmistakable. That Christ Himself possessed the power to forgive sins is, of course, undisputed by any Christian. When He healed the man sick of the palsy, for example, He said to him: "Son, be of good cheer, thy sins be forgiven thee"; and to the Scribes, who thought that He had committed blasphemy in saying this, He answered: "That ye may know that the Son of man hath power on earth to forgive sins, . . . Arise, take up thy bed, and go unto thy house." (*Matt.* 9). But Christ said also to His Apostles: "As the Father hath sent me, I also send you"; and *immediately after saying this, and in connection with those words,* He added: "Receive ye the Holy Ghost. Whose sins ye remit, they are remitted unto them; and whose sins ye retain, they are retained." (*Jn.* 20:21-24). In equally clear language did Jesus also say to St. Peter: "I will give to thee the keys of the kingdom of heaven, and whatsoever thou shalt bind on earth, it shall be bound also in heaven; and whatsoever thou shalt loose on earth, it shall be loosed also in heaven." Now if these words mean anything, they indicate that Jesus gave to His Apostles a commission to forgive sins in His name; and since that act would be impossible on their part if they did not know what sins had been committed, these must at first be made known to them through Confession.

It is also noteworthy that the duty to give or withhold the forgiveness of sins, as His representatives, is just as clearly stated as the duty to preach the Gospel. Since, however, it was manifestly impossible for the first Apostles themselves to go into all the world and bring the glad tidings to everyone, it cannot be supposed that the duty and the power of hearing confessions and giving absolution was limited to those men only, and that so marvelous a source of grace and mercy should be closed with the completion of the Apostles' lives. As we have seen, these chose their own successors, who in their turn selected others to succeed them, thus handing down from age to age their duties and prerogatives. Thus were the words of Christ in reference to Confession and absolution interpreted by the early Church, and thus have they been understood and acted on for nearly two millenniums. The system has the weight of ecclesiastical tradition, and is as old as Christianity itself.

St. Athanasius, for example, says: "He who confesses in penitence, receives through the priest by the grace of Christ the remission of sins. . . If our chains [of sin] are loosed, we shall go on to better things; if yours are not loosed, go and give yourself into the hands of the disciples of Jesus; *for they are here who can loose us, having received the power from the Saviour.*"

Confession, therefore, not merely to God alone, but also to His authorized representatives in the Church, is the system instituted by Christ, and bears with it the privilege of obtaining from them in His name the assurance of absolution. Now, as free agents, all men and women can accept this system, or reject it; but if they reject it, they cannot be communicating members of the Catholic Church. The question before me, therefore, was the following: "Will you do as Christ ordained that you should do, or will you not?" At first I tried evasively to argue that, as numberless Protestants, who believe themselves good Christians, confess their sins to God alone, so I could do the same. But I had come by this time to regard the Catholic Church as the only true descendant of the Church of the Apostles, and I wished to belong to that, or none. Yet to do this without submitting to the Sacrament of Penance was impossible. I asked myself, therefore, whether my prejudices and hostility to this Sacrament might not be groundless.

While trying to answer this question, I was reminded that the system of Confession and absolution is not exclusively Roman Catholic, but exists in the Eastern Orthodox Church, as well as in all the earliest separated Oriental bodies, Copts, Armenians, Maronites and others. To some extent also it exists both in principle and practice in the Anglican and Episcopal Churches. [Anglican and Episcopalian clergymen, not being true ordained priests, cannot of course confer valid absolution, even though they may go through the motions and say the correct words. On September 18, 1896 Pope Leo XIII, in the full *Apostolicae Curae,* declared that Anglican Orders are absolutely null and void.—*Editor, 1990.*] Opening the Anglican Prayer Book, I read the words which the clergy repeat every day in the service of Morning Prayer. The section is headed with the sentence: "The Declaration of Absolution or Remission of Sins" ("To be made by the Priest alone, standing, the people still kneeling"): "Almighty God, the Father of Our Lord Jesus Christ, who desireth not the death of the sinner. . .hath given power and commandment to His Ministers, to declare and pronounce to His people, being penitent, the Absolution and Remission of their sins." Moreover, in the directions given to Anglican clergymen for the visitation of the sick, we read in the Prayer Book of the Church of England the following: "Here shall the sick person be moved to make a special confession of his sins, if he feels his conscience troubled with any weighty matter. After which confession, *the Priest shall absolve him* after this sort: Our Lord Jesus Christ, who hath left power to His Church to absolve all sinners who truly repent and believe in Him, of His great mercy forgive thee thine offences; and by His authority committed to me, *I absolve thee from all thy sins,* in the name of the Father, and of the Son, and of the Holy Ghost. Amen."

The Church of England lays this duty of Absolution on its priests in the most explicit manner. Every one of her clergymen, individually, at the moment when he kneels and receives the laying on of the Bishop's hands, hears the words: "Receive the Holy Ghost. . .*Whose sins thou dost forgive, they are forgiven; and whose sins thou dost retain, they are retained.*" Either this means an awful reality, or it is blasphemy. Twice every day the Church of England bids her clergymen remind their congregations solemnly that God has given to *them* (the clergy) this power, and commanded them to use it! How, then, can any Anglicans and Episcopalians denounce the system of Confession and absolution practiced in the Catholic Church, when it is *not only permitted, but actually commanded in their own?* High Church Anglicans are, therefore, consistent when they institute auricular confession and private absolution in their churches. In 1891 it was estimated that there were in England 566 such churches.

Those who do not approve of auricular confession and absolution, claim that it is sufficient to pronounce a general absolution to the assembled congregation. Among so many participants each individual loses more or less the sense of personal responsibility and sorrow, such as the solitary penitent, face to face with his confessor, must experience. How little the soul of a contrite sinner is helped by a general confession and by a general absolution, and how it yearns to receive the latter from a competent priest, after a full confession, has been testified to repeatedly. One clergyman of the Church of England writes: "I believe that thousands of priests" (of the Anglican Church) "and tens of thousands of lay people would bear me out in saying that, for deepening the spiritual life, for checking habits of sin, for a safeguard against despair, and for promoting real contrition it [Sacramental Confession] is, to their certain knowledge, of the most unspeakable value." (*Newberry House Magazine,* Vol. 6, 1892).

The famous English divine, the Rev. J. Keble, also says: "Our one great grievance is the neglect of Confession." (Coleridge's *Life of Keble*). Still another Anglican clergyman writes: "The hearing of confessions is the very backbone and marrow of pastoral work...Experience shows the frequent unreality of spiritual intercourse, unless in some degree connected with Confession. Mere *religious conversation* with a priest...has simply encouraged sentimentalism and degenerated into religious gossip." (Rev. Charles Lowder to the Bishop of London).

Yet this attempt of High Church Anglicans to meet a heartfelt need *is only an imitation, and not the real thing.* In the Catholic Church the practice is regulated by a severe ecclesiastical training and a supervision which in the Anglican confession are unknown. Moreover, the idea of *married* clergymen acting as confessors, under solemn vows of secrecy, can hardly be entertained seriously, especially as Anglican clergymen are, compared with Catholic priests, men of the world, in the sense of mingling freely in worldly sports and fashionable society.

Of course all Protestant Non-conformists, who constitute (outside the Catholic Church) the great majority of Christians at the present time, repudiate the idea of private Confession and absolution. But it is difficult to see how they can reconcile their standpoint with the explicit utterances of Christ and the practice of the Church for centuries.

"But cannot one's sins be forgiven by confessing them to God alone?" I one day asked a Catholic friend. "Undoubtedly," was the reply; "and one ought every day to confess them thus to God in prayer; but Christ's own words to His Apostles plainly teach that this is not all that Christ intended should be done. St. Augustine says: 'To pretend that it is enough to confess to God alone, is to make void the power of the keys given to the Church, and to contradict the words of Christ in the Gospel.' "

Probably one reason why our Saviour did not think such private Confession to God to be sufficient lies in the fact that self-deception in such cases is so easy.

One is apt to consider remorse and repentance as one and the same thing! Remorse, however, is involuntary; repentance is voluntary, and includes a genuine sorrow for the act, *as sin.* Everyone is inclined to fancy that his penitence is sincere and that his sins are pardoned, if no one else is aware of them, and if no one else tests his professed sincerity, that is to say, *if he is himself both judge and criminal!* But a dispassionate confessor, understanding well, through many revelations of the human heart, the weaknesses of human nature, is certainly less liable to be deceived, particularly as he is bound by solemn vows to judge the case as the representative of God.

Moreover, there is something more than Confession in the Catholic Sacrament of Penance. That is only the fourth part of it; the other three factors are contrition, absolution and satisfaction. The last is very important. Catholic dogma claims that a certain amount of temporal punishment is due in this world, *even for sins that God has pardoned,* and that for these some "satisfaction" must be made, in the sense of reparation. When a Protestant confesses his sins to God alone, even though he be genuinely repentant, his only incitement to make reparation for his evil deeds is his own feeble will. The Catholic Church, however, has from the very beginning insisted that there should be some other judge of the repentance of the sinner than the man himself; and has demanded of the penitent *proofs* of his sincerity in the form of penance, reparation and good works. Such proofs the Protestant rarely thinks of giving, because he is not called upon to do so; and even if he should voluntarily impose upon himself some penance, such as the restitution of ill-gotten wealth, reconciliation with his enemies, retraction of a calumny uttered, the renunciation of some harmful pleasure, or the avoidance of persons or occasions tending to temptation, it would not be so easy for him to carry these duties into execution, as would be the case *if they were commanded by someone else, who subsequently would inquire with authority whether they had been done.*

Self-imposed penances, like private resolutions, are rarely adhered to long. The nature and amount of the penance imposed by a confessor is largely left to the discretion of the priest, who is specially trained for this function; for, while the *principle* of Sacramental Confession and Penance is very clearly laid down in the New Testament, the *precise details* of the way in which it is to be practiced are left to the decisions of the Church, and to the wisdom and experience of those to whom from age to age the care of souls has been confided.

The eloquent Father Burke said of the Sacrament of Penance: "Perhaps the devil never struck a more severe blow at man's happiness than when, through Luther's instrumentality, he deprived man of the consolations of Confession. The Catholic who has something on his mind, which is a source of mental anxiety, and the keeping of which is breaking his heart, knows that in the first priest he meets he has a friend, whom God has provided for him, and in whom he can place implicit faith." There is often in a guilty soul an unappeasable longing to unburden its load of sin to some living person, provided one can feel assured that none but God and the confessor will ever know what is avowed. Such a confession, made to a fellow human being, under the seal of that inviolable secrecy which no Catholic priest has ever broken, makes the penitence seem real, and gives a relief from sin's oppression, which mere subjective confession rarely can confer.

It scarcely needs to be said that, if Confession is to be of the slightest use, it must be thorough and genuine. It if be intentionally incomplete or falsified, God is aware of the deception, even though the priest should be induced to give absolution; and woe to him who seeks to cheat the Almighty! No Catholic is so ignorant of the rudiments of his religion as to imagine that absolution obtained by deceiving the priest has any value; and every Catholic child who knows his catechism is aware of the fact that, should one practice such a mummery, not only does one leave the confessional unshriven, but with the added sin of sacrilege. The confessional is the only tribunal before which both the accuser and accused are one, and to whose bar no witnesses are summoned. Hence the validity of the Sacrament does not depend on the confessor, but upon the penitent. The former is merely the channel through which sacramental grace flows; and this grace reaches the penitent only on certain well-defined conditions, which the latter must fulfill. The priest can pass judgment only on what is told him. One mortal sin, concealed intentionally, vitiates the whole confession.

As many Protestants have no knowledge whatever of the nature of a Catholic confession, it may be well to give a simple outline of it here. Upon the kneeling penitent the priest bestows his blessing in the words prescribed by the Roman ritual: "The Lord be in thy heart and on thy lips, that thou mayest truly and humbly confess thy sins, in the name of the Father, and of the Son, and of the Holy Ghost." After the penitent's enumeration of the sins of which he has been guilty since his last confession, he adds: "For these and all my other sins, which I cannot now remember, I am heartily sorry; I purpose amendment for the future, and most humbly ask pardon of God, and penance and absolution of you, my spiritual Father." The priest then usually warns, exhorts or advises the penitent, and gives him a penance to perform, or a definite task to accomplish. Then, if satisfied of the penitent's sincerity and true repentance, he utters the words: "May the Almighty and merciful Lord give thee pardon, absolution and remission of thy sins. Amen! Our Lord Jesus Christ absolves thee, and I, by His authority, absolve thee. . . from all thy sins in the name of the Father, and of the Son, and of the Holy Ghost. Amen!"

I once entertained the notion that a Catholic, by confessing to a priest, cleared his past record and could begin to sin again, certain of being once more pardoned at a subsequent confession. But even if that were true—which, of course, is not the case—how would his situation differ from that of the repentant Protestant, who has confessed to God alone? In both cases the penitent feels that he is pardoned, and has the assurance that his future sins will also, if truly repented of, be forgiven, provided he has at present no wish or intention to recommit them. But of the two penitents (their dispositions being supposed to be equally good), which has the stronger guarantee against continuance in some well-recognized path of sin?

Is it the Protestant, of whose vice no one, except perhaps a guilty partner, knows, and whose confession has been a purely secret and subjective one to God; or the Catholic, whose guilt is known to his confessor, whose contrition has been tested by an experienced and sympathetic friend, and to whom warnings, counsels and entreaties have been given, and on whom even penance has been laid? I have known Protestant men and women, who, counting on their ultimate salvation through being strictly orthodox in the faith, have—with brief intervals of repentance—continued in a course of sin for years, chiefly because their guilt was unsuspected by anyone. If they had ever confessed it to a priest, and had thus been aware of his abiding knowledge of it, receiving at the same time *his absolute refusal to give them absolution, with admission to the Holy Communion, if they persisted in their wrong-doing,* they might have changed their lives completely.

"The man you hate," says the proverb, "is the man you do not know." In nothing is this truer than in reference to the Catholic clergy. How many Protestants are able to judge of Catholic priests from a personal acquaintance with any of them? We think perhaps with repugnance of confessing to an unknown man, however devout, but actual experience of the Sacrament of Penance changes one's opinion. In the first place, the hearing of confessions is, for those who sit for hours in the confessional, often a terrible trial of patience and even of physical endurance. Since becoming a Catholic, I have known priests who, though still fasting before saying Mass, have sat in the confessional for hours of a winter morning, till they were numb with cold and well-nigh exhausted. On the other hand, what compensations must a conscientious priest possess, when it becomes his precious privilege to share the joy of the angels in God's presence, by welcoming a repentant sinner back into the Church of Christ, advising him, strengthening him, assuring him of his heavenly Father's pardon, and giving him permission to partake of the Holy Eucharist!

"But is not the system of Confession liable to abuse?" I asked myself for the thousandth time. "Undoubtedly," replied my conscience; "but, after all, what system and what course of action among sinful mortals *may* not be abused?"

In certain cases, and with certain persons, discretion should be used in selecting a confessor; but the same thing must often be done in the choice of a physician. Between the two, the chances are much less that an ordained priest, who usually partakes daily of the Holy Communion, will violate his sacred duty, and mar in any way a soul committed to his care. Moreover, it should be borne in mind that every priest must also confess his own sins. No Catholic is exempt from that duty, whether he be a humble country cleric, or the Pope of Rome.

Even if there are occasional lapses of unworthy priests, such cases are not restricted to the Catholic clergy only. At one time in my life, in order to wean a certain Protestant Church member from what I thought excessive admiration for the Non-Conformist ministry, I clipped, for a year or two, from the daily papers a startling number of well-verified accounts of clerical scandals in that body. I was induced to do this by going one Sunday to a Protestant church in a large American city, only to find the edifice closed, and the congregation standing about in horrified groups, discussing a discovery made the evening before, which had led to the elopement of their preacher with one of his flock, though both were married, and left behind them in their flight two families of children! The truth is, this is a painful subject, about which neither Protestants nor Catholics should make intolerant or sweeping statements. There are weak moments in even the purest institutions. To all ecclesiastical denominations is the sentence applicable: "He that is without sin among you, let him first cast a stone." There are tares among the wheat within the Church, but God does not apply the torch to the field...yet! Evil sometimes appears to triumph on this earth to the end of the chapter, but...there is another chapter!

It is a fatal error to renounce faith in the Church of Christ because some of its members are backsliders or hypocrites. That is the great mistake that Luther and the other Reformers committed. Even the faults of an unworthy priest are not to be ascribed to the Church itself, for *such a priest is a renegade from its precepts.* One should not judge of the fruit of a tree from the rotten apples which have fallen from it. I may not be edified by the conduct of some particular prelate, but *just as his virtues would not give me virtue, so his shortcomings should not rob me of it.* Another's sins cannot excuse my own. A consoling thought in this connection is the fact that a priest, by virtue of his consecrated office, *can* be a useful ministrant at the altar, irrespective of his character as a man, much as the sentence of a judge avails to hang a guilty murderer, whether the judge himself be a moral man, or not. It is the latter's official act, as a magistrate, that decides the validity of his sentence. The Sacraments derive their efficacy from Christ, not from the human channel that conveys them.

About this time I found the following statement in regard to the Catholic Church, which deeply impressed me: "Lax in discipline, morals and faith many of her members have been and now are; but if none but the good had obtained admission to her fold, and if none but the perfect had been her Pontiffs, then might she seem to owe her deathless life to merely human means. The fact that her rulers have been weak and sinful mortals like ourselves, reveals a power greater than that of any Pope, which has preserved her from decay and doctrinal error. By laying stress upon the frailty of the Church's human elements, her enemies bear testimony to the supernatural origin of her spirit, which still persists, in spite of human sins among her members. If half the scandals imputed to her rulers and her people are true, the continued vitality of the Church is all the more wonderful." It is a verification of the Apostle's words: "We have this treasure in earthen vessels, that the excellency may be of the power of God, and not of us."

If we are to repudiate Papal supremacy in the Church because some of her Popes have been immoral, sinful men, then, in order to be consistent, we ought to repudiate the glorious company of the Apostles, because Judas once belonged to it, or because its leader, Peter, wickedly denied his Lord. Human frailties will always exist in the Church, while it is a Church militant. Christ was doubted by one of His disciples, denied by another, betrayed by a third, and forsaken by all. Yet He finished the work which was given Him to do, and He will fulfill His promise to the Church He founded. The following lines from the valuable work, *Kirche oder Protestantismus,* Mainz, 1883, p. 136, footnote, are worthy of careful consideration: "If we are reproached with the Church's unworthy Popes, we reply as follows: First, that we Catholics have at all times frankly and honorably acknowledged, as well as deeply lamented, the unworthiness of those Pontiffs, and have never thought of surrounding them with an unjustifiable halo of sanctity, or a false prestige. Second, that, although unworthy Popes in their private lives, through human weaknesses and passions, fell into certain sins and errors, nevertheless in their office, as Popes *they never enunciated any doctrine contrary to Christian morals and never issued an immoral decree.* Third, that the essential dignity and majesty of the Papal office itself remain completely unaffected by the personal unworthiness of its individual representatives. . .Even the first Pope, St. Peter, sinned grievously by denying his Lord and Master; yet the exalted dignity which the Lord conferred upon him before all the other Apostles remained with him; and Pope Leo the Great truly said: 'The worthiness of St. Peter is not lost in one unworthy heir.' Fourth, that the number of unworthy Popes, as they appear before us in the course of eighteen hundred years, is very small; that the faults of which they were guilty were for the most part committed before their elevation to the Papacy; and that not only have those faults been often much exaggerated by hostile historians, but offences have been imputed to them of which they were wholly innocent. This fact has been pointed out, even in regard to the unworthy Pope Alexander VI, by the English Protestant authority Roscoe, in his great historical work: *The Life and Pontificate of Leo X.* Fifth, that in the history of the Papacy the faults of the few unworthy Popes fade into obscurity, compared with the heroic virtues of so many worthy, pious, great and holy Pontiffs. . .As little as the spots upon the sun can darken that great luminary, so just as little can the imperfections of the record of some individual Popes dim the bright sunlight of the Papacy, which has lighted up the earth for eighteen centuries."

Lest this should appear exaggerated eulogy, let me conclude this chapter by quoting a tribute to the Papacy from the famous historian Ferdinand Gregorovius, in his well-known *History of Rome in the Middle Ages.* He, though a Protestant Rationalist, writes that the story of the Papacy forms "the most sorrowful, the most glorious and the most exalted history that stands recorded in the annals of mankind." (Vol. 8, p. 644).

Chapter 17

REVERENCE SHOWN TO
THE BLESSED VIRGIN AND PRAYERS
TO HER AND TO THE SAINTS

Mother dearest! Mother fairest!
Mother purest! Mother rarest!
Help of earth and joy of Heaven!
Love and praise to thee be given!
     —FABER.

Let us, then, learn that we can never be lonely or forsaken
in this life. Shall they forget us because they are 'made perfect'?
Shall they love us less because they now have power to
love us more? *If we forget them not, shall* they *not remember*
us with God? No trial, then, can isolate us, no sorrow can
cut us off from the Communion of Saints. Kneel down, and
you are with them; lift up your eyes, and the heavenly world,
high above all perturbation, hangs serenely overhead; only a
thin veil, it may be, floats between. All whom we loved and
all who loved us, . . . are ever near, because ever in His presence,
in whom we live and dwell.—CARDINAL MANNING.

A GREATER DIFFICULTY than those which I have mentioned was the overcoming of a prejudice, instilled
into my mind from childhood, against the reverence
paid by Catholics to the Blessed Virgin.

This now appears to me so wicked and unfounded, that
I am ashamed to have been dominated by it so long. Nevertheless, it was to me for a time a serious difficulty, and is one
still no doubt to the majority of Protestants. "In the first
place," a Protestant lady asked me recently, "why do Catholics
always speak of the Mother of Christ as the 'Blessed Virgin'?"
"Can you find that strange," I answered, "when you recall

her own prophetic words? In St. Luke's Gospel (1:48) we read: 'From henceforth all generations shall call me blessed.' " "But are not those the words of Christ referring to Himself?" inquired my otherwise highly educated questioner in perfectly good faith! So little did she know the Gospel, which she and all Protestants are supposed to regard as the Revelation of God, and as their only standard of authority! This prophetic declaration of the Mother of the Saviour certainly entails on Christians an obligation to fulfill her prophecy, yet Protestants, as a rule, pay no attention to it. Indeed, I have heard them refuse to use the term "Blessed Virgin," because it was "too much like the Roman Catholics." But surely Catholics follow here the example given in the Gospel. The Archangel Gabriel, at the Annunciation, greeted her with the words: "Hail, full of grace! The Lord is with thee; blessed art thou among women"; and St. Elizabeth used the same expression: "Blessed art thou among women...Whence is this to me, that the Mother of my Lord should come to me?"

In any case, however, why should Protestants hesitate to call the Virgin Mary "Blessed?" What woman ever was, or could be, more entitled to that term, than she whom God selected out of all her sex to be the earthly vehicle of the Incarnation of His Son—of Deity? Can any greater honor be imagined for a mortal? Could any life be made more blessed than that which gave to mankind its Redeemer?

In those who disbelieve in Christ's Divinity the slighting of the Virgin Mother may be comprehensible; but why should *evangelical Protestants* object to designating as Blessed the Mother of their Saviour? Can anyone expect to please even an earthly son by showing a lack of reverence to his mother? How much less, then, can such a course be pleasing to the Son of God, who, while enduring agony upon the Cross, confided His Mother to His beloved disciple? Can there be any doubt that *Christ still loves and reverences His Mother now in Heaven,* to whom He was obedient on earth for thirty years out of the three-and-thirty of His life? Certainly, therefore, those who honor the Mother, honor the Son as well; and "Every crown that is wreathed for Mary is laid at Jesus' feet." Some well-known stanzas by Father Faber admirably express these sentiments:

Mother of mercies, day by day
My love for thee grows more and more;
Thy gifts are strewn upon my way,
Like sands upon the great seashore.

But scornful men have coldly said
Thy love was leading me from God;
And yet in this I did but tread
The very path my Saviour trod.

They know but little of thy worth
Who speak these heartless words to me,
For what did Jesus love on earth
One half so tenderly as thee?

Jesus when His three hours were run,
Bequeathed thee from the Cross to me;
And oh, how can I love thy Son,
Sweet Mother, if I love not thee?

Study of this subject revealed to me the following facts: Catholic doctrine does *not* place the Blessed Virgin on an equality with God, as is often asserted, but fully recognizes, in her case also, the infinite distance existing between creature and Creator. Yet who can fail to see that Mary, of necessity, occupies a unique position among all created beings? Christ had but one Mother. Incarnate God vouchsafed to tabernacle Himself in the flesh of no other mortal medium. She thus became the earthly Mother of Deity. Why should she not, then, be supremely honored among mortals?

Moreover, she alone, of all her race, was privileged to *cooperate* in the work of Redemption by her own free will and choice. For, when the holy mystery of the Incarnation was announced to her, she answered with humility: "Behold the handmaid of the Lord; be it done to me according to thy word." This being so, how is it possible to regard Christ's Mother as merely an "ordinary woman," as Protestants sometimes style her? What angel or what saint was ever so exalted? And to have been thus honored and selected out of all created beings, must not her character, her fitness and her holiness have been unique? If not, *why should Almighty God, who had the universe to choose from,* have selected HER? If in the whole world there had been a woman purer, sweeter, more devout and humble than the Blessed Virgin, is it conceivable that God would not have chosen that woman? Again and again I asked myself: Why have I never seriously thought of this before, instead of foolishly repeating the old Protestant and rationalistic shibboleths to her discredit, and brutally insisting on the humiliation of the Mother of Our Lord?

The schismatic Greek Church and most of the Oriental sects of Christendom agree with Catholics in reverencing Mary, and in praying for her intercession; and even Mohammedans pay her greater honor than do the majority of Protestant Christians! Yet those who thus ignore the love and intercession of the Blessed Virgin rob the religion of Christ of a legitimate tenderness and sweetness they can never know. Their strange hostility to the Mother of our Saviour is sometimes carried to almost incredible extremes. Rev. J. G. Sutcliffe, formerly curate in Great Yarmouth, England, testifies on this point as follows: "My vicar, preaching on the Mother of Jesus, taught us that she was 'no better than any respectable girl in our town!'" (*Roads to Rome*, p. 258). Surely such men forget, not only what unparalleled honor was conferred upon her by the Almighty, but also how intimately connected was her life with that of her Child, the Incarnate Son of God!

During thirty years of Christ's existence on this earth they were practically never separated, and rarely even during the remaining three. Mary had given to His human frame its flesh and blood; had nursed Him as an infant; had guided His first footsteps; had given Him instructions in the ways of life; had taken Him in flight to Egypt; and watched Him, always "subject to her," slowly and divinely grow to manhood. She was His loving confidante, and He no doubt was hers. What a wonderfully sanctifying influence must the holy presence of the Son of God have exercised upon her in the quiet home in Nazareth during those thirty years! She was, moreover, His companion to the last. She heard His touching parables and sermons, wondered at His words, and marveled at His miracles, the first of which He wrought at her request. She also watched in anguish His sufferings upon the Cross, and heard His tender words concerning her, uttered with His dying breath. She, too, it was who held and bathed His lacerated body, shared the joy of the disciples at His Resurrection, and was present with them on the day of His Ascension, and on the day of Pentecost, when the Holy Spirit came upon them.

"But," it may be urged, "why do Catholics go so far as to apply to the Blessed Virgin the title 'Mother of God?'" Yet does not that title correspond to the fact? Used by Catholics, it refers, of course, to Mary, as the Mother of Christ on earth. Catholic doctrine does not state that Mary was the Mother of the Godhead, the Divine Nature, self-existent from eternity; but that she was the Mother of Christ, who, though a single personality, had two natures (Divine and human), and was God as well as man. Since, therefore, the Blessed Virgin was Christ's Mother, she *was* assuredly the Mother of God, in the sense alluded to; and this exalted title, thus defined, was given to her formally by the Council of Ephesus, as early as the year 434. This does not mean, however, that the title had not previously existed among Christians, unofficially, for it was used by the Church Fathers: Origen, Eusebius, Athanasius, Ambrose and many more. In 434, however, on account of the Nestorian heresy, it was deemed necessary for the Church carefully to define the doctrine of the two natures in Christ, and for the Pope to proclaim it solemnly *ex cathedra,* in order to put it for evermore beyond the region of dogmatic controversy among Catholics. Since then innumerable pious lips in every century, in every country in the world, and on the loneliest expanses of the sea, have formulated those heart-moving words: *"Sancta Maria, Mater Dei, ora pro nobis peccatoribus nunc et in hora mortis nostrae!"* ["Holy Mary, Mother of God, pray for us sinners now and at the hour of our death."—*Editor*, 1990.]

As for the doctrine of the Immaculate Conception of the Blessed Virgin, most Protestants have erroneous notions of what it really signifies. It does not mean, of course, that Mary, like her Son, was immaculately conceived by the Holy Ghost, or that she was in any sense *divine*. It merely states that, as the mortal vehicle of Christ's Incarnation, the Blessed Virgin was, from the very moment of her conception, entirely uncontaminated by the taint of that *Original Sin,* through which the father of our race had forfeited for himself and his descendants many blessed privileges. It means that, having been chosen from all others to become the Mother of Incarnate God, to her was granted the special boon of being from the outset *freed from that blemish,* and that she thus was made a spotless vessel for the Saviour of mankind. If the truth of the Incarnation itself is once believed, is this additional doctrine difficult to accept? Do not the circumstances of the case almost inevitably presuppose such action on the part of God? Belief in the Blessed Virgin's exemption from the inherited evil in humanity seems a necessary part of our ideal of what the Mother of the perfect Son of God should be.

Although this doctrine of the Immaculate Conception was first officially proclaimed by Pope Pius IX in 1854, it had been held already in the Church for centuries. (See Cardinal Newman's *Development of Doctrine*, p. 145.) It was, however, then defined for the first time, as an essential dogma of the Faith, like several other doctrines, which from the first lay hidden in the Church's inspired consciousness, and which have been from time to time declared by its chief Pastor, whenever their promulgation has been needed to refute some heresy, or to rekindle Christian zeal.

Even the doctrine of the Divinity of Christ was not formally defined till the first Council of Nicaea, A.D. 325, the object being then to refute the Arian heresy; nor was the dogma of the Divinity of the Holy Ghost formally proclaimed until the Council of Constantinople, A.D. 381, to meet the heresy of Macedonius. In fact, whenever a Catholic dogma has been openly assailed, the Church has felt obliged to state authoritatively her decision in regard to it. Such solemn definitions are, however, indicative of the continued *life* of the Church, not, as some declare, of her decadence. Mallock well says of the Catholic Church: "Her doctrines, as she one by one unfolds them, emerge upon us like petals from a half-closed bud; they are not added arbitrarily from without; they are developed from within." If Protestants object to this unfolding of certain dogmas, which, like seeds, were necessarily included in the original deposit of Faith, given the Catholic Church by the Holy Ghost on the day of Pentecost, they should remember that the same is true of dogmas, *which they themselves hold* in common with Catholics. There was, for example, a progressive development of the doctrine of the Holy Trinity and the Atonement, no less than of the dogmas of Purgatory and the Immaculate Conception of the Blessed Virgin.

Objection is also often made by Protestants to the custom of *praying* to the Virgin Mother; but here, too, everything depends upon a proper understanding of the Catholic standpoint. The Catholic doctrine does *not* teach, but, on the contrary, *forbids, any adoration* of the Blessed Virgin. It states that to adore her, in the sense that God should be adored, would be idolatry, for adoration is for God alone. To love and reverence her, however, is both a duty and a privilege.

Moreover, prayers to the Blessed Virgin are always, in the last analysis, prayers for her *intercession*. Humbly, reverently and lovingly Catholics ask the Virgin Mother (and the Saints as well) to intercede for them, and to further their petitions to Almighty God, who is, of course, the final Source of every grace and blessing.

Why should we not pray thus to Christ's Mother and the Saints? Do we not often ask an earthly friend to pray for us, and have we not abundant warrant in the Bible for so doing? St. Paul writes: "Now I beseech you, brethren, for the Lord Jesus Christ's sake, . . . that you strive together with me *in your prayers to God for me.*" (*Rom.* 15:30). In *1 Thess.* 5:25 he writes: "Brethren, *pray for us.*" (See also *Eph.* 6:18, 19 and *Heb.* 13:18). But if it be a Christian duty to ask a friend on earth to pray in our *behalf, why not request the same friend, when he has left this world, to pray for us in Heaven?* One understands how Materialists repudiate the doctrine of the Communion of Saints, for they have no belief in the existence of such beings; but how is it possible for Protestants, who do believe in the reality of a spiritual world, to reject the beautiful and consoling idea of the helpful influence of the Angels of God and of the Saints in Heaven? Why admit the agency of evil spirits, yet deny the influence of good ones? On what authority? Certainly not on that of the Bible. Scripture teaches us that souls in Heaven retain their love for us, and that they are, to some extent at least, aware of what transpires here. Jesus Himself assures us that "joy shall be in heaven over one sinner that repenteth, more than over ninety and nine just persons which need no repentance." He also tells us: "There is joy in the presence of the Angels of God over one sinner that repenteth." But how can they rejoice over our repentance, *unless they know of it?* And since sorrow for sin is an affair of the soul, how can they know of it, unless they are cognizant of our thoughts and wishes? St. Paul tells us that we are compassed about with a "great cloud of witnesses"; and in the *Book of Revelation* (8:3), we read of an Angel, whose duty it is to "offer the prayers of all saints upon the altar which was before the throne. And the smoke of the incense, which came *with the prayers of the saints,* ascended up before God." Moreover, in the same book (5:8), we read of "golden vials full of perfumes, which are the *prayers of saints.*"

Now the prayers of Saints and Angels can hardly be for

themselves, but must rather be for those who need their prayers, that is, for the poor sinners *in this world.*

It is unquestionable that from the very first days of the Church, Christians invoked the intercession of the Saints; for in the subterranean aisles of the Catacombs we find funereal inscriptions, appealing to deceased Christians to remember them in Heaven. Thus, one such reads: *"Ask for us in thy prayers, for we know thou art with Christ."* The Fathers of the early Church themselves maintained the practice of praying for the intercession of the Saints. St. Chrysostom, for example, said: "Not on this festal day only, but on other days also let us invoke these Saints; let us implore them to become our patrons; for they have great power, not merely during life, but also after death; yea, much greater after death." Few Christian customs are, in fact, so completely justified by Scripture and tradition as this.

Just how the Saints and Angels are made aware of our petitions need not concern us. That is a part of the mystery of the spirit world. We know that we are urged by Scripture and counselled by the Church to pray to them; to God we leave the rest. But, if it be proper to invoke the aid and intercession of the Saints and Angels, how much more should we invoke the help and intercession of Christ's Blessed Mother!

Jesus, though seated at the right hand of His Father, is still her Son, and cannot fail to hear with love and tenderness her prayers for those for whom He died, and whom she also loves for His dear sake. Such prayer in no sense weakens Christ's essential attributes as Mediator, for *every prayer to her is really based upon the mediation of her Son.* There are moments in the lives of most of us when, either through the realization of our own unworthiness and insignificance, or of the awe-inspiring majesty of God, we long to have supporters in our supplications, some tender, human souls to intercede for us; and these the Catholic finds in the Blessed Virgin and the Saints. It is the teaching of the Catholic Church that the Mother of Christ is a most potent advocate, and also that "the Saints, reigning with Christ, offer their prayers for men to God, and that it is good and useful to call upon them, and to have recourse to their prayers, help and assistance, in order to obtain benefits from God through Jesus Christ, who alone is our Redeemer and Saviour." Millions of prayers ascend thus daily to the Blessed Virgin, for her aid and intercession, from every portion of the Christian world.

Among the many names of endearment by which she is addressed in these petitions, one of the most beautiful is "Stella Maris," in token of her watchful care over those who find themselves exposed to danger on the deep. How many touching prayers and poems has this thought inspired! Among the latter is the "Evening Song to the Blessed Virgin," by Mrs. Hemans, the singing of which made upon me many years ago an ineffaceable impression.

> *Ave sanctissima!*
> *'Tis nightfall on the sea;*
> *Ora pro nobis,*
> *Our souls rise to thee.*
>
> *Watch us while shadows lie*
> *O'er the dim waters spread;*
> *Hear the heart's lonely sigh,*
> *Thine too hath bled.*
>
> *Thou, that hast looked on death,*
> *Aid us when death is near!*
> *Whisper of Heaven to faith,*
> *Sweet Mother, hear!*
>
> *Ora pro nobis!*
> *The wave must rock our sleep;*
> *Ora, Mater, ora,*
> *Star of the deep!*

The beneficial influence of the Blessed Virgin in the history of Christianity for nineteen hundred years can hardly be exaggerated. From Catholic writers it would, of course, be easy to bring abundant evidence of this; but theirs perhaps would not be so impressive to non–Catholics as the testimony of the eminent historian William H. Lecky, who, though a Rationalist, wrote the following: "The world is governed by its ideals, and seldom or never has there been one which has exercised a more salutary influence than the medieval conception of the Virgin. For the first time woman was elevated to her rightful position, and the sanctity of weakness was recognized, as well as the sanctity of sorrow. No longer the slave or toy of man, no longer associated only with ideas of degradation and of sensuality, woman rose, in the person of the Virgin Mother, into a new sphere, and became the object of a reverential homage, of which antiquity had no conception. . . A new type of character was called into being; a new kind of admiration was fostered. Into a harsh and ignorant and benighted age this ideal type infused a conception of gentleness and purity, unknown to the proudest civilizations of the past. In the pages of living tenderness, which many a monkish writer has left in honour of his celestial patron; in the millions who, in many lands and in many ages, have sought to mould their characters into her image; in those holy maidens who, for the love of Mary, have separated themselves from all the glories and pleasures of the world, to seek in fastings and vigils and humble charity to render themselves worthy of her benediction; in the new sense of honour, in the chivalrous respect, in the softening of manners, in the refinement of tastes displayed in all the walks of society; in these and in many other ways we detect its influence. *All that was best in Europe clustered around it, and it is the origin of many of the purest elements of our civilization.*" (*History of Rationalism,* Vol. 1, p. 225). Again, in his *History of European Morals,* the same writer says: "It is remarkable that the Jews. . .should have furnished the world with its *supreme ideal;* and it is also a striking illustration of the qualities which prove most attractive in woman, that one, of whom we know nothing except her gentleness and her sorrow, should have exercised a magnetic power upon the world, *incomparably greater than was exercised by the most majestic female portraits of paganism.*" Such were

a few of the considerations which made the reverence paid
to the Blessed Virgin by the Catholic Church not only comprehensible to me, but also natural and beautiful.

It was about this time in my journey towards the Church
of Rome that I wrote the following verses:

IN RETROSPECT

*How could I live so long without communion
With Thee, Almighty and Omniscient God,
How could I bear no hope of a reunion
With vanished loved ones, sleeping 'neath the sod?*

*How could I trace, the midnight skies exploring,
Vast stellar systems with their perfect laws,
Yet still continue foolishly ignoring
Their great Designer, Framer and First Cause?*

*How could I scorn Thy wondrous Revelation,
Deny that God had visited His earth,
Suggest a better scheme for man's salvation,
And doubt the doctrine of Christ's virgin birth?*

*How could I live so long without discerning,
Dear Virgin Mother, what thou really art?
Why was my soul, alas! so late in learning
The priceless treasure of thy loving heart?*

*How could I doubt that thou, God's own selection,
Wast from thy first conception undefiled,
Pure, full of grace, endowed with all perfection,
A stainless temple for thy Holy Child?*

*How could I live with mind and heart united
In bitter conflict with this Christian Faith,
Content to linger in a world benighted,
With life a mystery and God a wraith?*

*Because—a tiny drop in God's vast ocean
Presumed to criticize the boundless sea,
Because an atom wished to guide Earth's motion,
And teach its Maker what His world should be!*

Chapter 18

MIRACLES, ANCIENT AND MODERN

*The moment that, in our pride of heart, we refuse to accept the condescension of the Almighty, and desire Him, instead of stooping to hold our hands, to rise up before us into His glory, God takes us at our word; He rises into His own invisible and inconceivable majesty; He goes forth upon the ways which are not our ways, and retires into the thoughts which are not our thoughts; and we are left alone. Then presently we say in our vain hearts—There is no God!—*RUSKIN.

Why should it be thought a thing incredible with you that God should raise the dead?—ST. PAUL: ACTS 26:8.

In a miracle, God, for one moment, shows Himself, that we may remember it is He that is at work, when no miracle is seen.—F. W. ROBERTSON.

ANOTHER OBSTACLE in my path, as I approached the Catholic Church, was what I conceived to be her attitude towards modern miracles.

In dealing with this subject, I looked at it first from my old standpoint of a sceptic, who holds that all miracles, whether ancient or modern, are incredible, and that belief in them is an evidence of ignorance and credulity. In reality, however, I had now passed beyond that point; had lost a little of my arrogance; and had perceived that with God all things are possible, and that the inconceivable difference between a finite, ignorant creature and the infinitely wise Creator and Preserver of this boundless universe warrants no rash assertions. I had also realized that the startling discoveries, constantly being made in the realm of science, call for the utmost circumspection in the face of facts, of which we hitherto have had no inkling. Beyond our present limited comprehension lies a sphere, within which God can work, of course, as easily as in our own. Of this vast, extra-sensible sphere we know comparatively nothing. We live and move and have our being in a labyrinth of mysteries, from which we find no exit by the paths of science.

It is true, we discover certain uniform "laws," or methods, in the working of those mysteries; and minds which look exclusively at Nature's regularity are apt to be annoyed by any suggestion of exceptions to the rule. Hostility to miracles becomes thus sometimes among scientists an "obsession," quite as great as any which the scientists condemn. As we have seen in a previous chapter, the evidence is incontrovertible that Nature's "laws," or methods of procedure, are governed by a Supreme intelligence and will. Why, then, is it not possible (nay, under certain circumstances probable) that the Creator and Maintainer of the universe should sometimes wish to change the usual operation of the "laws" which *we* know, and to make use of others, of which we are not yet aware, but which are also of His making? "God," says St. Augustine, "does not do anything contrary to Nature, when He works a miracle; but merely does something contrary to the usual course of Nature, *as we know it*"; and we have seen already from the words of Darwin and Lord Kelvin how little of that course we really know. Even Huxley acknowledged that we know too little of Nature to say that a miracle *cannot* be wrought by laws with which we are unacquainted.

Is God the slave of His own creation, or is He a divinely free and independent Will? Science assures us that our earth and the sidereal system which we see must once have had a beginning, as it must have an end. If this be so, however, and if the "germs" of this potential state of things ever began to evolve, there must have been performed, *at that initiatory stage at least,* a miracle. Whether or not there were at subsequent epochs more Divine interpositions *does not affect the fact of that initial one;* and the length of time which has elapsed since then has nothing to do with it. How long ago, or with what speed, the will of God may work, does not affect the character of the deed. The first creative impulse given to the universe must have been miraculous, and we can say the same of the origin of life.

Science confesses its absolute inability to solve the problem of life's origin. Its source is evidently independent of matter. Professor Tyndall says: "I affirm that no shred of trustworthy experimental testimony exists to prove that life in our day has ever existed independently of antecedent life." (*Nineteenth Century*, 1878, p. 507). Professor Huxley also declares that the doctrine of "life only from life" is "victorious along the whole line at the present time." (*Critiques and Addresses*, p. 239). Professor Virchow calls the doctrine of the production of life from non-living matter utterly discredited. Numerous other scientists state that "all really scientific experience tells us that life can be produced from a living being only." (*The Unseen Universe*, p. 229).

Whether, therefore, life be given at every birth, or is conferred through a long line of evolved parents and their offspring, it is evident that, at all events, *the first* living being in the series did not derive its life-principle from inheritance, for it had no progenitors, but received immediately and for itself this precious gift from the Giver of all life—the Intelligent Creator. But why should we limit God's power to work miracles to these two solitary instances—the first creative impulse to the universe and the origin of life?

Because, it may be said, all miracles are contrary to experience. But to whose experience? To our own? Possibly; though many persons, in respect to answers to prayer, would assert the contrary. To the experience of the majority of mankind? Probably; for, to be a miracle at all, it must be an unusual occurrence. To universal experience? But to say that begs the question. Millions have believed that miracles have occurred, and have testified to the fact. We should always remember that comprehension is not always a condition of knowledge. We hold as verities many things which we do not understand. We know, for example, and believe in the inconceivable velocity of light, the infinitude of space, and the existence of an interstellar ether—but who can comprehend these wonders? We may not, therefore, comprehend *how* God can work a miracle, and yet believe that He has done so.

To deny the *possibility* of God's intervention in His own world is to make matter independent of its Maker, and the machine superior to its Constructor. God would thus be thrust into the background of His universe! What would He be in that event? Matter! The universe is now interpreted for the most part in terms of Force; and this we see in a million forms, not acting blindly, but in a definite direction, and evidently guided by Intelligence. What is such Force except another name for the action of God's will? Cannot God work on matter by His will, as easily as we ourselves work on the matter of our bodies by *our* wills? Incomprehensible? But can we comprehend how, by a mental, immaterial volition, we make our fingers fly along the keys of a piano or the strings of a violin in difficult arpeggios? The *way* in which the human mind works upon matter, arresting or changing the ordinary course of its laws, may be incomprehensible, but the fact is indisputable. It is not a miracle, but it sufficiently resembles one to make the denial of the possibility of a miracle on such a ground unreasonable. How dare we say that God cannot control and intercept the ordinary course of natural laws, if in His infinite wisdom He sees fit to do so?

In our attitude towards the miraculous everything depends upon our conception of God Himself. If we regard Him as *our Father,* we find it natural that He should sometimes intervene in behalf of His children; and if He wishes to do this, how can He reveal Himself to us, instruct us, warn us, save us and assist us, without using what seem to us supernatural means, because we know only "natural" means?

If we believe in answers to our prayers, we ought to have no difficulty in believing properly attested miracles. All who pray with faith must logically admit their possibility. It is true, the Rationalist sneers at prayer; but, as we saw in the previous chapter, he does so in defiance of the fact that the soul of every spiritual man, consciously or unconsciously, longs for communion with his Maker. In fact, the want of such communion is the cause of that impatient restlessness and discontent which make material, irreligious lives so full of ennui, disillusion and despair. Sceptics object that God knows all our wants before we ask Him, and that He needs not either our petitions, or those of others for us; yet prayer remains not only a divinely implanted instinct of the soul, but is also a part of the Divine scheme of things; and though we may have cynically argued against prayer a thousand times, nevertheless, in hours of danger and distress, our hearts spontaneously turn to God. It is the supreme distinction of man that he is able to commune with God; not with an unknown, vague, impersonal "Infinite" and "Absolute," a "Something, not ourselves, that makes for righteousness," for man needs— and according to Christ can find—in God a *personal Father.*

Hence man instinctively desires to go to Him in prayer. The historian Guizot has well said: "Alone, of all living beings here below, *man* prays. There is not, among all his moral instincts, a more natural, a more universal, a more invincible one than that of prayer. The child betakes himself to it with ready docility; the aged man returns to it, as a refuge amid decay and isolation.

"Prayer arises spontaneously, alike upon young lips that scarce can lisp the name of God, and on expiring ones that have hardly strength enough left to pronounce it. Among every people, celebrated or obscure, civilized or barbarian, acts and formulae of invocation meet us at every step. Everywhere, where there are living men, under certain circumstances, at certain hours, under certain impressions of the soul, eyes are raised, hands are clasped, and knees are bent, to implore or to thank, to adore or to appease. With joy or with terror, publicly or in the secrecy of his own heart, it is to prayer that man turns, as a last resource, to fill the void places of his soul, or to bear the burdens of his life. It is in prayer that he seeks, when all else fails him, a support for his weakness, comfort in his sorrows, and hope for his virtue. This universal and natural act of prayer witnesses to a natural and universal faith in the abiding and ever-free action of God upon man and his destiny." (*L'Eglise et la Société chrétienne,* pp. 22-24).

Nothing is taught more clearly in every portion of the Bible than that God desires to have His children pray to Him. Christ's words are unmistakable on this point. Not only did He teach mankind the prayer which bears His name, but He particularly said: "Whatsoever ye shall ask in My name that will I do"; and "All things whatsoever ye shall ask in prayer, believing, ye shall receive"; "Pray for them that despitefully use you"; "Watch ye, therefore, and pray always." The Epistles of St. Paul and St. John are also full of admonitions to pray, and we may well conclude from them that

Prayer is the Christian's vital breath.

Certainly nothing unites the soul to God so firmly and so tenderly as prayer, and nothing is more horrible to think of than a prayerless world! Poor, ignorant, ephemeral creatures— we, who do not know whether we shall draw another breath, how dare we lift our puny heads defiantly towards starlit space, and sneeringly refuse to kneel before the Infinite Creator of the universe—too proud to ask Him for His aid, or thank Him for His mercies!

The attitude of the Bible toward miracles is also unequivocal. From beginning to end it takes for granted the existence of an unseen, spiritual world, peopled with spiritual beings, who are often close to us, and influence our minds and deeds. It teaches also that under certain conditions and to certain persons those spiritual beings manifest themselves by visions, words or dreams, as messengers from God, and as angelic helpers of our poor humanity. Do those who read these lines dismiss the Bible's picture of the universe as childish? Let

them remember that, whereas, fifty years ago, men scoffed
at everything pertaining to the supernatural, and laughed at
the idea of any spiritual world and psychical phenomena, today
some of the ablest scientists are working hard to obtain, if
possible, convincing evidence of the existence of spiritual beings, and of their intimate connection with our minds.

Nothing that either the Bible or the Church has ever told
of miracles, of angels' admonitions, of warning dreams and
visions, or of direct communications from the spirit world,
is more incredible than much that leading scientists now relate as facts, or reckon with as possibilities! They ask us to
accept, as true, statements which, made by theologians, would
be greeted with derision.

Moreover, the miracles recorded by the Bible and the Church
have at least the noble background of a religion dating back
for thousands of years, and have invariably for their object
some important aim connected with the kingdom of God,
with the advent of His Son upon our earth, or with the assistance of His Saints in the promulgation of the Gospel. But
the marvels, certified to by modern psychic investigators, seem
purposeless and relatively valueless.

When St. Joseph, for example, was warned in a dream to
take the young Child and His Mother and go into Egypt,
there was a most important reason for that warning, connected with the life and safety of the Christ-Child. But the
dreams mentioned by the Society for Psychical Research are
usually admonitions or announcements *to some private individuals
about trivial worldly matters,* and hence must be regarded as being
far less worthy of credence than a warning relative to the
Son of God. I do not deny the truth of many of the remarkable communications said to have been made, or of the appa-
ritions of the dead, at the very moment of their decease, to
relatives thousands of miles away. I only claim that if the
Psychists ask from us respect and credence for *their* assertions, they should be equally tolerant towards the assertions
of the Bible and the Church. This is, however, seldom the case.

Let any scientist state that several thousand atoms can find room and to spare on the point of a needle, and his declaration will appear to many people as being far more credible than that the Son of God restored a blind man's sight, or multiplied five loaves of bread and two small fishes for a famished multitude. Yet the atomic theory rests entirely on inference. No one has ever seen an atom, or ever will see one, however absolutely he may believe in its existence. Can we not, therefore, also by inference, if from nothing more, believe in a spirit world, though we have never actually seen a disembodied spirit? The readiness of certain people to believe some supernatural facts, which they *wish* to believe, and then unwillingness to accept other facts, just as credible, which they do *not* wish to believe, is a peculiarity of human nature often to be met with, quite apart from the piety or infidelity of the individual. Modern disbelievers in Christianity are wont to scoff at the "superstition of Catholics," because of their belief in miracles; yet frequently these critics are themselves more superstitious than the objects of their criticism.

How can men flippantly denounce believers in Christianity as superstitious and credulous, when *dis*believers in Christianity never were more credulous and superstitious than they are today? That many of these accept, as real communications from the spirit world, the twaddle and inanity said to be brought to them by "little Indian maidens" and even by distinguished personalities, who have left this life, and apparently have lost whatever intelligence they possessed here, is as sad as it is amazing. What plummet line has also ever fathomed the abysmal depths of the credulity of many who dabble in the "occult"? What nonsense, too, is often swallowed blindly by the dazed disciple of some Indian "Mahatma," sent to Europe or to America to make converts! In these days, when individual "private judgment" is declared to be the unique test of truth, a man has only to proclaim what is apparently incredible, and he will find believers. Or let a woman wrap herself in veils of sufficient mystery and speak an almost unintelligible language, and thousands will be found to hail her as a prophetess, make pilgrimages to her home, as to a shrine, and build fine churches in her honor. Effrontery, grandiloquence and mystery are all that is required to create new cults, especially if they are announced as being destined to replace Christianity!

I have a friend who disbelieves in the Resurrection of Christ and mocks at the doctrine of Transubstantiation, yet he believes that a dead professor sends dictations from the spirit world to his former housekeeper, who gives them out as scientific articles from ghostland! He ridicules the Angels' message of good will at Bethlehem, yet holds as something probable the theory of a scientist whose strange experiments are supposed to prove that certain magnetic emanations (visible to the initiated) stream forth from men, women, animals and metals! From human beings blue flames emanate from the right side of the body, and yellow flames from the left; and similar emanations issue from photographs, revealing to "sensitives" in a darkened room the information whether the pictures are those of males or females; while "flames" from a letter also indicate the sex of the writer! This sort of thing convinces one that many sceptics of the Bible believe what is asserted in the name of Science with a docility and faith which are conspicuously absent when they have to deal with the Revelation of Almighty God!

Whether God actually made this Revelation, has been already considered in a former chapter. That is a matter for man's reason to determine, with the help of God. But when we are convinced that such a Revelation *has* been made, then Faith must necessarily accept what that Divine Revelation tells us, even though the atmosphere of mystery, which everywhere surrounds us here, is not thereby entirely removed. Those who decline to believe in the miraculous on the ground that they "accept nothing on the testimony of others," forget that they do practically nothing else than take the testimony of others their whole life long. What do they know, *from personal inspection of the original documents,* of any one of thousands of historical and biographical statements, which nevertheless they implicitly believe on the testimony of strangers—mostly dead? What do they know, *from actual experience,* of many portions of our earth, which bold explorers have described? What do they know, *from personal examination,* of the truth of countless marvelous assertions made in reference to astronomy, biology, chemistry, and a score of other fields of investigation in the natural world?

M. Pouchet, for example, an honored member of the Institute of France, in his book *The Universe* tells us that by means of a modern microscope it is possible to enlarge a surface *fifty-six million times!* That by this instrument animalcules, invisible to the unaided vision, can be seen and studied separately, although *ten thousand* of them could be ranged along the length of an inch! He also states that the chalk cliffs of England, and indeed whole mountains in other parts of the world, as well as thousands of miles of coral reefs, are composed of the skeletons of tiny creatures, *millions of whose corpses would not have filled the space of a cubic inch;* that a drop of water sometimes contains more atomic bodies than there are inhabitants on our planet; that a common fly, which we so lightly kill, has eight thousand eyes, and certain butterflies twenty-five thousand, and that a fly's wings vibrate, in a rapid flight, 3,600 times in a second! If we accept these and countless other inconceivable statements as correct, it is evident that the vast majority of us do so on faith, depending solely on the assertions of a very few individuals, most of whom we have never seen. We are all disciples of someone, and many of us accept the declarations of the "Popes of Science" quite as submissively as Catholics receive an *ex cathedra* utterance of the Holy See. Those scientific Popes, however, are not infallible, and they confess themselves unable to explain the whence, why and wherefore of the marvelous phenomena which they record. Hence, in the last analysis, it is as true of Science as of Religion that "we walk by faith, and not by sight."

In fact, our latest Science teaches us the *reality of the Unseen,* and asks us to believe in forces which are not only invisible, but almost inconceivable. We are assured that heat in all things, including our own bodies, is caused by the intensely rapid vibration of their molecules; that we are being whirled through space at a speed of eighteen miles a second, though we are utterly unconscious of any motion at all; and that a constant warfare, on which our very lives depend, is going on between two mighty armies of millions of bacilli in our blood! When shall we learn that, in thinking of the Supernatural and our relations to it, we are (aside from what God's Revelation teaches us) like a colony of ants, discussing the circumference of the earth, or the climate of the North Pole? Yet we insist on measuring infinity with our poor human standards, refusing to believe there may be other standards, which the Infinite can use at will!

★　★　★

When I approached this subject from the standpoint of the Christian believer, I found its solution naturally much easier; for the believing Christian not only admits the *possibility* of miracles, but accepts as true the statement that they actually occurred at certain times in the course of God's relations with the human race. Some of the accounts of miraculous appearances, recorded in the Old Testament, may perhaps be looked upon as allegorical, but no true Christian doubts the miracles which accompanied the birth, death, resurrection and earthly ministrations of the Saviour of mankind. For what are the Gospels, for the most part, but records of the Supernatural— from the song of the Angels before Bethlehem to the Ascension of the world's Redeemer?

The figures of the early Christian history move constantly before a background necessarily miraculous. Jesus Himself confirms and sanctions this conception of the universe. In fact, if miracles are impossible, so is Christianity. Stripped of its supernatural elements, the story of Christianity is a deception, and (what is worse) its Founder was Himself a deceiver. It is impossible to escape from the conclusion that either Jesus wrought the miracles ascribed to Him in the Gospels, or else that He intentionally deceived His disciples in regard to them; for *He Himself repeatedly appealed to those miracles, as proofs of His Divine mission.* In direct answer to the question: "Art thou he that should come, or do we look for another?" He replied: "Go and show John again those things which ye do hear and see: the blind receive their sight, and the lame walk, the lepers are cleansed, and the deaf hear, the dead are raised up, and the poor have the Gospel preached to them." (*Matt.* 11:4-5). Again He said: "If I do not the works of my Father, believe me not. But if I do, though ye believe not me, believe the works." (*John* 10:37-38). Again: "I have greater witness than that of John; for the works which the Father hath given me to finish—*the same works that I do, bear witness of me that the Father hath sent me."* (*John* 5:36). Now if Christ really performed those works of healing, if He did actually raise the daughter of Jairus, and Lazarus, and the son of the widow of Naim from the dead, the objections of the Rationalist fall to the ground. But if He did *not* raise them from the dead, then—since He claimed to do these deeds, as proofs of His Divinity—He was in truth the blasphemous impostor that the chief priests said He was. Anyone who, though really only human, induces men to worship him as God, is both a conscienceless trickster and a promoter of idolatry.

In considering the credibility of Christ's miracles, we should also not forget that they were often wrought in the presence of hostile and sceptical observers. The whole ninth chapter of St. John's Gospel is an illustration of this fact. There were at first the neighbors, who had doubts about the identity of the blind man whom Christ had cured; then came the Pharisees, who questioned critically both the blind man and his parents; there were also the Jews, who were determined, if possible, to discredit Jesus, and to expel from the synagogue anyone who should believe in Him; and finally there were those who cursed the man who had regained his sight, drove him from their midst, and excommunicated him. Mark the conclusion. "Jesus heard that they had cast him out, and when He had found him, He said unto him: Dost thou believe on the Son of God? He answered and said: Who is He, Lord, that I might believe on Him? And Jesus said unto him: Thou hast both seen Him, and it is He that talketh with thee. And he said: Lord, I believe. And he worshipped Him."

Many attempts have been made to explain away Christ's miracles, but it is a significant fact that the early opponents of Christianity did not try to deny their reality. Admitting the facts, they sought to account for them by saying that Jesus had made use of magic. Celsus, for example, ascribed them to Christ's acquaintance with occult philosophy, acquired by Him in Egypt! There is even a party among modern Rationalists, which claims that the works attributed to Christ were not sufficiently striking and convincing to command men's credence! These critics say that the miracles should have been much more spectacular. If Christ, they argue, had descended from the Cross, or if an attestation of His Godhead had been written on the sky in flaming letters, *then* no one could have doubted, and there would have remained an overwhelming proof of His Divinity; whereas now. . .! But such objectors seem to forget that practically *no miracle* CAN *convince those who are unwilling to believe.*

Not one of Christ's bitter enemies was convinced of His Divinity by any of the miracles which they knew He wrought. On the contrary, because He did perform them, they desired to kill Him! The chief priests and Pharisees made His miracles their principal reason for destroying Him, saying: "What do we? for *this man doeth many miracles.* If we let him thus alone, all men will believe on him." They even wanted to put innocent Lazarus to death, because his resurrection had made many converts! (*John* 12:10-11). If there is such a thing as a "will to believe," there is also a will *not* to believe. A message flashed across the heavens, to the effect that Jesus was the Son of God, would probably have been described, twenty-four hours after its disappearance, as a "curious cloud-effect"; even a descent from the Cross would have been thought a fantasy by all who had not actually seen it; and some even of those eyewitnesses would probably have subsequently let themselves be persuaded that the event had not occurred "objectively." Plausible "explanations" of any miracle can be made, and, as a matter of fact, always have been made, by the incredulous. Renan even suggests that Lazarus, instead of really rising from the dead, had not died at all, but had caused himself, to gratify some morbid fantasy, to be wrapped in cerements and shut up in the family tomb! So, when the sepulchre of Christ was found to be empty, the Jews declared that His disciples must have come by night and stolen the body. *Sic erat in principio, nunc est, et semper erit.* ["As it was in the beginning, is now, and ever shall be." —*Editor*, 1990.]

It is evidently not God's purpose to *compel* men to believe in the supernatural; nor will He use such overpowering means for that object as shall destroy their freedom of will. Miracles are not intended to be like blows from a bludgeon, to reduce men to subjection; they are invitations to faith. Considering, then, that there were the best of antecedent reasons why miraculous events should herald and accompany the life of the Son of God on earth, the testimony for them in the Gospels is amply sufficient. If we refuse to believe it, it is not likely that we should do so "even though one rose from the dead."

Now, if we grant that God at one time did work miracles, in order to convince and to convert men, there is no *a priori* reason why such proofs of His assistance and protection should not be repeated. It is, in fact, more difficult to believe that God would work one miracle only and no more, than that He should work many.

Upon what ground do Protestants assert that the "age of miracles is past?" The Bible does not say so. On the contrary, it relates that Jesus said to His disciples: "Verily, verily, I say unto you, he that believeth in Me, the works that I do shall he do also, and greater works than these shall he do, because I go to the Father." If, therefore, the Church which Christ established still exists, and if its mission is not ended, why should not God employ at times the same miraculous means to strengthen faith, to rivet man's attention, and to convince an unbelieving race? There is no reason why He should not do so.

Examining my own position, in the light of these considerations, I found it reasonable to believe that the Creator had worked miracles at the beginning of this universe, as we know it, and also at some subsequent stages of its development, notably at the epoch of the origin of life. I believed also that in connection with the most stupendous fact in history—the Incarnation—the Miraculous became necessary, and that its absence, under the circumstances, would have been incongruous. I believed, too, in the Resurrection of Christ, not merely from historical evidence, but also because the occurrence of that great event was absolutely essential, in order to put God's seal forever on the whole redemptive drama. I believed, moreover, that God has, since that time, worked many miracles in response to prayer among the Saints of the Church, and also among private individuals. I saw, therefore, nothing improbable in the idea that miracles may, at any time, be wrought by the will of God for the Church's inspiration, comfort and increase of faith.

But *whether all the modern miracles which are alleged to have occurred really did occur, and are capable of verification, is a matter of opinion, not of faith.* The Church forces on no one a belief in any particular modern miracles. For most of these she assumes no responsibility, and may pronounce no formal condemnation of them, unless she sees that they are really incredible, and liable to do harm. She recognizes that even in the credulity of many simple souls there lies the germ of the great truth of the *possibility* of miracles. What she requires of her children is a full belief that God in the past *has* wrought miracles, and *can* work more. Belief in modern miracles is, therefore, chiefly an affair of evidence. To one good Catholic a miracle at Lourdes appears to be well proved; another equally good Catholic may not find it so. So long as the Church has not settled the question, her children are free to believe what they like in regard to it.

There was, however, one modern miracle of which I personally could not doubt—my own conversion! Two years before I began to write this book I should have said it was as probable that a dead tree could bloom again, or a descending river turn back in its course, as that I ever could believe in Christ's Divinity and in His Church. That was to me the miracle of miracles. If God could call and bring me once more to Himself, after so many years of infidelity, why should I doubt the story of Christ's healing of the blind man? Like him, I now exclaimed: "One thing I know, that whereas I once was blind, I now see."

Chapter 19

THE VENERATION OF IMAGES
AND RELICS

He who is indifferent to a picture, a letter, or any personal
memento of a departed friend, never really loved him.

I love it, I love it; and who shall dare
To chide me for loving that old Armchair?
I've treasured it long, as a sainted prize;
I've bedewed it with tears, and embalmed it with sighs;
'Tis bound by a thousand bands to my heart;
Not a tie will break, not a link will start;
Would ye learn the spell?—A mother sat there;
And a sacred thing is that old Armchair.
                                        —ELIZA COOK.

THE SO-CALLED "Worship of Images" in the Catholic Church presented to me no special difficulty, and
I should hardly think it worthy of mention here,
did not some Protestants entertain upon the subject a prejudice which is as unjustified as it is surprising. There stand
before me in my library, as I write, two marble busts—one
of the Emperor Marcus Aurelius, the other of Dante. When
I read the *Meditations* of the former, or the *Divine Comedy* of
the latter, I often raise my eyes towards those two works
of art with satisfaction. Upon my desk, too, is a picture of
my sainted mother. How often have I looked upon this through
a mist of tears, and even spoken words to her, whose features
thus confronted me. But if I thus enjoy these likenesses of
an admired moralist, a famous poet, and my beloved mother,
why should I not find consolation and enjoyment in the contemplation of two further objects which adorn my walls—a
finely carved Tyrolean crucifix and a copy of one of Raphael's

Madonnas? If I feel love and reverence for Jesus and the Blessed
Virgin, why should I not enjoy appropriate representations
of them, at least as much as I enjoy the bust of Dante or
the portrait of my mother? If the memorials of those we love
on earth are precious, should souvenirs of those we love in
Heaven be less so?

The Catholic Church condemns idolatry as an abomination; but she maintains that proper reverence for sacred images is not idolatry. The notion that a Catholic worships the
image itself is too absurd for refutation. The most ignorant
peasant knows too much for that; and to the most uneducated Catholic a sculptured crucifix or picture of the Blessed
Virgin stands as a symbol only of the Person represented by
it. Let those who talk of the "worship" of images and pictures ask a Catholic whether he or she "worships" the figure
itself! Clear, definite instruction is given on this point in Catholic catechisms and in the declaration of the Council of Trent.
The latter says: "The holy bodies of martyrs and of others
now living with Christ—which bodies were once living members of Christ, and temples of the Holy Ghost, and which
by Him are to be raised to eternal life and to be glorified—are
to be *venerated* by the faithful . . . Moreover the images of Christ
and of the Virgin Mother of God, and of the Saints, are to
be had and retained particularly in temples, and due honor
and veneration are to be given them; *not that any divinity or
virtue is believed to be in them on account of which they are to be
worshipped, or that anything is to be asked of them,* or that trust
is to be reposed in images, as was of old by the Gentiles,
who placed their hope in idols; but because the honor which
is shown them is referred to the prototypes which these images represent . . . If any abuses have crept in among these
holy and salutary observances, the Holy Synod ardently desires
that they may be utterly abolished."

The English Penny Catechism says explicitly: "We should
give to relics, crucifixes and holy pictures an inferior and relative honour, so far as they relate to Christ and His Saints,

and are memorials of them. *We may not pray to relics or images, for they can neither see, nor hear, nor help us."* In other words, praying to a picture or image is categorically forbidden. The accusation that Catholics worship these objects is, therefore, a calumny. When we lay wreaths at the pedestals of the statues of national heroes, or bare our heads before them during a patriotic speech, are we "worshipping" the bronze or marble figures themselves? To ask the question is to answer it. The touching and consoling fact that God once took upon Himself for us a human form, enables us reverently to represent that form in art, as a memorial of His condescension; and it is owing to this fact that the world's greatest masters, from Raphael to Leonardo, and from Michelangelo to Albrecht Dürer, have enriched the world with so many beautiful reminders of Our Lord and of His Mother.

It has always seemed strange to me that Protestants use so sparingly those handmaids of religion—painting and sculpture. Formerly, indeed, their prejudice against all symbols of Christianity was so intense that they not only stripped old churches, monasteries and cathedrals of their crosses, crucifixes, statues of the Apostles, and pictures of the Blessed Virgin, but actually mutilated sculptured carvings over the portals of the noblest sanctuaries, struck off the noses from the statues of bishops on their tombs, and whitewashed frescoes of religious subjects upon cloister walls! Even in our own times some Protestants have thought it consonant with the worship of God to make the walls of their churches as bare and unattractive as possible. Most of them even now will not erect a cross on their church steeples, and those who do concede to this pathetic symbol of Christ's Passion a place upon the altar, will not permit the figure of the Crucified to hang upon it!

What is the cause of this aversion to the image of Our Lord in those who claim to love Him, and who sing such hymns as "In the Cross of Christ I glory," and "When I survey the wondrous Cross, on which the Prince of Glory died"? Does it not lie in an unreasonable hatred of the Catholic Church, which has for ages held this symbol as the most sacred object in the world? When people tell me that such memorials are unnecessary, they speak the truth perhaps so far as they themselves are concerned, but they assuredly cannot speak for all. Many there are who find such things a blessing. It is a matter of feeling and association, rather than of intellect. I, for example, though an educated man, and having attained an age when life is seldom influenced by sentimental emotions, confess to a feeling of genuine pleasure in seeing near me, when in church or in my home, some beautiful memento of the Son of God, or of His Mother, or the Saints. I do not pray to them, of course, yet often during prayer or religious meditation I love to turn my gaze to them, as aids to a devotional frame of mind.

How inconsistent are those Protestants who, while condemning the Catholic use of images and pictures, adorn their own church windows with stained-glass representations of Christ or of the Saints, or let their children carry in Sunday school processions banners adorned with figures of the Saviour and His Apostles! In any case it should be borne in mind that Mother Church does not *compel* her children to kneel or pray before any statue. They may, if they choose to do so, offer up their prayers to God in the darkest corner of a vast cathedral, apart from any fair memorial of Saint or Saviour. The Church endeavors to adapt herself to *all* her children, and to respond to every rightful yearning of the human soul. Like a wise and devoted mother, she provides milk for her babes, as well as meat for men. Like Jesus, she makes use of parables and figures, as well as of the deepest theological philosophy, and her great hopes and precious consolations are for all sinning, suffering creatures of this evil world. No two intelligences are absolutely alike, and hence in the Catholic Church the intellectually superior must kindly tolerate the simplicity of the less learned. Charity and unity are the two essentials, which make the close association of such dissimilar human elements possible within one fold.

Though to a Catholic peasant and to a Catholic scholar the same words of the liturgy may convey a meaning different in degree, the difference is not of *kind,* for the essential thought contained in those words must be to both of them identical. The attitude of the two men towards those words may be as dissimilar as that of a rustic looking at a planet with the naked eye, and an astronomer gazing at it through a telescope. Both see it, yet how differently! The peasant probably knows at most that the satellite moves about the sun; but the observer with the telescope sees the planet's moons, reckons its speed, and analyzes its component elements through the irised spectrum [i.e., broken into the rainbowed colors of the spectrum.—*Editor,* 1990.]. But both believe the essential fact that it is part of God's creation. That for the peasant is sufficient; for what the other's telescopic vision and deep study have revealed to him might fill the rustic's mind with doubt and dread. Thus do extremes of thought and culture meet fraternally beneath the Church's roof, and furnish further evidence of her impressive unity.

The democratic spirit, so proverbial and universal in Catholicism, leads one also to look with greater sympathy and comprehension on the inartistic ornaments of many humble Catholic chapels. These I had once been inclined to ridicule, but now I realized that the Catholic Church is not for rich and cultured people only, but also for the poor and ignorant. The greatest masters of the ages, it is true, have worked for her; but if mosaics, priceless paintings and imposing statues are conspicuous in her grand cathedrals, equally precious in God's sight are humble wayside shrines and the simple offerings of the poor. We do not sufficiently consider how the Catholic religion embellishes the commonplace of life, and changes into poetry the prosaic lives of those whose only spiritual home and source of inspiration is the House of God. The memories of artistic objects connected with their religion, crude and primitive though they often are, exert a lasting influence upon their characters. An English writer has well said of their effect upon the Catholic peasant: "Associated with the fondest recollections of his childhood, and with the music of the church bells. . . painted over the altar where he received the companion of his life, around the cemetery where so many whom he loved are laid, on the stations of the mountains, on the portal of the vineyard, on the chapel where the storm-tossed mariner fulfills his grateful vows, keeping guard over his cottage door, and looking down upon his humble bed, forms of tender beauty and gentle pathos forever haunt the poor man's fancy, and silently win their way into the very depths of his being. More than any spoken eloquence, more than any dogmatic teaching, they transform and subdue his character, till he learns to realize the sanctity of weakness and suffering, the supreme majesty of compassion and gentleness." (Lecky's *History of European Morals,* Vol. 2, p. 106).

A word may be said in this connection in reference to the use of *relics* among Catholics, since this, too, forms a stumbling block to many. It is needless to say that reverence for Christian relics is as old as Christianity itself. St. Jerome speaks of "the venerable sepulchres of the martyrs," and St. Augustine says: "In this place we have not made an altar to St. Stephen, but we have made of the relics of St. Stephen an altar to God; for such altars are pleasing to God." But, apart from history and tradition, this is an impulse common to human nature. Are we not all more or less relic-hunters? Against such souvenirs in themselves no possible objection can be made. Whoever has preserved a lock of hair from the head of some loved friend or parent, long since dead; whoever cherishes a watch, a ring, or any real memorial of one whose death has left a wound that time can never heal; whoever looks with awe upon the sword of Washington, or the pen with which the martyred Lincoln signed the Act that freed the slaves; knows that a love and reverence for relics, personal or historic, forms one of the strongest and most universal characteristics of mankind. If, then, the relics of some saintly servant of the Church lend an additional sanctity to a Christian altar, is it a matter for reproach, or even for surprise? And if those relics, in response to prayer, are sometimes made the medium of grace and healing to the penitent, is that fact in itself incredible or absurd? Surely, if we believe that God does answer prayer, and does at times work miracles of healing, can we conceive of any more likely means for Him to choose for doing so, than the revered memorials of a body which, while on earth, had toiled and suffered, and it may be died, to prove fidelity and love to Christ?

We read, for example, in *Acts* 19:12, that handkerchiefs and aprons which had touched the body of St. Paul cured people of diseases, since "God wrought special miracles" by these means; and in *Acts* 5:15-16, it is said that similar cures were made, if but the shadow of St. Peter fell upon the sick. Nevertheless (and this is the point to bear in mind), *belief in the genuineness of relics is merely a matter of opinion.*

The Church, like a loving mother, often tolerates indulgently what she does not formally authorize or approve. Hence this imagined "difficulty" ought to offer no real obstacle to anyone desiring admission to the Church of Rome; and, as a matter of fact, it offered none to me.

Chapter 20

PERSECUTIONS FOR HERESY BY CATHOLICS AND PROTESTANTS

The oppression of any people for opinion's sake has rarely had any other effect than to fix those opinions deeper, and render them more important.—HOSEA BALLOU.

Religion is to be defended by dying ourselves, not by killing others.—LACTANTIUS.

Les seules causes qui meurent sont les causes pour lesquelles on ne meurt pas. [The only causes which die are the causes for which people do not die.]—LOUIS VEUILLOT.

We hate some persons because we do not know them, and we will not know them because we hate them.—COLTON.

The Religion that fosters intolerance needs another Christ to die for it.—BEECHER.

THE NOTION that the acceptance or rejection of a creed is something to be settled by the individual's free and independent judgment is of comparatively recent date. The Reformers, it is true, *talked* much of the right of private judgment in such matters, but their intolerance and persecutions show how little liberty they gave to anyone. For centuries in every country the prevalent religion was looked upon as an essential characteristic of the nation—often its most precious treasure, guarded and guaranteed by the State itself. Hence every attack that was made upon the Church, and every doubt that was cast upon her doctrines, was looked upon as a threat to national security. Sceptics were, therefore, regarded as traitors to the State, and were amenable, not only to ecclesiastical, but also to civil punishment.

272

When, little by little, in the disintegrated Protestant countries, dogmas came to be of less public importance, and Church and State drew further away from each other, a change took place. Their jurisdictions gradually became distinct, and punishments grew less severe. Already early in the nineteenth century, corporal chastisement had almost wholly disappeared from legal tribunals, and to a great extent from schools and families. On the whole, the result has been beneficial, except perhaps in the abolition of the whipping post for certain cases of brutal cruelty; but it remains a fact that we of the present generation have grown up in this milder atmosphere, and are indignant when we read of many of the punishments of former times, since we are quite unused to anything like them. Hence, in our estimate of persecutions for heresy, we must be careful not to take with us into former centuries the sentiments of this present age, with its more lenient civil and religious penalties, and its indifference to creeds. We should be guilty thus of an anachronism, which would infallibly prejudice our judgment. In other words, in order to decide the question fairly, we must transport ourselves as far as possible into the ways of thinking and acting which then prevailed. So doing, we shall at once perceive that the age in which "religious" persecutions flourished was, *in respect to punishments of every kind,* a cruel and a barbarous one.

Even in civil cases, having nothing to do with religion, the application of torture in the examination of prisoners and even of witnesses was a common occurrence; and penalties, varying from mutilation to death, were inflicted for the smallest offences. Some misdemeanors were punished by slitting the nostrils with scissors; others by the lopping off of ears; while many criminals were mercilessly whipped in public, in the presence of a brutal crowd. To witness the flogging or the execution of some poor wretch formed one of England's popular amusements far into the eighteenth century. Dr. Dodd, a clergyman who was hanged in London for committing forgery, was, before being taken to the gallows, exhibited at two shillings a head! Debtors were kept for years in fetid dungeons, heavily loaded with chains, until released by death. In England, as late as 1577, the theft of a sum of money exceeding a shilling in amount was punishable with death; and no longer ago than 1832, death was the legal penalty for stealing a sheep, or the sum of five shillings from a shop! And what was true in this respect of England was equally true of other countries at that time. When, therefore, we read of the horrors of "religious" persecutions, we should remember that, fearful though they were, they were not exceptional, but in accordance with the general spirit of the age.

We sometimes think of those old ancestors of ours, and thank God that we are not like them, but whatever may be said against their persecutions for heresy, *they* at least had for their motive a firm belief that the maintenance of certain Christian dogmas was essential for man's salvation. Modern atrocities, like those of the Congo, for example, have, on the contrary, no higher motives than greed for gold, a sadistic lust to witness torture, or a relentless hatred of weaker races, usually of a different color! Moreover, we must not conclude that, because the ancient mode of persecution for religion's sake has disappeared, the *spirit* of intolerance has entirely vanished. Buckle, writing in 1857 in his *History of Civilization* (Vol. 1, p. 264), says: "In Sweden, which is one of the oldest Protestant countries in Europe, there is—not occasionally but habitually—an intolerance and a spirit of persecution, which would be discreditable to a Catholic country, but which is doubly disgraceful when proceeding from a people who profess to base their religion on the right of private judgment." In England also, as late as 1850, Father Faber wrote as follows of the treatment which he and his fellow priests received when they had founded in London the Brompton Oratory: "All over the walls you see: 'Don't go to the Oratory!' 'No Popery!' 'Down with the Oratorians!' 'Beware of the Oratorians!' We are cursed in the streets. Even 'gentlemen' shout from their carriages at us." About the same time, the

British Press and Bishops of the Church of England were publishing against the Tractarian leaders and especially against Newman—one of the clearest thinkers and most brilliant writers of the nineteenth century, as well as one of the finest specimens of an English gentleman—such vile invectives as the following: "Agents of Satan," "Snakes in the grass," "Men polluting our Church's sacred edifices, and leaving their slime about her altars," and "Miscreants, whose heads may God crush"! From such manifestations of hatred and hostility it would be easy to pass to acts of violence, were a popular catchword found, and a fanatical demagogue bold enough to utter it.

What now prevents religious persecution, with its rack and stake, is not so much an amelioration in man's brutal nature, as a general state of unbelief and indifference towards religious things. It is easy to be tolerant when one does not care; but every faith, believed in with intensity, undoubtedly inclines to persecute antagonistic creeds. This is but natural. Whoever believes that his own salvation and that of his friends depend on holding a certain faith, is not disposed to witness with indifference an effort to destroy that faith; and since the interests of eternity infinitely outweigh those of time, it is almost inevitable that he should adopt stern measures to repress what he believes will put men's souls in danger of perdition.

Religious persecution usually continues till one of two causes rises to repress it. One is the sceptical notion that all religions are equally good or equally worthless; the other is an enlightened spirit of tolerance, exercised towards all varieties of sincere opinion. This latter sentiment is not really Indifferentism. It is inspired rather by the conviction that it is useless to endeavor to *compel* belief in any form of religion whatsoever. Unhappily this enlightened, tolerant spirit is of slow growth, and never has been conspicuous in history; but *if it be asserted that very few Catholics in the past have been inspired by it, the same thing can be said of Protestants.*

This fact is forgotten by Protestants. They read bloodcurdling stories of the Inquisition and of atrocities commit-ted by Catholics, but *what does the average Protestant know of Protestant atrocities in the centuries succeeding the Reformation?* Noth-ing, unless he makes a special study of the subject; for in the controversial sermons which he hears, nothing is said of them; and in the books and papers which he reads (all Prot-estant publications, as a rule), nothing is written of them. Yet they are perfectly well known to every scholar, and can be verified by anyone. If I do not enumerate here the perse-cutions carried on by Catholics in the past, it is because it is not necessary in this book to do so. This volume is ad-dressed especially to Protestants, and Catholic persecutions are to them sufficiently well known. The other side of the question, however, they do *not* generally know.

Now, granting for the sake of argument that all that is usually said of Catholic persecutions is true, the fact remains that *Protestants, as such, have no right to denounce them,* as if such deeds were characteristic of Catholics only. People who live in glass houses should not throw stones. In fact, the highest Authority tells us that only those who are without sin should ever throw them at all. Not, therefore, to indulge in lapida-tion, but only to reveal to certain Protestants how much glass is incorporated in the framework of their own Church, I cite a few from many facts which influenced my own mind strongly, and may have some effect on theirs. First of all, it should be borne in mind that *politics* often played a greater part in the so-called "religious" persecutions than religion itself; for, during the wars engendered by the Reformation, all Governments took sides for one religion or the other, and almost every nation was not only menaced by its neighbors, but often was divided against itself. This is seen with fright-ful distinctness in the history of the religious Civil Wars, which desolated England, France and Germany. We have already, in the chapter on the Church of England, seen how persecu-tion and confiscation were employed against those of the peo-ple of England who wished to remain Catholics. But it should be remembered also, as indicating the degree of Protestant intolerance then prevailing, that those atrocities were not inflicted upon Catholics only.

Such of the Protestants as did not conform to the Anglican Church, but wished to "protest" a little on their own account, were also persecuted. Among these were the Puritans, who in their turn, later on, were to persecute those who protested against them! The treatment given to Dissenters by Elizabeth was less severe than that inflicted upon Catholics, for the former were regarded as misguided brethren, who had fallen from grace; but it was bad enough. Presbyterians, for example, were often branded, exposed in the pillory, imprisoned, banished, mutilated and even put to death. A few Anabaptists and Unitarians were burned alive. Of the Bishops of the Church of England, Bucke, in his *History of Civilization* (Vol. 1, p. 308), says: "Its Bishops witnessed with composure the most revolting cruelties, because the victims of them were the opponents of the English Church. Although the minds of men were filled with terror and with loathing, the Bishops made no complaint. But the moment James proposed *to protect from persecution* those who were hostile to the Church...the hierarchy became alive to the dangers with which the country was threatened from the violence of so arbitrary a Prince! ...The proximate cause of that great revolution, which cost James his crown, *was the publication by the King of an edict of religious toleration!* We ought never to forget that the first and only time the Church of England has made war on the Crown, was when the Crown had declared its intention of tolerating and in some degree protecting the rival religions of the country!" And this toleration and protection the King had wished to give *to Protestants, whom other Protestants were persecuting!*

Space does not permit a statement here of the Protestant persecutions of Catholics in France, where indeed they had much less opportunity to show intolerance, since the religion of the land was mostly Catholic; but instructive information can be gained on that point by consulting the work of Buckle, mentioned above (Vol. 2, pp. 50-61), whose remarks are the more noteworthy because he, as a well-known Rationalist and critic of the Roman Catholic Church, cannot be suspected of being a partisan of the Catholics.

We cannot, however, pass over in silence the awful record of the horrors perpetrated by Protestants in Ireland, the "Island of the Saints." In 1578, the Bishop of Killala was executed; in the same year the Archbishop of Cashel was burned at the stake in Dublin; in 1585, the Archbishop of Armagh was beheaded at the Tower of London; in 1611, the Bishop of Down, more than eighty years of age, suffered martyrdom at Dublin. Of the deaths and sufferings of the lesser clergy, space fails to give a description. The same oppressive laws, which were enacted against Catholics in England, were carried out with still greater severity in Ireland. In 1652, an attempt was made to exterminate the entire Irish Catholic priesthood. An Act signed by the Commissioners for the Parliament of England decreed that every Romish priest should be deemed guilty of rebellion, should be sentenced to be hanged until he was half dead, and then should be beheaded and his body quartered, his bowels drawn out and burned, and his head fixed on a pole in some public place. The punishment of those who entertained a priest was by the same Act declared to be confiscation of their goods and an ignominious death on the gallows. The same price (five pounds) was set by these Commissioners on the head of a Romish priest as on that of a wolf, the number of wolves in Ireland being then large! Finally, scarcely a Catholic prelate was left on the whole island to bless, ordain or confirm. Nevertheless some Catholic Bishops still remained at their posts, although in hiding, meeting their flocks in solitary glens, much as the early Christians gathered in the Catacombs. (See *The Book of Erin,* by J. M. Davidson, *Curr's Review,* etc.)

From 1692 to 1800 not a single Catholic member set foot in the Parliament of Ireland, because they were asked, as a condition of entry there, to affirm that "the sacrifice of the Mass is damnable and idolatrous"; an easy way of securing a Protestant majority! After 1709, a reward of fifty pounds was offered for the discovery of an Archbishop or Bishop! The price for a simple priest was raised from five to twenty pounds! Professional "priest-catchers" did a lucrative business.

But Anglican persecution of Catholics in Ireland was not confined to priests. It was extended to schoolmasters as well. From 1695 to 1782, by order of the British Parliament, every Catholic schoolmaster discovered instructing the Irish people in religion, or even in the simple elements of education, was transported. Large rewards were offered for their apprehension, and hundreds of Catholics were banished from Ireland for teaching Irish boys in remote valleys or behind hedges, while others stood on watch to give the alarm. It comes, therefore, with poor grace from anyone to sneer at the ignorance of many of the Irish people of those days.

Dissenters in Ireland, though better treated than Catholics, also endured appalling miseries at the hands of the Anglicans. The sect of Presbyterians seems to have been particularly obnoxious to the leaders of the National Church, and when the fire of persecution burned with special violence they were hunted over the mountains of Ireland like wild beasts. Instances are recorded of Dissenters whose fingers were wrenched asunder, whose bodies were seared with red-hot irons, and whose legs were broken in their boots! Their wives were also whipped in public and driven through the streets before a hooting mob. It is not strange, therefore, that multitudes of Non-Conformists fled from Ireland and England to America; but what *is* amazing is the fact that, after such experiences, those fugitives did not learn the lesson of toleration, and did not grant to those who differed from them in religious views, a freedom similar to that which they themselves had always claimed.

So long as *they* had suffered persecution, they had appealed to the principle of religious liberty; but when they found themselves in a position to persecute, they tried to outdo what they had endured! They had crossed the sea to seek in the New World "freedom to worship God," but they themselves wished a monopoly of that liberty. Among those whom they thus attacked was that mildest of all Christian sects, the Society of Friends—otherwise known as Quakers. They had already suffered much from Protestants in England, and during many years there were seldom less than a thousand of them always in English prisons. On the accession of James II, this number reached 1,460. Some also were transported, and many died in captivity. George Fox, the founder of the sect, endured everything short of martyrdom. In America he was beaten by a mob and left for dead, and was repeatedly incarcerated. How he escaped mutilation is remarkable, for according to the laws of Massachusetts the punishment for a Quaker's first conviction was the loss of an ear; a second conviction deprived him of the other ear; and the third was punished by the boring of his tongue with a hot iron. For the hopelessly obstinate death was reserved.

In Boston three Quaker men and one woman were hanged; and one woman, stripped to the waist, was scourged through three towns of Massachusetts. But Quakers were not the only Non-conformists whom the "defenders of the right of private judgment" persecuted in America. The eminent Baptist clergyman Roger Williams, founder of the State of Rhode Island, was banished from Massachusetts in mid-winter into the icy wilderness, where he wandered for fourteen weeks among the Indians on the bleak New England coast, until he secured a place of refuge in the region, where he subsequently founded the city of Providence, associated with his name. As late as 1750, an old man is said to have been publicly scourged in Boston for non-attendance at the Congregational form of worship. (Wilberforce, *History of the American Church,* p. 146.).

Of the persecution of "witches," which became an epidemic in New England at one time, it is sufficient to say that Protestants in the town of Salem hanged numbers of persons accused of being witches, and in the neighboring town of Charlestown a poor old clergyman was, for the same reason, crushed to death between two slabs of stone! This cruel deed was even publicly commended by the Protestant ministers of Boston and Charlestown. John Wesley, the founder of Methodism, was one of the bitterest persecutors of "witchcraft," and declared: "The giving up of witchcraft is in effect giving up the Bible." In England, under James I, a law was passed subjecting witches to death on the first conviction, even though they had done no harm. Twelve Anglican Bishops voted for this law! The last witch was hanged in Scotland in 1727, but in 1733 the Associated Presbytery reaffirmed its belief in witchcraft, and deplored the fact that many had begun to doubt it.

One feature of these persecutions—whether they were directed against Catholics or denominational "heresies," is the fact that *their instigators were not fanatical mobs, but Protestant leaders,* whom naturally the people only too readily followed. That these leaders were often conscientious clergymen and magistrates, does not shift from them the responsibility. The proof of this is found in every history, and Longfellow has portrayed the hideous truth in his *New England Tragedies.* It is unquestionable also that the champions of Protestantism—Luther, Calvin, Beza, Knox, Cranmer and Ridley—advocated the right of the *civil* authorities to punish the "crime" of heresy.

When Calvin burned Servetus because of his views about the doctrine of the Trinity, the cruel deed was applauded by almost all European Protestants, including Melancthon and Bullinger. Hence, *whatever may be said of Catholic persecution, the spirit of Protestantism in this respect was just as intolerant.* Rousseau says truly: "The Reformation was intolerant from its cradle, and its authors were universal persecutors." The Protestant historian Hallam, in his *Constitutional History* (Vol. 1, Chap. 2), affirms: "Persecution is the deadly original sin of

the Reformed churches, which cools every honest man's zeal
for their cause, in proportion as his reading becomes more
extensive." Auguste Comte also writes: "The intolerance of
Protestantism was certainly not less tyrannical than that with
which Catholicism is so much reproached." (*Philosophie Positive,* Vol. 4, p. 51).

What makes, however, Protestant persecutions specially
revolting is the fact that *they were absolutely inconsistent with
the primary doctrine of Protestantism—the right of private judgment
in matters of religious belief!* Nothing can be more illogical than
at one moment to assert that one may interpret the Bible
to suit himself, and at the next to torture and kill him for
having done so!

Nor should we ever forget that, in the conflict precipitated
by the Reformation, *the Protestants were the aggressors,* the
Catholics were the defenders. The Protestants were attempting to destroy the old, established Christian Church, which
had existed fifteen hundred years, and to replace it by something new, untried and revolutionary. The Catholics were up-
holding a Faith, hallowed by centuries of pious associations
and sublime achievements; the Protestants, on the contrary,
were fighting for a creed which was not only an affair of
yesterday, but which already was beginning to disintegrate
into hostile sects, each of which, if it gained the upper hand,
commenced to persecute the rest! The Catholics punished people for *abandoning* their ancestral Faith; the Protestants punished
them for *not* abandoning it, or even for preferring some more
recent brand of Protestantism than that of their persecutors!
The Catholics contended for an old religion, in which they
all—both Protestants and Catholics alike—had been baptized
and reared; the Protestants insisted on a creed, which had
as yet no history and not a single claim upon men's gratitude
for services rendered to humanity. All religious persecution
is bad; but, in this case, of the two parties guilty of it, the
Catholics certainly had the more defensible motives for their
conduct.

At all events, the argument that the persecutions for heresy perpetrated by Catholics constitute a reason why one should not enter the Catholic Church, has not a particle more force than a similar argument would have against one's entering the Protestant Church. In both there have been those deserving of blame in this respect, and what applies to one applies also to the other. If it be urged, however, that on account of the persecutions, common to them both, one should not enter *either* of the great divisions of Christianity, it may be answered that one ought not to condemn an entire Church because in bygone ages some of its members have, in error, disobeyed the precepts of their Master. When we remember that in the hour of His betrayal and arrest the merciful Founder of that Church bade His impetuous disciple sheathe his sword, and that His last prayer on the Cross, in supplication for His torturers, was: "Father, forgive them; they know not what they do," we may feel sure that the excesses, which a portion of His professed followers—both Catholics and Protestants—have at times committed through mistaken zeal, He would be the first to rebuke.

Chapter 21

THE FINAL STEP

There is by God's grace an immeasurable distance between late and too late.—MADAME SWETCHINE.

Thou hast created us for Thyself, O God, and our heart is restless till it rests in Thee.—ST. AUGUSTINE.

NOW THAT so many difficulties had been overcome, and so many reasons found why I should not return to any of the Protestant sects, I had to face the solemn question, whether I should not humbly seek at once admission to the one and only Apostolic Catholic Church, whose spiritual shepherd is the Pope of Rome? Yet still my evil genius made me ask: "What is the need of joining *any* Church? Why is it not permissible to lead an individual religious life apart from any ecclesiastical body?" But, I reflected, if that be permissible and equally good for the soul, why had Christ taken such pains to found a Church, to institute its Sacraments, and to promise it His abiding presence till the world should end? *He certainly would not have done this had it not been needful.*

The truth is, such an institution as the Church is necessary for a true religious life. Solitary thinkers are sterile. Only a company of believers can survive and propagate itself; and religion, though in one sense the affair of the individual soul, cannot exist as a complete and permanent unity, unless it have some sort of organization, some unity of faith, some common form of worship, and some accepted rules of conduct. "Neglect not the assembling of yourselves together," is a precept which the Church has always observed.

"But if I join a Church," I asked myself, "must I do so publicly? Why may I not remain before the world a so-called

Protestant, though secretly a Catholic?" Such a procedure seemed, however, cowardly and insincere.

"But," I still further queried, "is not salvation possible outside of the Catholic Church? Why not take the chances, and avoid disagreeable experiences?" It is true, the Catholic Church believes that many souls outside her fold may certainly be saved, although she does not recommend them to remain there. [More accurately, whereas *no one* may be saved outside the Catholic Church, it is nevertheless possible to be saved by belonging to the Church in an invisible manner; this could be the case with a truly sincere Protestant or even a truly sincere non-Christian. Such persons would indeed belong to the Church, though in an extraordinary manner.—*Editor,* 1990.] She holds that there are many non-Catholics who believe the fundamentals of Christianity, yet are prevented from accepting the Divine Commission of the Catholic Church itself, not through selfish interests, fear of worldly criticism, or hostile treatment, but through what is called *"invincible ignorance,"* since they have never had an adequate chance of knowing thoroughly her claims and truths. Such Christian believers are not united to the visible *body* of the Church, but they are united to her *soul* by a true spiritual communion of faith and love to God. [Since the publication of the encyclical *Mystici Corporis* (1943), theologians recognize that it is better to speak of such persons as belonging to the Church in an invisible manner, rather than as belonging only to her "soul."—*Editor,* 1990.] No Catholic has a right to judge of the eternal destiny of any individual. Pope Pius IX said: "Far be it from us to dare to set bounds to the boundless mercy of God; . . .we must hold, as of faith, that out of the Apostolic Roman Church there is no salvation, and that she is the only ark of safety. But we must also recognize with certainty that those who are in invincible ignorance of the true religion, are not guilty of this in the eye of the Lord. And who will presume to mark out the limits of this ignorance of our most holy religion, according to the character and diversity of peoples, countries and minds?" Again he wrote: "It is known to us that those who are in invincible ignorance of our most holy religion, but who observe carefully the natural law and precepts graven by God upon the hearts of all men, and who, being disposed to obey God, lead an honest and upright life, may by the light of Divine grace attain to eternal life; for God, who sees clearly, and searches and knows the heart, the disposition, thoughts, and intention of each, in His supreme mercy and goodness by no means permits that anyone suffer eternal punishment, who has not of his own free will fallen into sin."

But *when a man is thoroughly convinced that the Catholic Church is the true Church of God,* established here on earth for the salvation of men, yet still refuses to belong to her communion through a fear of social ostracism, business injury or political detriment, then the situation is entirely different. Such a man sins undoubtedly against his conscience, insults his Saviour, and imperils his soul.

"There is probably no point," says the Protestant writer Mallock, "about which the general world is so misinformed and ignorant, as the sober but boundless charity of what is called the 'anathematising' Church. So little indeed is this charity understood generally, that to assert it seems a startling paradox. . . Yet it is the simple statement of a fact. Never was there a religious body, except the Roman, that laid the intense stress which she does on all her dogmatic teachings, and yet had the justice that comes of sympathy for those who cannot receive them. The holy and humble men who do not know her, or who in good faith reject her, she commits with confidence to God's uncovenanted mercies, and these she knows are infinite." [Cf. the bracketed comments two paragraphs above.—*Editor,* 1990.]

A Catholic writer, Mgr. Baunard, in his *"La Foi et ses victoires,"* has said: "Admire the compassionate breadth of the heart of the Catholic Church. We Catholics believe that beyond and outside of the eternal *body* of the Church, formed by its pastors and their faithful flock, there is, in addition, its *soul;* which, overflowing these limits [Cf. bracketed comments on p. 285.—*Editor,* 1990], embraces the universal society of the just, the reunion of all those, who, profiting by the all-sufficient grace which God refuses to no one to effect his salvation, form around the Cross of Christ at various distances an immense family; invisible, it is true, to mortal eyes, but visible to those of Him who is their Father in Heaven. To be a part of that soul, one thing alone is needed. It is that every man, faithful to the amount of light which he has been able to receive, should believe, hope and love, according to the measure of those gifts; should conform his moral life to what he knows of the Divine law; and should desire to approach as nearly as possible to the pure and entire truth. Such a one belongs to the Church by his intentions; he will belong to it in Heaven through blessedness; and to say what is the number of these invisible citizens of the City of God is the work of God alone. All that we know is that God has an infinite love for souls, that He possesses a thousand Divine secrets of reaching them, and that His mercy is a fathomless sea, whose limit one must never think has been attained."

It follows that no pagan is lost except through his own fault. God gives to all sufficient grace for their salvation, and will not judge unfairly any man who does the best he can. This being so, I naturally asked myself: "What is the use of joining the Catholic Church, if I can be saved just as well without it?" But could I plead, as an excuse, "invincible ignorance?" No; for I *was* no longer ignorant of the convincing truth of the claims of Catholicism. Moreover, even if I were eventually pardoned for neglecting what I *knew* to be my duty, I certainly should not be saved "just as well." If Christ, the Son of God, came to this planet to seek and to save those who were lost; if for that purpose He founded a Church, against which He declared the gates of Hell should not prevail; and if He promised to abide with that Church until the end of the world: then *it cannot be a matter of indifference to*

*Him, or to the human beings whom He desires to save from sin
and its consequences, whether they join that Church or not.* The
awful drama of the Incarnation, Passion, Death and Resurrection of the Word made flesh is not a thing to treat indiffer-
ently, or to accept in part. Christ's precepts, if Divine, are
meant to be obeyed. Otherwise the love and mercy of the
Infinite would be subject to the whims and criticisms of His
ignorant but arrogant creatures! Whatever God's immeasurable love may do, it is difficult to think that it can be the
same in point of pardon and privilege, here or hereafter, for
those who did not join His Church on earth, if fully aware
of what they were doing. [The imperative for joining the
Catholic Church comes from Our Lord Himself, who said:
"He that believeth and is baptized, shall be saved: but he
that believeth not shall be condemned." (*Mark* 16:16). The
need to belong to the Roman Catholic Church for salvation
is basically twofold: First, in the Catholic Church alone are
to be found *all* the truths necessary for men to know and
to follow in order to achieve salvation; and secondly, in the
Church one has access to the Seven Sacraments, which im-
part the graces needed to enable him to become acceptable
to God and to help him work out his salvation.—*Editor, 1990.*]

Nor is it possible for those who wish to lead a godly
life, to find elsewhere so many aids to spirituality as those
which are included in the blessed influences of that Church's
Sacraments; for God communicates His grace through certain sacramental channels, instituted by Christ Himself, and
*the Church to which He gave those Sacraments is the Catholic
Church, which alone dates from the beginning.* Wise with two
thousand years of spiritual experience, she guides and teaches,
disciplines and comforts us, points out the way to Heaven,
and gives us strength to walk in it. She is the helpful shepherd of our souls, and she still retains the keys of Heaven,
as her Founder gave them to her. To this Church Jesus stated
that He stood in the relation of the Vine to the branches,
and those who know this, and yet still remain outside of

that blest union, do so at their peril.

I found, therefore, no reason which could justify me either in becoming a Protestant, or in concealing my entry into the Church of Rome. Yet intellectually to perceive this, or emotionally to feel it, was not enough. Reason could lead me to the limit of decision, but reason alone could not compel me to step over it. A merely mental change of view is not a real conversion. In addition to an intellectual conviction and an emotional desire, *a definite act of the will is needful.* That act can be, however, instantaneous, and hence the final step in the journey from Agnosticism to Faith is frequently the shortest of all. It consists merely in the *free determination* to do what the Prodigal Son did, when, "having come to himself," he resolved to leave his empty and unsatisfying life, and to arise and go to his father, saying to him: "Father, I have sinned against heaven and in thy sight, and I am no more worthy to be called thy son." Through God's grace I was enabled to take that final step, and to arise and go to the Father of my soul.

Then, on the 28th of September, the eve of the Feast of St. Michael, my wife and I, as quietly and unobtrusively as possible, made our submission, and were received into the Church of Rome. Perhaps I cannot express my feelings, when long suspense had given place to certainty, and when the arduous struggle had been followed by a sense of perfect peace, better than in the following lines, which were written shortly after our first Communion.

AVE ECCLESIA!

Time-hallowed Church, whose truth divine
Endures unchanged from age to age,
What joy to feel that we are thine,
Nor lost our priceless heritage!

Blest hour, when altercation ends,
When rival sects their efforts cease,
And Christ His welcoming arms extends
And breathes His benison of peace!

Peace, for the Church on Peter's Rock
Speaks with a sanction, hers alone,
Protecting from Time's rudest shock
The Faith the Saviour made her own.

How sweet now to devoutly kneel
Where oft our feet so lightly trod,
And in her lamplit shrines to feel
The presence of the Son of God!

To hear her immemorial prayers,
Unaltered, in that ancient tongue,
Whose sense each kneeling suppliant shares,
Though softly read, or grandly sung!

To find in Christian Art a spell
That only those who love her know,
New tenderness in Raphael,
New strength in Michelangelo;

New splendor in those works sublime
Which bear Christ's emblem towards the sky,
And lift the soul from things of time
To visions of eternity!

What joy, amid the irised light
That floods those miracles in stone,
To walk by faith as well as sight,
The faith those builders made their own!

As ships which angry billows toss
Seek shelter from the stormy blast,
So 'neath the standard of the Cross
We, too, have reached the port at last.

Dear Mother Church, with grateful tears
We find the blessèd fold of Rome,
Sad from the long past's wasted years,
But thankful to have reached our home.

Chapter 22

SOME CATHOLIC PRIVILEGES
AND COMPENSATIONS

*Too late have I sought Thee, O Ancient Truth; too late have
I found Thee, O Ancient Beauty; for Thyself Thou hast created
us, O God, and our hearts are restless till they rest in Thee.*
—ST. AUGUSTINE.

*The convert Carl Ernst Jarcke, formerly Professor of Jurispru-
dence in Berlin and Bonn, stated to Pater Stern on his deathbed:
"When I am dead, say to all who will hear, that I found my
supreme happiness in the infallible Roman Catholic Church.'"*
—SCHERER: Warum liebe ich meine Kirche? p. 150.

Quam pius es petentibus!
Quam bonus te quaerentibus!
Sed quid invenientibus!

THE SOURCES of happiness open to the Catholic convert are numerous, but all of them are not to be
described. I am no friend of intimate spiritual
disclosures. "The gods approve the depth, but not the tumult
of the soul," and the soul's depths should rarely be exposed
to human gaze. In general, the convert's life is changed from
tumult to tranquillity, but sentiment is unreliable. Both exal-
tation and depression often depend on purely physical causes.
It is unwise to lead a neophyte to expect some strange and
rapturous ecstasy. Joy, peace, relief and gratitude, together
with a sense of duty done, these he will certainly experience;
but no one should forget that, just as long as we are in this
world, the struggle against sin and doubts will not be ended.
The Cross will still remain the Cross; and earth is not, and
never will be, Heaven.

Still, in addition to the pure subjective happiness which God's grace gives in never-to-be-forgotten moments, there are some special sources of delight and quite exceptional privileges peculiar to the Catholic Church which may be mentioned without indiscretion. These are not all perceived at first. It takes some time to grow accustomed to this wonderful inheritance. Sometimes we are impressed with one feature of it, sometimes with another.

One of these is the realization that *wheresoever in the whole world we may find ourselves, we have in every Catholic church a spiritual home.* Wherever the Catholic goes, in any land, in any city, he finds awaiting him the well-known altar before which he can worship with an unchanged ritual in a changeless faith. Moreover, at any hour of the day, on entering a Catholic sanctuary, he finds therein the Blessed Sacrament perpetually present, and, as a witness to the fact, the ever-burning lamp. There, too, he kneels before familiar shrines, and greets with love and reverence the customary representations of the Saviour, the Blessed Virgin and the Saints. If Mass is being said, or Vespers sung, or the Benediction given, the ceremony is the same, the Latin words identical. Truly, if the Church can say with her Founder, "My Kingdom is not of this world," she can also say in reference to her universality: "The world is my kingdom." Not only is the language of the Mass everywhere the same; every movement of the celebrant, his vestments, and his various positions at the altar are so identical with those to which the visitor is accustomed, that, even though he should not hear a word, a glance at the officiating priest enables him to understand just what part of the service has been reached, and thus he can immediately join in it. [This was true of the Traditional Latin Mass, universally used in the Latin Rite until approximately 1965-1967. However, at the time of this edition, 1990, most Catholic Masses are said in the vernacular, though some well-informed Catholics think the Church will one day return to the ancient Latin Liturgy.—*Editor,* 1990.]

Another source of spiritual blessing to the convert is the fact that the Catholic Church presents *more means of help to lead a pious life* than any other body of Christianity. Not only are her churches open to the worshipper from dawn to dusk, but there are in them daily many services. Among the most beautiful of these are the "May Devotions," meetings for prayer and song, held every evening during the month of May in honor of the Blessed Virgin. Similar ones are celebrated in honor of the Sacred Heart of Jesus in many places daily during the month of June; while special preparatory services are always held before the greater festivals of the Church, such as those of Epiphany, Easter, the Immaculate Conception, Corpus Christi, Pentecost and Christmas. The Saints' days also are commemorated faithfully, and how superlatively rich the Church is in memorials of her hallowed dead! Their feasts succeed each other through the year, like beads upon a rosary. No day is wholly wanting in such sacred associations, and many days are crowded with reminders of her saints and martyrs. Wisely does the Church ordain that these inspiring festivals shall be observed, for they excite her children to increased devotion, and bid them bear in mind that they are by inheritance "Children of the Saints."

By these means Catholics are kept near to God and constantly in touch with sacred things. In striking contrast to such stimulating souvenirs, Protestant Non-conformists, as a rule, pay no attention to these festivals, not even to Easter and Good Friday! Anglican and Episcopalian Churches, it is true, observe the religious year to some extent, but far less thoroughly than the Church of Rome. How many of them ever think that *all the Saints,* whose names are mentioned in their Prayer-Book, and whose prayers are found in Anglican devotional books, were Catholics? Since the date of their withdrawal from the Mother Church, the Protestants have had no Saints; at least have claimed none; but even in comparatively modern times the Catholic Church has numbered in her fold such holy men and women as St. Ignatius Loyola,

St. Francis Xavier, St. Vincent de Paul, St. Philip Neri, St. Aloysius, St. Charles Borromeo, St. Francis of Assisi, St. Theresa, St. Catherine of Siena, and many more. Yet all these saints would have heartily repudiated the schismatic Church of England, since it rejected many of the Sacraments so dear to them, and since it has actually denounced the Sacrifice of the Mass as idolatrous!

Another advantage, soon appreciated by the convert, is the realization that *Christian art* can now be enjoyed by him as never before. The noble music of the Church, especially that included in her chants and requiems, is now peculiarly his own, since his is now the faith which prompted and inspired it. The grand cathedrals also of Christianity, all built originally for the Catholic Church, in the ages of faith, hope and love, and formerly used for centuries exclusively for her magnificent ritual, are now no longer to the convert merely architectural masterpieces. Each of them is a stately portion of his Father's house, a shrine, within which dwells the Presence of the Son of God, and all are different expressions of the aspirations of the Catholic Faith, since every architect and workman once employed in their construction was a Catholic.

So is it also in the spheres of sculpture and painting; for, from the dawn of the Renaissance down to the present time, practically every work of art connected with the Christian religion has been the production of a son of the Catholic Church. In fact, the entire realm of Christian art abounds in representations of saintly persons whom Catholics love, revere and honor, yet many of whom appeal as little to the average Protestant as do the characters in Greek mythology. How differently do we, as converts, look upon such works!

The Sistine Madonna, for example, seems no more to us, as formerly, merely a wonderful portrayal of majestic motherhood. This it still is, but we discern in the triumphant Mother also a representation of our Lady of Heaven, honored above all womankind by God's selection as the Mother of His Incarnate Son.

Only a Catholic can fully enter into the spirit of Raphael's pictures of the Blessed Virgin. She has been truly called the theme of Raphael's life, the golden thread which is interwoven with the whole fabric of his art. No less than fifty of his paintings were consecrated to her portrayal. For centuries also many other painters vied with one another in doing homage to the Mother of God, a fact which brings us to another source of consolation, happiness and spiritual aid, peculiar to the Catholic Church, *the love and homage paid to the Virgin Mother,* as well as her responsive love and care for us. This seems particularly precious to the convert, since he has hitherto known nothing of it.

The feminine element, wholly wanting in Protestant worship, is in the Catholic Church one of its most beautiful and tender features. All hearts are not alike. Some unimpassioned souls prefer to pray to God alone, the awe-inspiring, omnipresent and omniscient Deity. Others are moved to hold communion with their Saviour only, who in His earthly life was subject to our infirmities, and "was in all points tempted like as we are, yet without sin." And there are others still, lone, orphaned hearts, who crave a mother's love and care, and find the greatest surcease of their pain by coming to the Mother of their crucified Redeemer, and begging her to comfort and to plead for them. There are in every life some moments when a mother's tenderness outweighs the world, and prayer to Mary often meets this want, especially when one's earthly mother is forever gone. The Blessed Virgin's sympathy answers a definite craving of the human heart. Let us rejoice that in the Catholic Church this craving is appeased, and that unnumbered millions have obtained through Mary's heavenly compassion a consolation nothing else could give.

But of the many compensations which await the convert, in return for any loss and persecution he may have experienced, the greatest surely is the precious privilege of the *Holy Mass.* To those who do not understand the Mass, it is an empty spectacle.

To those who comprehend it, it is the very soul of Catholicism, and the essence of Christianity. Slowly but irresistibly its beauty, mysticism and solemnity drew me to the Blessed Sacrament and to the Church that shelters it. The steps by which my faltering feet ascended to its altar were its *ancient prayers.* These, as I read them and appreciated their significance, *in connection with the ceremony itself,* filled me with awe and admiration.

Deny that Jesus was the Son of God, sent to redeem mankind from sin and punishment by His atoning sacrifice, and there can be no meaning in the Mass. Believe it, and the rite becomes at once the greatest spiritual privilege, and the highest act of human adoration. It is the re-enactment of the sacrifice of Christ, the celebration of His death upon an altar, typifying Calvary; and these to the repentant worshipper bring sanctifying grace. What first impressed me, as a non-Catholic, in the Mass was not its lighted altar, incense, music, priests and acolytes; these are indeed impressive, beautiful, frequently sublime. But that which often overpowered me was the thought of its *universality.* It thrills one, as he kneels before the elevated Host, to recollect that there is not a country, scarcely a city or hamlet, in the civilized world, *where this same ritual of the Mass is not said daily, often many times a day;* and not an island rises from the sea, if it be tenanted by man, from which the supplication of the Mass does not ascend to God each day, like incense from an altar. Other religious rites are local; this is universal. Like an unbroken chain, it clasps the rounded globe, and holds it fast to God. Its service never ends. Its continuity sweeps round our planet, like the moving tides. At every moment, *somewhere,* as the earth revolves, the rising sun is shining on the emblem of Christ's sacrifice, upheld by the adoring celebrant, and on this Holy Eucharist that sun can never set. Somewhere before a Catholic altar the words are always being uttered: *"Agnus Dei, qui tollis peccata mundi, miserere nobis"!* ["Lamb of God, Who takes away the sins of the world, have mercy on us!"] Yes, these identical words are used in every land, dear to the Saints and Martyrs of remote antiquity, and hallowed since by generations of faithful usage, a type of the Church's universality and unity.

Nevertheless, to every worshipper is given perfect liberty to participate in the Mass as he prefers. Thus, one may follow the service step by step, in Latin, or in the vernacular translation [This is true of the Traditional Latin Mass, which is said largely in a subdued voice.—*Editor,* 1990.]; another may use some prayers, submitted as appropriate substitutes; a third may whisper his own private supplications, inspired by his individual needs. In any case, however, the spirit of the Mass presents unqualified unity, for the prayers suggested are based upon the canon of the Mass, which has remained essentially unaltered since the death of Pope Gregory the Great in 604. [This is true of the Traditional Latin Mass.—*Editor,* 1990.] What an impressive history stands behind those words repeated daily in the Mass! In their essential features all have been guarded jealously by Mother Church for centuries, and are now set imperishably in her Missal, like jewels in a crown. How sweet for the communicant, as he receives the Blessed Sacrament, to hear from the lips of the servant of God the immemorial prayer which has for ages soothed the hearts of millions: *Corpus Domini nostri Jesu Christi custodiat animam tuam in vitam aeternam!* ["May the body of Our Lord Jesus Christ preserve your soul unto life everlasting!"—*Editor,* 1990.] Up through that stately ritual, by its successive stages of the Confession, the *Gloria in excelsis,* the Epistle, the Gospel and the Creed, all linked into a golden rosary of prayers, one reaches finally a moment, which to the soul that understands, believes and worships, is almost overwhelming.

The bell rings thrice, and an impressive silence fills the church, as the officiating priest utters the awe-inspiring words: "THIS IS MY BODY." For, as this solemn sentence is pronounced, the mystery of Transubstantiation is effected. Divinity is there! Kneeling, the priest adores the Sacred Host; then, rising, while the thrice-rung bell again commands attention, he elevates the Blessed Sacrament before the kneeling congregation, which adores therein the Presence of the Son of God! If its significance is rightly understood and thoroughly believed in, there is no moment in a human life so wonderful as this; unless it be when the celebrant brings the Holy Eucharist to the kneeling supplicant, with the words: "Behold the Lamb of God; behold Him who taketh away the sins of the world!" Beside this solemn celebration of the sacrifice of Calvary, all other Christian services fade into unrealities. *The Mass alone seems real.*

Which is of greater benefit to the soul, the stately High Mass, with its noble music, clouds of incense, and additional clergy, or the still, unobtrusive Low Mass, where few words are audible? That depends largely on the mental and spiritual condition of the individual. Many prefer the quiet Mass to the more imposing ceremony save as a rare indulgence. Certainly it is delightful occasionally to assist at a High Mass, for it uplifts one, as if carried heavenward on powerful wings; but the tender, simple, Low Mass, with its concluding Benediction, is like the shady grove, the clear, cool streamlet, and the wayside halt, which makes life's dusty highway sweet and bearable. Of either ceremony the following lines are true:

> *There's the sight of a Host uplifted,*
> *There's the silver sound of a bell,*
> *There's the gleam of a golden chalice,*
> *Be glad, sad hearts, 'tis well;*
> *He made, and He keeps love's promise*
> *With His own all days to dwell.*
>
> *The priest comes down to the railing,*
> *Where heads are bowed in prayer;*
> *In the tender clasp of his fingers*
> *The Host lies pure and fair;*
> *And the hearts of Christ and the Christian*
> *Meet there, and only there.*

O Love that is deep and deathless!
O Faith that is strong and grand!
O Hope that will shine forever
O'er the wastes of a weary land!
Christ's Heart finds an earthly heaven
In the palm of the priest's pure hand.
                              —FATHER RYAN.

When I am asked what I have found within the Catholic Church superior to all that Protestantism gave me, I find that language is inadequate to express it. One thinks of the familiar metaphor of a stained glass window in a vast cathedral. Seen from without by day, this seems to be an unintelligible mass of dusky glass. Viewed from within, however, it reveals a beautiful design, where sacred [his]story glows resplendently in form and color. So is it with the Church of Rome. One must enter it to understand its sanctity and charm. When I reflect upon that Church's long, unbroken continuity extending back to the very days of the Apostles; when I recall her grand, inspiring traditions, her blessed Sacraments, her immemorial language, her changeless creed, her noble ritual, her stately ceremonies, her priceless works of art, her wondrous unity of doctrine, her ancient prayers, her matchless organization, her Apostolic authority, her splendid roll of Saints and Martyrs reaching up like Jacob's ladder, and uniting earth and Heaven; when I reflect upon the intercession for us of those Saints and Martyrs, enhanced by the petitions of the Blessed Mother of Our Lord; and, last, not least, when I consider the abiding Presence of the Saviour on her altars; I feel that this One, Holy, Apostolic Church has given me certainty for doubt, order for confusion, sunlight for darkness, and substance for shadow. It is the Bread of Life and the Wine of the Soul, instead of the unsatisfying husks; the father's welcome, with the ring and the robe, instead of the weary exile in the wilderness of doubt. It is true, the prodigal must retrace the homeward road, and even enter the doorway of the mansion on his knees; but, *within, what a recompense!*

Favored are those who, from their childhood up, are nurtured in the Catholic Church, and to whom all her comforts, aids and Sacraments come no less freely than the air and sunshine. Yet I have sometimes wondered whether such favored Catholics ever know the rapture of the homeless waif, to whom the splendors of his Father's house are suddenly revealed; the consolation of the mariner, whose storm-tossed vessel finally attains the sheltered port; the gratitude of the lonely wanderer, long lost in cold and darkness, who shares at last, however undeservedly, the warmth and light of God's great spiritual HOME!

If you have enjoyed this book, consider making your next selection from among the following . . .

Prices guaranteed through June 30, 1996.

Miraculous Images of Our Lady. *Cruz* 20.00
Raised from the Dead. *Fr. Hebert* 15.00
Love and Service of God, Infinite Love. *Mother Louise Margaret.* 10.00
Life and Work of Mother Louise Margaret. *Fr. O'Connell* 10.00
Autobiography of St. Margaret Mary 4.00
Thoughts and Sayings of St. Margaret Mary 3.00
The Voice of the Saints. *Comp. by Francis Johnston* 5.00
The 12 Steps to Holiness and Salvation. *St. Alphonsus* 7.00
The Rosary and the Crisis of Faith. *Cirrincione & Nelson* 1.25
Sin and Its Consequences. *Cardinal Manning* 5.00
Fourfold Sovereignty of God. *Cardinal Manning* 5.00
Dialogue of St. Catherine of Siena. *Transl. Algar Thorold* 9.00
Catholic Answer to Jehovah's Witnesses. *D'Angelo* 8.00
Twelve Promises of the Sacred Heart. (100 cards) 5.00
Life of St. Aloysius Gonzaga. *Fr. Meschler* 10.00
The Love of Mary. *D. Roberto* 7.00
Begone Satan. *Fr. Vogl* 2.00
The Prophets and Our Times. *Fr. R. G. Culleton* 11.00
St. Therese, The Little Flower. *John Beevers* 4.50
St. Joseph of Copertino. *Fr. Angelo Pastrovicchi* 4.50
Mary, The Second Eve. *Cardinal Newman* 2.50
Devotion to Infant Jesus of Prague. *Booklet* 75
Reign of Christ the King in Public & Private Life. *Davies* 1.25
The Wonder of Guadalupe. *Francis Johnston* 6.00
Apologetics. *Msgr. Paul Glenn* 9.00
Baltimore Catechism No. 1 ....3.00
Baltimore Catechism No. 2 ....4.00
Baltimore Catechism No. 3 ....7.00
An Explanation of the Baltimore Catechism. *Fr. Kinkead* 13.00
Bethlehem. *Fr. Faber* 16.50
Bible History. *Schuster* 10.00
Blessed Eucharist. *Fr. Mueller* 9.00
Catholic Catechism. *Fr. Faerber* 5.00
The Devil. *Fr. Delaporte* 5.00
Dogmatic Theology for the Laity. *Fr. Premm* 18.00
Evidence of Satan in the Modern World. *Cristiani* 8.50
Fifteen Promises of Mary. (100 cards) 5.00
Life of Anne Catherine Emmerich. 2 vols. *Schmoeger* 37.50
Life of the Blessed Virgin Mary. *Emmerich* 15.00
Manual of Practical Devotion to St. Joseph. *Patrignani* 13.50
Prayer to St. Michael. (100 leaflets) 5.00
Prayerbook of Favorite Litanies. *Fr. Hebert* 9.00
Preparation for Death. (Abridged). *St. Alphonsus* 7.00
Purgatory Explained. *Schouppe* 13.50
Purgatory Explained. (pocket, unabr.). *Schouppe* 7.50
Fundamentals of Catholic Dogma. *Ludwig Ott* 20.00
Spiritual Conferences. *Tauler* 12.00
Trustful Surrender to Divine Providence. *Bl. Claude* 4.00
Wife, Mother and Mystic. *Bessieres* 7.00
The Agony of Jesus. *Padre Pio* 1.50

Prices guaranteed through June 30, 1996.

Is It a Saint's Name? *Fr. William Dunne* 1.50
St. Pius V—His Life, Times, Miracles. *Anderson* 4.00
Who Is Teresa Neumann? *Fr. Charles Carty* 2.00
Martyrs of the Coliseum. *Fr. O'Reilly* 16.50
Way of the Cross. *St. Alphonsus Liguori* 75
Way of the Cross. *Franciscan version* 75
How Christ Said the First Mass. *Fr. Meagher* 16.50
Too Busy for God? Think Again! *D'Angelo* 4.00
St. Bernadette Soubirous. *Trochu* 16.50
Passion and Death of Jesus Christ. *Liguori* 8.50
Treatise on the Love of God. 2 Vols. *St. Francis de Sales* 16.50
Confession Quizzes. *Radio Replies Press* 1.00
St. Philip Neri. *Fr. V. J. Matthews* 4.50
St. Louise de Marillac. *Sr. Vincent Regnault* 4.50
The Old World and America. *Rev. Philip Furlong* 16.50
Prophecy for Today. *Edward Connor* 4.50
The Book of Infinite Love. *Mother de la Touche* 4.50
Chats with Converts. *Fr. M. D. Forrest* 9.00
The Church Teaches. *Church Documents* .15.00
Conversation with Christ. *Peter T. Rohrbach* 8.00
Purgatory and Heaven. *J. P. Arendzen* 3.50
Liberalism Is a Sin. *Sarda y Salvany* 6.00
Spiritual Legacy of Sr. Mary of the Trinity. *van den Broek* 9.00
The Creator and the Creature. *Fr. Frederick Faber* 13.50
Radio Replies. 3 Vols. *Frs. Rumble and Carty* 36.00
Convert's Catechism of Catholic Doctrine. *Fr. Geiermann* 3.00
Incarnation, Birth, Infancy of Jesus Christ. *St. Alphonsus* 8.50
Light and Peace. *Fr. R. P. Quadrupani* 5.00
Dogmatic Canons & Decrees of Trent, Vat. I. *Documents* 8.00
The Evolution Hoax Exposed. *A. N. Field* 6.00
The Primitive Church. *Fr. D. I. Lanslots* 8.50
Ven. Jacinta Marto of Fatima. *Cirrincione* 1.50
The Priest, the Man of God. *St. Joseph Cafasso* 12.00
Blessed Sacrament. *Fr. Frederick Faber* .16.50
Christ Denied. *Fr. Paul Wickens* 2.00
New Regulations on Indulgences. *Fr. Winfrid Herbst* 2.50
A Tour of the Summa. *Msgr. Paul Glenn* .18.00
Spiritual Conferences. *Fr. Frederick Faber* 13.50
Latin Grammar. *Scanlon and Scanlon* 13.50
A Brief Life of Christ. *Fr. Rumble* 2.00
Marriage Quizzes. *Radio Replies Press* 1.00
True Church Quizzes. *Radio Replies Press* 1.00
St. Lydwine of Schiedam. *J. K. Huysmans* 7.00
Mary, Mother of the Church. *Church Documents* 3.00
The Sacred Heart and the Priesthood. *de la Touche* 7.00
Revelations of St. Bridget. *St. Bridget of Sweden* 2.50
Magnificent Prayers. *St. Bridget of Sweden* 1.50
The Happiness of Heaven. *Fr. J. Boudreau* 7.00
St. Catherine Labouré of the Miraculous Medal. *Dirvin* 12.50
The Glories of Mary. (pocket, unabr.). *St. Alphonsus Liguori* 9.00

Prices guaranteed through June 30, 1996.

At your Bookdealer or direct from the Publisher.

Prices guaranteed through June 30, 1996.

NOTES

NOTES

NOTES

NOTES